CAMPAIGNS
Cases in
Political Conflict

Walt Anderson
San Fernando Valley State College

Goodyear Publishing Company, Inc.
Pacific Palisades, California

This book is dedicated to Mauriça
and so am I.

I want to express my thanks to Ned Lazzaro for his valuable contribution to the research and writing of Chapter Thirteen.

CONTENTS

v

IV

V

VI

VII

INTRODUCTION

This book is primarily a look at fourteen American election campaigns—
the men who took part in them, the tactics that were used, and some of
the events, expected and unexpected, which influenced their results. It is
also, secondarily, a look through the window of political campaigning at
American history itself. It is designed for use in political science or history
courses, and emphasizes three subjects of contemporary importance—
the political status of Negroes, radicalism and reaction in political campaigns, and the influence of the mass media.

The selection of campaigns is also intended to give the reader an
acquaintance with the variations in political conflict in different regions—
the South, the Midwest, the Far West, the Eastern Seaboard—and in different kinds of elections. Two mayoral campaigns, three senatorial campaigns,
six gubernatorial campaigns, and three presidential primary campaigns are
included. Of the presidential primary chapters, two—Chapter 10, on John
Kennedy in West Virginia, and Chapter 14, on Eugene McCarthy in New
Hampshire—focus on the primaries of a single state, and one—Chapter 4,
on the 1912 battle between William H. Taft and Theodore Roosevelt—
follows the campaign through several states, since the subject matter is the
development of the presidential primaries themselves as well as the campaign.

In general, I have allowed the requirements of the subject to shape
the form of the chapter. Most chapters emphasize a single election; others
span a longer period of time before and after the election which is the
pivotal point of the study. Chapter 3, for example, sketches the career of
"Pitchfork Ben" Tillman over a period of some 20 years, to document the
course of the Tillman movement and its consequences for the black citizens
of South Carolina; Chapter 5 deals with several of Floyd B. Olson's political campaigns in order to illustrate his changing style of radical leadership.

Political campaigns have a way of running somewhat obliquely to
what academicians regard as the hard realities of history, and analysts of

political change frequently prefer to look elsewhere than in the campaigns themselves—with their omissions, emotionalism, inaccuracies, and deliberate distortions of fact—for their information. Campaign oratory, especially, is likely to be ignored in favor of more rational data: demographic information, financing, party organization. This is a serious omission: campaign oratory, for better or worse, is an important factor in the American decision-making process, even though the issues as defined in a campaign may not be the same as conditions which can be empirically verified. For example, the real threat of communism to the internal security of the United States in the 1950's may have been negligible; but, whether or not it was real, the threat attained a political importance which affected the outcomes of several major elections and helped to determine the course of American foreign policy.

The style of political oratory has changed enormously in the past century, and several of the chapters in this book illustrate the evolution. Chapter 1, on the Lincoln-Douglas senatorial campaign in Illinois, examines in some detail the emergence of an issue and its treatment in a campaign. Each man, in the series of debates which became the core of the campaign, used the issue of slavery, trimmed the issue to fit his own political needs, and worked hard to create misconceptions about the exact nature of his opponent's position. But whatever the shortcomings of the debates, they did provide an exhaustive examination of possible positions on the issue of slavery and forced each candidate to state his own position more clearly than he might otherwise have done—certainly clearly enough to remove them both from consideration as presidential candidates acceptable to the South.

In this campaign for the first time teams of reporters traveled with the candidates and sent dispatches to newspapers outside the state. The influence of the mass media is an essential part of the historical importance of the campaign: through the mass media, both men were able to campaign to a national constituency, and both Lincoln and Douglas—but particularly Douglas, who wanted to hold a southern political base—had to sacrifice their effectiveness in a future national election in trying to win a sectional one. (A little less than a hundred years later Hubert Humphrey, making a television broadcast from West Virginia, would err in the opposite direction: neglecting the local campaign in order to appeal to the national constituency.)

The Lincoln-Douglas campaign, which heightened national interest in an issue and moved the country a step closer to Civil War, stands as a supreme example of the potential explosiveness of head-on political debate, and its lesson has been clearly comprehended by professional politicians: In one way or another, much of political campaigning is a strategy of avoiding issues. Professionals of the machine variety sought to avoid the dangers of debate by organizing sizable blocks of voters who had an allegiance to the machine and were uninterested in political speechmaking; the new professionals, the public-relations men, campaign by issue control. Issues are chosen and positions shaped on the basis of public-opinion polls, and the successful campaign runs on a small number of issues. One of the forms political conflict takes in such a campaign is a struggle over which issues shall dominate, and a campaign manager of the public-relations persuasion often considers the battle won when he succeeds in making his client's opponent respond to his statements and thus, in effect, consent to debate with the issues he has chosen. Chapter 6 deals with one of the most long-lived and powerful of the urban machines, Tammany Hall, and Chapters 7, 8, 9, and 12 offer examples of campaigns managed with a strong public-relations influence.

The campaign run by the supporters of Governor Frank Merriam in opposition to the challenge of Upton Sinclair in California (Chapter 7) is generally accepted to be the first major campaign staged by a professional campaign-management firm. As a result of their 1934 performance, Whitaker and Baxter became extremely successful operators with the ability to pick and choose clients from among some of the most powerful figures in California politics; they profited from numerous books and articles—mostly unfavorable—about their work; and Sinclair himself, who in his various writings about the campaign assigned them an important role in his defeat, undoubtedly contributed to the growth of their notoriety.

Although their kind of political enterprise has been most successful in California, giving rise to a number of competing firms including Spencer-Roberts (Chapter 12), it has not been restricted to that state; Whitaker and Baxter themselves have operated outside of California, most notably as coordinators of the complex and costly AMA campaign against Medicare, and similar entrepreneurs are currently operating throughout the country and at all levels of politics.

The PR-oriented campaign manager practices a form of issue control which is relatively new in American politics and the effects of which upon the workings of the democratic system are still undetermined. Its main elements are selection and simplification. A campaign is conducted on the basis of a few strong issues; it aims to construct and communicate a dominant image of the candidate, his stand, and his opposition.

This type of campaign thrives in a climate of public excitement about a coming election, and PR campaign managers will try whenever possible to create this kind of excitement if it does not already exist. News media increase their attention to a candidate's activities in response to public interest in a contest, and stimulating free publicity is a major part of a public-relations man's job. This kind of campaign also relies on a heavy *paid* use of the news media. The more intensive a campaign becomes, the more a candidate will be required to spend for advertising, and the higher will be the profit to the agency through which the advertising is placed. The corporate structure of Whitaker and Baxter included an advertising agency which received a 15 per cent commission on all advertising expenses. Nearly all contemporary campaign-management firms are also advertising agencies with an understandable preference for the highly publicized and extremely costly elections which are becoming increasingly familiar in American politics.

This is far different from the preferences of the machine-oriented campaign manager. The machines functioned best when the public did not become too excited about elections; surges of public excitement—such as the periodic reform movements in New York City—tax a machine's resources. In New York Tammany's strength lay in control of a solid core of votes that, even if occasionally overwhelmed, could be counted upon to return the machine to power when the furor subsided and keep it there until the next reform movement should come along; the machine's forte, in short, was not persuading the undecided but delivering the dependable. The 1950 senatorial campaign in Maryland (Chapter 9) offers one example of what can happen when the two styles of campaign-management collide: The Republican candidate's media-oriented campaign did not convert substantial numbers of the Democratic faithful, but it did stimulate a high voter turnout, and the masses of new voters—who *were* influenced by the media campaign—determined the outcome of the election.

It cannot be coincidental that so many campaigns in which communism has been a dominant issue have also been campaigns managed by public-relations professionals. When the impetus is toward simplification and clarification of issues, the radicalism or questionable loyalty of an opponent provides a ready focus for a campaign. Furthermore, anti-Communist campaigns have often been well funded—making extensive advertising possible—and supported by one or many newspapers—facilitating the task of finding an outlet for press releases.

We may also learn something about the handling of issues in political campaigns by considering how radical candidates themselves have fared as campaigners. Floyd B. Olson, running as the candidate of a political party which was committed to Socialist principles, was elected governor of the state of Minnesota; but Upton Sinclair, who had left the Socialist party and had won the nomination of the Democratic party—the majority party —in California, was defeated. The effectiveness of the campaign *against* Sinclair has already been noted, but we should not overlook the strategy of Sinclair's own campaign, which was—at least until Democratic party leaders stepped in—to give maximum exposure in great detail to his plans for radical changes in the state government. Olson, on the other hand, played down Socialist ideas in 1930, and campaigned as a reformer rather than as a radical; his conflict was with ideologues in his own party who believed—correctly—that he was compromising party doctrine in order to win over middle-of-the-road voters. This is quite similar to the dispute which has always separated the pragmatists from the purists in the British Labour party. It raises the strategic question of how much information about his own position on issues a candidate can safely inject into a campaign. Many campaign managers, such as Murray Chotiner, have advised their clients to be extremely selective in introducing even material of public record—such as their own voting histories—into a campaign (see page 142).

Five of the chapters in this book deal primarily with the Negro in American politics. The Lincoln-Douglas senatorial campaign was dominated by the question of the place of black people in American society, not only in terms of the issue of slavery, but also in terms of the equally divisive question of what might be the legal status of freed slaves. The texts of the debates—particularly Lincoln's struggles to find a defensible position on that explosive question—tell volumes about the fears of white Americans as they confronted or tried to avoid confronting the implications of a multiracial democratic society.

Chapters 2 and 3 deal with Reconstruction—more specifically, with the two phases of the end of Reconstruction in the state of South Carolina. In the first phase, as exemplified in the campaign which elected former Confederate General Wade Hampton to the governorship, power passed from the hands of the Reconstructionists and was regained by essentially the same class which had controlled the state before the Civil War. In the second phase, marked by the rise of Ben Tillman, power passed to a new generation of southern leaders who were suspicious of the old aristocracy and the urban financial interests, and fearful of the potential political power of the freed blacks. It was the second phase which resulted in the disenfranchisement of the southern blacks whose presence made them a continuing threat to political stability. Ben Tillman and later southern politicians like him dispensed with the rhetoric by which southern aristocrats sometimes represented themselves as protectors and uplifters of the Negro race, and frankly proclaimed their own belief in white supremacy as a matter of plain political survival.

As we come to two more recent campaigns—Lester Maddox' for the governorship of Georgia in 1966 and Carl M. Stokes's for the mayoralty of Cleveland in 1967—we see some striking changes and also some striking absences of change. After a hundred years of emancipation blacks in the state of Georgia were still unable to exert sufficient political influence to win themselves a real choice in the state election: The choice offered them by the two parties in 1966 was between one avowed white supremacist and another—between a Goldwater Republican and a Wallace Democrat. Many observers doubt that the Maddox victory was "significant" in view of his subsequent inability to convert much of his ideology into legislation. This overlooks some important considerations: The fact that one man was able to capitalize on resistance to integration and become governor of a southern state is in itself significant. And perhaps even more significant, in view of the above observations about the advisability of radical candidates' soft-pedaling their ideologies in order to win votes, is the fact that Lester Maddox did not compromise with his ideas at all; no one doubted where he stood. In the 1960's no candidate as outspokenly radical as Lester Maddox is outspokenly reactionary attained a comparable political victory.

Blacks in the North are frequently characterized as occupying a political role similar to that of recent immigrants, and that is a fairly accurate and useful comparison in spite of what it implies about relegating to such a status a people who have lived on this continent for centuries. Waves of immigration have had a definite affect on the shape of American politics and are still identifiable as distinct political groupings: the "old Americans" from England and Western Europe, the Irish during the potato famine years, the Jews and Eastern Europeans after the Civil War. The phases through which immigrant groups seem to pass are, first, a stage of political inefficacy and exploitability; second, a move into power in local politics; third, a degree of political acceptability or respectability characterized by the ability of members of the group to become candidates for national office. Chapter 6 reflects the growing power of newer ethnic groups—the Italians and the Jews—in New York in the 1930's, as they began to dislodge the Irish from domination of the machines. And Chapter 13, on Carl Stokes's campaign in Cleveland, shows the Eastern European groups—the Cosmos—giving way to the new political power of the blacks. There is a fascinating compression of American history and interplay of ethnic groups in that campaign: first Stokes in the primary, running against a Rumanian-born incumbent with a Polish campaign manager; then Stokes in the final, his campaign offices staffed with prosperous liberal Jews from the suburbs as he campaigns against Seth Taft, the grandson of a President.

Chapter 10 shows an Irish Catholic, the descendant of potato famine immigrants and urban machine politicians, establishing his acceptability as a presidential candidate. The chapter raises a question that may need more attention as candidates of Jewish, Eastern European, and Negro origin campaign for national office: What part do the mass media play in determining the acceptability of candidates of various ethnic backgrounds?

Chapter 10 is one of three chapters on the presidential primaries—the most media-dominated of all American elections. In somewhat the way that Los Angeles is a different kind of city because it grew after the invention of the car, the presidential primary is a different kind of political phenomenon because it grew after a time when it had become possible for the entire nation to follow election campaigns as they unfolded. The 1912 Roosevelt-Taft campaign was mainly an effort of Roosevelt's to score a public-opinion victory over Taft; as the 1934 Upton Sinclair campaign was the prototype for the professionally managed PR campaign, the 1912 presidential primaries set the style for the development of a curious kind of politicking in which candidates would attempt to manipulate the impact of primary victories as a way of obtaining delegate support. Ironically, in both these developments which increased the influence of the mass media in politics the Progressive movement played a part. The presidential primaries were a Progressive innovation and so were the various reform laws in California which set the stage for the emergence of Whitaker and Baxter. The reforms of the Progressives, designed to obstruct the workings of the political machines, created conditions favorable to the emergence of mass-media politics.

In this Introduction I have tried to indicate some of the main themes that are stressed in each chapter. No campaign, however, conveniently restricts its significance to a single frame of reference, and therefore several different classifications of the contents, with some overlapping of chapters, are possible. I would suggest the following possible ways of choosing material according to course emphasis:

The Negro in Politics: Chapters 1, 2, 3, 11, and 13. To this could be added Chapter 10, as a comment on the "minority" aspect of Catholicism, and Chapter 12, the California election in which public reaction to the Watts riots was a factor.

The Presidential Primaries: Chapters 4, 10, and 14.

Radical Movements and the Political Use of Anti-Communism: Chapters 5, 7, 8, 9, and 14.

Professional Campaign-Management and Influence of Mass Media in Campaigning: Chapters 1, 4, 7, 8, 9, 10, and 12.

Progressivism and Reform: Chapters 4, 5, and 6.

Agrarian Revolt: Chapters 3 and 5.

Political Trends of the 1960's: Chapters 10, 11, 12, 13, and 14.

Finally, I would like to point out that election laws can be extremely important in influencing both the style of a campaign and its final effect. Students of American government should have some acquaintance with the great range, historical and geographical, of election systems. Among those cited in this book are the various presidential primary laws enacted during the era of Progressivism; the system of crossfiling (another idea of the Progressives) which was still in effect in California during the Richard Nixon–Helen Gahagan Douglas campaign of 1950; the "unit vote" system in Maryland which gave John Butler the Republican nomination with a popular-vote minority; the complex of Georgia election laws which enabled Lester Maddox to become governor without ever having won a general election; and the presidential primary law in New Hampshire which gave Eugene McCarthy 20 out of 26 convention delegates although he had won only 42.2 per cent of the Democratic vote.

The consequences of the New Hampshire primary still cannot be fully appraised. It undoubtedly influenced Johnson's decision to retire, and Kennedy's to enter the race. The specific issue of the Vietnam war which dominated that campaign was, I believe, less important than the more general issues involved—the problem of America's struggle to find a role in world affairs acceptable to its own citizens, and the problem of the wavering faith of many Americans in the value of traditional party politics as a way of effecting social change. These questions, which were implied in that campaign conducted in the latter part of the past decade, are the ones I believe will dominate the politics of the 1970's.

A
HOUSE
DIVIDING

I

1

1858
Illinois
Stephen Douglas vs. *Abraham Lincoln*

In 1858 the Democratic party, which had begun as the party of Thomas Jefferson and had dominated American politics since the time of Andrew Jackson, was, like the country itself, being torn apart by the issue of slavery. Part of its membership had already broken away to join with former members of the collapsed Whig party in the new Republican party, and those Americans who still called themselves Democrats had been forced by the Kansas controversy into one or another of two camps—one supporting the Buchanan administration, one supporting Senator Stephen A. Douglas of Illinois.

The immediate cause of the split was the dispute over whether Kansas should be admitted to statehood with a constitution which had been written by proslavery settlers—a minority group—in the territory. But the dispute represented more than simply the question of Kansas: It was evidence of the divisiveness of the slavery issue and of the failure of the Democratic party to hold together in a single political framework the increasingly incompatible positions of its northern and southern members.

Douglas' position, embodied in the Kansas-Nebraska Act of 1854, which he had authored as chairman of the Senate committee on territories, was based on the principle of "squatter sovereignty"—the right of the settlers in new territories to determine for themselves whether or not slavery would be permitted. This principle had been weakened by the Dred Scott decision, coming out of a southern-dominated Supreme Court, which held that

3

slaveholders had a full legal right to take their slaves into new territories and use them there—that, in effect, where the United States flag went, slavery went also. Southerners had praised the decision, abolitionists and free-soilers had condemned it, and Douglas, in the interests of party unity, had accepted it. Squatter sovereignty, he said, would still survive in the territories on a *de facto* basis, and when the territories were ready for statehood they could choose to be admitted with antislavery constitutions.

Not so long before, the Missouri Compromise of 1820 had tried to settle the dispute another way, by prohibiting slavery in the area north of the line 36° 30′ with the exception of Missouri, which was admitted as a slave state. But Douglas' Kansas-Nebraska bill had repealed this, leaving the question of slavery up to the territorial settlers, and the Dred Scott decision in 1857 had declared that the Missouri Compromise was unconstitutional to begin with—that neither Congress nor territorial legislatures had the right to exclude slavery from territories.

The Dred Scott decision, the panic of 1857—which seemed to indicate a weakness in the North's economy—and the influence of strong-minded Southerners in the cabinet of the wavering President were all things that could give Southerners a feeling of confidence. But there were also good reasons for Southerners to believe that their section and its institutions were threatened. The balance of states, with Missouri admitted as a slave state, stood at sixteen free and fifteen slave; Minnesota and Oregon were ready for admission as free states, and other territories which would want statehood soon were filling with settlers who had no liking for slavery—either because they felt it economically unsuitable, or because they did not want their areas populated with blacks. Many Southerners hoped the United States would acquire territories in Central or South America that might be fit for plantation farming, and followed with interest the filibustering expeditions of Tennessee-born William Walker, whose first act upon becoming President of Nicaragua was to repeal its antislavery law.[1] But for the present, the only real prospect for a new slave state was Kansas.

For years, proslavery and antislavery forces had been competing in Kansas. The first settlers who came in merely crossed the border from neighboring Missouri—some bringing slaves with them. Soon farmers from free states were entering the new territory also,

[1] See William Walker, *War in Nicaragua* (Mobile, Ala.: Goetzel, 1860).

and abolitionists in New England, hoping to keep slavery out of
the territories, organized the New England Emigrant Aid Company,
which had one purpose: settling Kansas with a maximum number
of abolitionists. But New England was too far away, and the
process of recruiting settlers was slow. The proslavery Missourians
had more effective techniques: whenever there was an election in
Kansas, Missourians by the thousands would cross the border to
vote. When the territorial legislature was chosen in 1855, some
three-fourths of the votes were cast by border-crossers.[2] The antislavery Kansans boycotted this territorial government—which had its
capital in Lecompton—and set up a government of their own in
Topeka. They had a growing majority, as more and more settlers came
in from the North, but the Lecompton forces had the recognition
of Washington and control of the actual machinery of government.
The antislavery Kansans believed that time was on their side; the proslavery Kansans believed so too, and were eager to get the territory admitted as a slave state while they still had the power.
It was their drive for admission which led to the open break
between Senator Douglas and President Buchanan.

In 1857, an election was held in Kansas to choose delegates
to a constitutional convention—the constitution to be the basis
on which the territory would apply for statehood. At the time,
the population was overwhelmingly antislavery. Governor Robert
J. Walker, estimating the total number of settlers at 24,000, figured
the strength of the various political factions to be: "Free State
Democrats 9,000, Republicans 8,000, Proslavery Democrats 6,500,
Proslavery Know-Nothings 500."[3] But most of the antislavery settlers were not registered to vote and a good number of those who
were eligible would have no part of the election anyhow; their
numbers were further reduced by gerrymandering and crooked
election-administering by the Lecompton officials. In the final count
there were some 2,200 votes, and the men certified as delegates to
the convention were nearly all proslavery. As for their general character, the *Emporia Kansas News* described them as "brokendown
hacks, demagogues, fire-eaters, perjurers, ruffians, ballot-box stuffers
and loafers."[4]

[2] Paul M. Angle, *Created Equal? The Complete Lincoln-Douglas Debates of 1858* (Chicago: University of Chicago Press, 1958), p. xiii.
[3] Allen Nevins, *The Emergence of Lincoln*, I: *Douglas, Buchanan, and
Party Chaos, 1857–1859* (New York: Charles Scribner's Sons, 1950), 153.
[4] Quoted in *ibid.*, p. 230.

Douglas saw his party and his policies on trial in Kansas: If the territory were admitted with a proslavery constitution—especially one that did not even have the sanction of the residents of the territory—his doctrine of "squatter sovereignty" would have become a farce. He let it be known that any constitution which came out of Lecompton would have to be approved by the voters of Kansas in a fair election before it could be accepted by Congress. The President had also advocated a popular vote. In a letter to Governor Walker he wrote: "On the question of submitting the constitution to the bona fide residents of Kansas, I am willing to stand or fall. It is the principle of the Kansas-Nebraska Bill, the principle of Popular Sovereignty, and the Principle at the foundation of all popular government." [5] However, President Buchanan had a way of changing his mind.

The delegates who assembled in the town of Lecompton in 1857 were being pressured from all sides; they debated over whether or not to submit the constitution to the voters and finally came up with a compromise. The constitution itself would not be submitted for a popular vote, but there *would* be an election on a separate section having to do with slavery. The separate section, however, did not include the question of whether existing slave ownership would be protected; that was written into the main body of the constitution, in a passage which stated: "The right of property is before and higher than any constitutional sanction, and the right of the owner of a slave to such slave and its increase is the same and as inviolable as the right of the owner of any property whatever." [6]

The convention also placed its own chairman, John Calhoun, in charge of the election. Thus it was certain that there would be at least partial slavery in Kansas, and with the election machinery in the right hands, it was likely that the full proslavery section of the constitution would be passed as well. Free-soilers and abolitionists throughout the North denounced the convention and its work, but Buchanan now shifted his position. In a speech before both houses of the new Congress, he said that Kansas had "for some years occupied too much of the public attention." The best way to end the conflict would be to admit Kansas to statehood. "When

[5] *Ibid.,* p. 169.
[6] *Ibid.,* p. 234.

once admitted to the Union, with or without slavery, the excitement beyond her own limits will speedily pass away . . ." [7]

Douglas could not accept this. "We must stand on the popular sovereignty principle," he had written the previous month, "and go wherever the logical consequences may carry us, and defend it against *all assaults* from whatever quarter." [8]

While Douglas was preparing to defend the concept of popular sovereignty in Washington, antislavery settlers were defending it another way in Kansas. Defying the convention, they called for a plebescite on the entire constitution. Two separate elections were held in the territory. The one called by the convention was held on December 21; the one called by the dissenting settlers was held on January 4. In the first election, supervised by Calhoun, the vote ran 6,226 in favor of slavery, 569 against. In the second, 10,226 voted against the entire constitution, 138 for the constitution with slavery, and 24 for the constitution without slavery.[9]

Thus, depending on which election you chose to regard as legal, the territory had voted to apply for admission as a slave state, or it had rejected both slavery and the proslavery constitution. The Buchanan administration chose to accept the Lecompton constitution and the first election. The President forwarded the constitution to Congress early in 1858, calling it a law "as fair in its provisions as any that ever passed a legislative body for a similar purpose." He backed down from his previous statement about a public election by explaining: "I then believed, and still believe, that, under the organic act, the Kansas convention were bound to submit this all-important question of slavery to the people. It was never, however, my opinion that, independently of this act, they would have been bound to submit any portion of the constitution to a popular vote, to give it validity." As for the present status of Kansas under the Dred Scott decision, he said, "Kansas is . . . at this moment as much a slave state as Georgia or South Carolina." [10]

The Lecompton constitution, then, was the specific issue which split the Democratic party. Southerners were determined not to let

---

[7] John Basset Moore, ed., *The Works of James Buchanan* (Philadelphia: J.P. Lippincott, 1908–11), X, 151.

[8] Letter to John A. McClernand, November 25, 1857; Nevins, *op. cit.,* p. 250.

[9] Nevins, *op. cit.,* p. 269.

[10] Moore, *op. cit.,* pp. 184–90.

Kansas slip away from them; many threatened that the consequence of such a loss would be secession from the Union. And most Northerners, aligning themselves behind Douglas, were determined to block the Lecompton constitution. Buchanan, who could be as stubborn on some occasions as he was erratic on others, counted on party discipline to get the Lecompton constitution passed. Douglas, "the little giant," one of the most powerful men in the Senate and the party, was ready for a direct confrontation with the administration. "By God, sir," he is reported to have said, "I made Mr. James Buchanan, and by God, sir, I will unmake him." [11]

The administration's influence was strongest in the Senate. Douglas rallied Republican votes to his side, but even with their support the constitution, after much speechmaking, passed easily, 33 to 25. In the House, the opposition was stronger. A dispute over referring the bill to a committee turned into a fist fight between two members which in turn led to a free-for-all involving thirty or so Representatives. There had been fights in Congress before, but in this case the battle was clearly sectional, Northerners against Southerners. Representative Alexander H. Stephens of Virginia, noting the fact, wrote: "All things here are tending to bring my mind to the conclusion that the Union cannot or will not last long." [12]

The Buchanan administration applied every kind of pressure to keep northern Democrats in line: threats and promises, withholding of patronage and government contracts, flattering social invitations from the President and other leaders. But most of the northern Congressmen, for whom anti-Lecompton sentiment in their home states was a stronger form of political pressure than anything that could be exerted by the President, held firm. Finally, in a Senate-House conference committee, a compromise was worked out: The people of Kansas would have a chance to vote on the entire constitution, but there were some peculiar conditions involved: If the constitution passed, Kansas would be eligible for generous grants of federal land; if it did not pass, the territory's admission to statehood would be delayed for approximately two years. Douglas was at first inclined to accept the compromise, then denounced it before the Senate as a bribe. The compromise passed anyway, and in a carefully supervised election three months later the people of Kansas rejected the

---

[11] Nevins, *op. cit.*, p. 250.
[12] *Ibid.*, p. 288.

Lecompton constitution by a vote of 11,812 to 1,926.[13] The compromise bill had been of some face-saving value to the administration, but the President, and southern Democrats, never forgave Douglas. Republicans, however, particularly in the East, praised Douglas for his gallant stand and recommended to fellow Republicans in Illinois that he should be allowed to run for reelection to the Senate without opposition.

This was a curious development, because the Republican party was, as much as anything else, an organized reaction to the policies of Stephen Douglas. The passage of his Kansas-Nebraska Act of 1854, easing the way for expansion of slavery into the Great Plains, had led to anti-Nebraska meetings throughout the North. One of these, held in a Congregational church in Ripon, Wisconsin, on February 28, 1854, is generally commemorated as the birth of the Republican party. The "Republican" party title, only tentatively adopted at first, was felt to be less controversial than—and hence preferable to—"Free-Soil party," which had been the designation of an earlier antislavery political movement.

It was a time of political chaos, and in each election new parties or coalitions appeared and usually disappeared with equal speed. Most politicians who wanted to take some stand against further extension of slavery were afraid of becoming identified with the abolitionists—the militant, religious opponents of slavery who were strongest in New England but were rapidly growing into a national movement. There was another radical movement, prohibition, which also had its stronghold in New England but some strength throughout the country, North and South. And then there were the Know-Nothings, so-called because of the vow of secrecy required of their members, who were alarmed at the rapid rise in immigration to the United States, mainly from Ireland and Germany. In the midst of all this the Republican party arose, a nervous alliance of former Whigs and anti-Nebraska Democrats, free-soilers, abolitionists, and prohibitionists—teeming with radicals in its rank and file and led by politicians who wanted more than anything else to avoid the taint of radicalism.

The party grew rapidly. Horace Greeley, publisher of the *New York Tribune,* joined its ranks, and in 1855 Salmon P. Chase, a Republican candidate, was elected governor of Ohio. That same year

[13] *Ibid.,* p. 301.

Thurlow Weed and Senator William H. Seward, leaders of the New York Whig machine, joined the Republicans. In 1856 the party held its first national convention in Philadelphia and nominated John C. Fremont—explorer, Senator from California, and son-in-law of Missouri's Thomas Hart Benton—as its presidential candidate. Fremont, an attractive man whom Ambrose Bierce had described as having "all of the qualities of genius except ability," [14] ran surprisingly well in 1856, with 114 electoral votes to Buchanan's 174—and the Republican party was suddenly a force in national politics, with growing state organizations throughout the North.

In Illinois former Congressman Abraham Lincoln, who had considered himself a Whig until 1855, used his political contacts and political persuasiveness to coax other Whigs and free-soil Democrats into the new party, and he was the leading contender when Illinois Republicans met in Springfield in 1858 to nominate a senatorial candidate to oppose Stephen Douglas. The Illinois Republicans, who knew Douglas and did not trust him, were ignoring the advice of Horace Greeley and others who felt the best course for Republicans would be to support Douglas and possibly entice him into the party. They believed Douglas could be defeated, but they also knew it would be difficult to oppose a man of his reputation—and particularly so in 1858, while he was fresh from the battle with Buchanan, enjoying the praise of the northern press and letting himself be talked of as an 1860 presidential candidate. Normally, since the Senator was elected by the state legislature, no Republican nomination would be made until the legislature convened in November. The June convention was called in order to select a candidate in advance and give him time to make himself known. It turned out to be a momentous decision.

Lincoln won the nomination easily, as had been expected, and launched his campaign with an acceptance speech to the assembled delegates on the evening of June 16. In his speech Lincoln went dangerously beyond mere free-soil doctrine—he argued that the institution of slavery must not merely be contained to its present boundaries but must also, someday, be done away with entirely:

> *A house divided against itself cannot stand. I believe this government cannot endure, permanently half slave and half free.*

[14] George H. Mayer, *The Republican Party 1854–1966* (New York: Oxford University Press, 1967), p. 42.

> *I do not expect the Union to be dissolved—I do not expect the house to fall—but I do expect it will cease to be divided. It will become all one thing, or all the other. Either the opponents of slavery, will arrest the further spread of it, and place it where the public mind shall rest in the belief that it is in course of ultimate extinction; or its advocates will push it forward, till it shall become alike lawful in all the states, old as well as new —North as well as South.*[15]

From this high level of rhetoric, Lincoln descended to a distorted description of Douglas' position, charging his opponent with being part of a conspiracy to extend slavery. The struggle over the Lecompton constitution, Lincoln said, was only superficial; beneath it one could see the Dred Scott decision, the policies of Buchanan, and the policies of Douglas, all fitting together, as if the authors had "all understood one another from the beginning, and all worked upon a common plan or draft drawn up before the first lick was struck." The next logical addition, he suggested, would be a Supreme Court decision

> *. . . declaring that the Constitution of the United States does not permit a state to exclude slavery from its limits. . . . We shall lie down pleasantly dreaming that the people of Missouri are on the verge of making their state free; and we shall awake to the reality, instead, that the Supreme Court has made Illinois a slave state.*[16]

A few weeks later, Douglas returned from Washington to begin his campaign. At Chicago he was welcomed like a hero; there were banners proclaiming "Douglas, the Champion of Popular Sovereignty," draped from buildings alongside United States flags, and a crowd estimated at thirty thousand gathered outside his hotel to cheer him as he appeared on the balcony.[17] In that speech, Douglas called the congressional compromise on Lecompton a "moral victory," and said he regarded "the great principle of popular sovereignty as having been vindicated and made triumphant in this land as a permanent rule of public policy in the organization of territories and the admission of new states." [18]

The issue, Douglas argued, was not slavery, but the right of people to choose their own institutions:

[15] *Illinois State Journal,* June 18, 1858, quoted in Angle, *op. cit.,* p. 1.
[16] *Ibid.,* pp. 6–7.
[17] *Chicago Times,* July 10, 1858, quoted in *ibid.,* p. 11.
[18] *Ibid.,* p. 14.

*My objection to the Lecompton contrivance was that it under-
took to put a constitution on the people of Kansas against their
will, in opposition to their wishes, and thus violated the great
principle upon which all our institutions rest. It is no answer
to this argument to say that slavery is an evil and hence should
not be tolerated. You must allow the people to decide for
themselves whether it is a good or an evil. You allow them to
decide for themselves whether they desire a Maine liquor law
or not; you allow them to decide for themselves what kind of
common schools they will have; what system of banking they
will adopt, or whether they will adopt any at all; you allow
them to decide for themselves the relations between husband
and wife, parent and child, the guardian and ward; in fact,
you allow them to decide for themselves all other questions,
and why not upon this question? Whenever you put a limita-
tion upon the right of any people to decide what laws they
want, you have destroyed the fundamental principle of self-
government.*[19]

Then—while Lincoln, who was seated among the dignitaries on
the Tremont House balcony, listened—Douglas addressed himself
directly to the "house divided" speech, which he said was really a
clear and bold advocacy of "a war of sections, a war of North against
the South, of the free states against the slave states—a war of ex-
termination—to be continued relentlessly until the one or the other
shall be subdued and all the states shall either become free or become
slave." [20] Douglas also touched on the question of Negro citizenship:

*I am opposed to negro equality. I repeat that this nation is a
white people—a people composed of European descendants—
a people that have established this government for themselves
and their posterity, and I am in favor of preserving not only
the purity of the blood, but the purity of the government from
any mixture or amalgamation with inferior races. I have seen
the effects of this mixture of superior and inferior races—
this amalgamation of white men and Indians and negroes; we
have seen it in Mexico, in Central America, in South America,
and in all the Spanish-American states, and its result has been
degeneration, demoralization, and degradation below the
capacity for self-government.*
     *I am opposed to taking any step that recognizes the negro
man or the Indian as the equal of the white man. I am opposed
to giving him a voice in the administration of the government.
I would extend to the negro, and the Indian, and to all de-*

[19] *Ibid.*, p. 17.
[20] *Ibid.*, p. 18.

pendent races every right, every privilege, and every immunity consistent with the safety and welfare of the white races; but equality they never should have, either political or social, or in any other respect whatever.[21]

This was to become an important issue in the campaign, and one which would put Lincoln on the defensive. There were strong anti-Negro sentiments in Illinois, particularly in the southern part of the state, and everywhere the consideration which did the most to place abolitionists outside the boundaries of political respectability was the question of what would be the role of freed blacks if slavery should be outlawed. The next day Lincoln tried to put the issue away with humor:

We were often—more than once at least—in the course of Judge Douglas' speech last night, reminded that this government was made for white men—that he believed it was made for white men. Well, that is putting it into a shape in which no one wants to deny it, but the Judge then goes into his passion for drawing inferences that are not warranted. I protest, now and forever, against that counterfeit logic which presumes that because I do not want a negro woman for a slave, I do necessarily want her for a wife. My understanding is that I need not have her for either, but as God made us separate, we can leave one another alone and do one another much good thereby.[22]

This got laughs and cheers in the appropriate places from his Chicago audience, but before the campaign was over Lincoln would find it necessary to make stronger statements about the Negro question elsewhere in the state.

This exchange of speeches had opened the campaign and stated the basic themes which would be heard in it, but there was not yet any formal agreement between the two candidates about a debate. That came a few weeks later, after both had made appearances in Bloomington and Springfield.

In the 1850's—a time when election campaigns were followed with intense interest, when political speeches served as drama, spectator sport, and public entertainment—speaking tours were obligatory and debates were common. They made it easier for rural voters to hear both candidates, and also assured both sides of larger audiences than they might have had otherwise. It was Lincoln who

[21] *Ibid.*, p. 23.
[22] *Ibid.*, p. 39.

issued the challenge, in a letter to Douglas inviting him to "divide time and address the same audiences." [23]

There has been much historical speculation about why Douglas accepted the challenge, and whether it was wise of him to do so. Certain things about the decision, at any rate, are clear: One is that Douglas had great confidence in his own ability as a speaker; another is that he had considerable respect for Lincoln's talents as well— he had called him "the strong man of his party, the best stump speaker in the West." [24] Also, Douglas had his eye on the presidency in 1860: He knew that such a debate would be widely publicized, that by debating in Illinois he could present himself and his positions to the entire country.

Douglas agreed to debate Lincoln in seven towns, one in each of the congressional districts in which they had not already appeared. The towns chosen were Ottawa, Freeport, Jonesboro, Charleston, Galesburg, Quincy, and Alton. The first meeting would be at Ottawa, on August 21, and the last would be at Alton, on October 15. As for the time limitations, it was agreed—and the agreement is an impressive sign of the staying power of both audiences and candidates in those days—that the first speaker would have an hour, the second an hour and a half, and the first another half-hour for reply. The farmers and townspeople who would assemble for the events, then, would be guaranteed a good solid three hours of political oratory.

The campaign, it must be remembered, was a campaign on behalf of candidates for the state legislature, who would in turn elect a United States Senator. It was believed that the Republicans had a fair chance of winning a majority.

They had put up a good showing in the previous election, and their numbers were increasing; but they were at a disadvantage in that the heaviest Republican vote was in the fast-growing urban north of the state, which was underrepresented—the legislature had not been reapportioned since 1852, and as the apportionment stood the rural southern counties had a definite advantage. It was expected that the northern part of the state would elect Republicans and the southern part Democrats. The uncertain area was the middle, popu-

---

[23] Nevins, *op. cit.*, p. 374.
[24] Carl Sandburg, *Abraham Lincoln: The Prairie Years and the War Years* (1-vol. ed.) (New York: Harcourt, Brace & World, Inc., 1954), p. 138.

lated mostly by former Whigs whose behavior in a contest between Democrats and Republicans could not be predicted.[25]

Although Lincoln had no national reputation, the news that Douglas had agreed to debate a Republican candidate captured the public imagination. One of the reasons the campaign found its way so quickly into American legend is the fact that it was a national news event of prime importance even while it was happening. It received unprecedented journalistic attention—for the first time, newspapermen traveled with the candidates, filing stenographically recorded reports of the speeches and "color" stories about the towns and the lighter campaign incidents.[26]

The first debate took place in the town of Ottawa, in the northern part of the state, on a broiling hot August day. According to the correspondent of the *Chicago Press and Tribune*:

> *Before breakfast Ottawa was beleaguered with a multiplying host from all points of the compass. At eight o'clock the streets and avenues leading from the country were so enveloped with dust that the town resembled a vast smoke house. Teams, trains and processions poured in from every direction like an army with banners. National flags, mottoes and devices fluttered and stared from every street corner. Military companies and bands of music monopolized the thoroughfares around the court house and the public square. Two brass twelve pounders banged away in the centre of the city and drowned the hubbub of the multitude with their own higher capacities for hubbub.*[27]

Douglas spoke first, and for an hour the crowd of 12,000 (about twice the population of the town) stood in the sun in the public square and listened to the short, dynamic Senator as he accused Lincoln of "following the example and lead of all the little Abolition orators, who go around and lecture in the basements of schools and churches." Where Lincoln had a few weeks before tried to persuade the voters that Douglas' policies would lead eventually to slavery in Illinois, Douglas now told them that Lincoln's policies would lead to citizenship for freed Negroes in Illinois:

> *We have provided that the negro shall not be a slave, and we have also provided that he shall not be a citizen, but protect*

[25] Angle, *op. cit.*, pp. xxiii–xxiv.
[26] *Ibid.*, p. xxiv.
[27] Weekly issue, August 26, 1858, quoted in *ibid.*, p. 102.

*him in his civil rights, in his life, his person and his property,
only depriving him of all political rights whatsoever, and refusing to put him on an equality with the white man. That
policy of Illinois is satisfactory to the Democratic party and to
me, and if it were to the Republicans, there would then be no
question upon the subject; but the Republicans say that he
ought to be made a citizen, and when he becomes a citizen he
becomes your equal, with all your rights and privileges."* [28]

Lincoln, then, was forced to deny that he was an abolitionist,
and also to clarify his position toward Negroes. He said:

*I have no purpose directly or indirectly to interfere with the
institution of slavery in the states where it exists. I believe I
have no lawful right to do so, and I have no inclination to do
so. I have no purpose to introduce political and social equality
between the white and the black races. There is a physical difference between the two, which in my judgement will probably
forever forbid their living together upon the footing of perfect
equality, and inasmuch as it becomes a necessity that there
must be a difference, I, as well as Judge Douglas, am in favor
of the race to which I belong, having the superior position. I
have never said anything to the contrary, but I hold that notwithstanding all this, there is no reason in the world why the
negro is not entitled to all the natural rights enumerated in the
Declaration of Independence, the right to life, liberty and the
pursuit of happiness. I hold that he is as much entitled to these
as the white man. I agree with Judge Douglas he is not my
equal in many respects—certainly not in color, perhaps not in
moral or intellectual endowment. But in the right to eat the
bread, without leave of everybody else, which his own hand
earns, he is my equal and the equal of Judge Douglas, and the
equal of every living man.* [29]

And, although Lincoln had refused to be called an abolitionist,
he did repeat the basic argument of his "house divided" speech.
Slavery, he said, had always "failed to be a bond of union, and, on
the contrary, been an apple of discord and an element of division."
The fact that the nation had been able to exist so far with some
states free and some slave—a point which Douglas had not failed to
emphasize—he accounted for "by looking at the position in which
our fathers originally placed it—restricting it from the new territories

[28] *Ibid.,* pp. 111–12.
[29] *Ibid.,* p. 117. Italics, etc., are as used in the original (1860) published
version of the debates, using as text Lincoln's scrapbook, which contained the
Chicago Press and Tribune reports of his speeches.

where it had not gone, and legislating to cut off its source by the abrogation of the slave trade, thus putting the seal of legislation *against its spread*. The public mind *did* rest in the belief that it was in the course of ultimate extinction." [30]

Both candidates, at the end of the debate, were wildly cheered by their supporters, and Lincoln was carried away on the shoulders of a group of his admirers. Newspaper reports of the outcome of the contest were equally partisan. The *Philadelphia Press* said of Lincoln: "Poor fellow! he was writhing in the powerful grasp of an intellectual giant. His speech amounted to nothing." [31] The *New York Evening Post* reporter, on the other hand, described how Lincoln's bony countenance seemed to come alive as he talked, so that:

> *every lineament, now so ill-formed, grows brilliant and expressive, and you have before you a man of rare power and of strong magnetic influence. He* takes *the people every time, and there is no getting away from his sturdy good sense, his unaffected sincerity, and the unceasing play of his good humor, which accompanies his close logic and smoothes the way to conviction.*[32]

In the five intervening days between the first debate and the second Lincoln made three speeches and Douglas, who was having trouble with his throat, made one. The debaters came together again on August 27 in Freeport, near the northern border; the crowd was as large as before, and the weather was cold with occasional drizzling rain. In the Freeport debate—probably the most extensively discussed and quoted of the entire series—Lincoln spoke first, answering some questions which had been raised earlier by Douglas, and then asking Douglas some questions.

The questions Lincoln answered had to do with his views on the fugitive slave law, the admission of new slave states to the Union, the abolition of slavery in the District of Columbia, the prohibition of the slave trade between states, and the prohibition of slavery in the territories. Lincoln stated that he was in favor of retaining the fugitive slave law, at least for the present; that he was not opposed to admitting new slave states if the people in the territory clearly desired the institution, although he would "be exceedingly glad to know that there would never be another slave state admitted into

---

[30] *Ibid.,* p. 119.
[31] Sandburg, *op. cit.,* p. 139.
[32] Nevins, *op. cit.,* p. 377.

the Union"; that he favored gradual elimination of slavery from the District of Columbia if it could be done fairly, with compensation to slaveowners; that he was not ready to take a stand about the constitutionality of prohibiting the slave trade between states; and that he was "impliedly, if not expressly, pledged to a belief in the *right* and *duty* of Congress to prohibit slavery in all the United States territories." [33]

Lincoln then put to Douglas four questions, of which the second was the most explosive: "Can the people of a United States territory, in any lawful way, against the wish of any citizen of the United States, exclude slavery from its limits prior to the formation of a state constitution?" [34] The question attacked Douglas at one of his weakest points. He was the champion of popular sovereignity, yet he had supported the Dred Scott decision, which obliged territories to recognize the legal property rights of slaveowners. The two, it would seem, were incompatible, and any answer which threatened the future of the Dred Scott decision would undoubtedly hurt Douglas —if not in Illinois in 1858, then certainly in the South in 1860.

Actually, Lincoln had a good idea of what Douglas' answer would be. Over a year earlier, Douglas had stated in a speech at Springfield that there would still be *de facto* prohibition of slavery in the territories because the right to own slaves "remains a barren and worthless right, unless sustained, protected and enforced by appropriate police regulations and local legislation prescribing adequate remedies for its violation." [35] And when he rose to reply to Lincoln at Freeport Douglas made essentially the same statement:

> *It matters not what way the Supreme Court may hereafter decide as to the abstract question whether slavery may or may not go into a territory under the Constitution, the people have the lawful means to introduce it or exclude it as they please, for the reason that slavery cannot exist a day or an hour anywhere, unless it is supported by local police regulations.*[36]

But if Douglas' answer to the celebrated "Freeport question" was not new to Douglas, it was news to many of the people who read about it around the country, and it is an example of the effect the

33 Angle, *op cit.*, pp. 140–43.

34 *Ibid.*, pp. 143–44.

35 Don E. Fehrenbacher, "Lincoln, Douglas, and the Freeport Question," *American Historical Review,* LXVI (April 1961), 610.

36 *Ibid.*, p. 600.

debates were to have on Douglas' political fortunes. Although he was holding his own against Lincoln in Illinois, he was being forced by a clever opponent to make statements that would complete his estrangement from the Buchanan administration and the Democrats of the South.

After Freeport more than two weeks elapsed before the next debate, and both campaigners used their time to make speeches throughout the critical central portion of the state.

The third debate took place in Jonesboro, at the far southern tip of the state. It was an area where proslavery sentiment was strong, where there were few Republicans and the Democrats were more of the Buchanan than the Douglas variety. The turn-out was small, and for the most part both candidates confined themselves to restatements and elaborations of their views on the issues that had been raised in earlier speeches. There was, in fact, little introduction of really new material into the campaign after the first two debates; there were any number of other questions that might have been argued, but the candidates and the public were in the grip of one single issue, and the debates were, finally, an exhaustive process of examining as many of its moral and legal aspects as the politics of the time allowed.

So at Jonesboro the candidates argued about slavery, and on September 18 they met for the fourth time, at Charleston, and argued about slavery again. The Charleston crowd was nearer the size of the first debates, twelve to fifteen thousand, and the *Chicago Times* reported the Democratic parade which escorted Douglas into town:

> *It was a glorious sight to see the long line of teams filled with men, women, and children, extending across the prairie as far as the eye could reach, the flags gaily flying in the morning breeze, and the brass instruments of the numerous bands gleaming in the sun. At every house and every cross-road the procession received accessions, until when entering Charleston, it was nearly two miles long. On the outskirts of the town it was met by the citizens of Charleston and the delegations from the western part of Coles and the adjoining counties, who carried several large and splendid banners, upon one of which appeared, "Edgar county good for five hundred majority for the Little Giant," and on another, "This government was made for white men—Douglas for life."* [37]

[37] *Chicago Times*, Sept. 21, 1858, quoted in Angle, *op. cit.*, pp. 232–33.

The pro-Lincoln *Press and Tribune,* however, talked only of
the Republican procession, "the most formidable array of the campaign," with innumerable banners which "fluttered in the wind farther
than the .eye could reach," and dismissed the Douglas escort as, by
comparison, "a very puny affair." [38]

Lincoln, whom Douglas had successfully placed on the defensive about the matter of racial equality, opened his speech with what
he described as a brief clarification of his position:

> *I will say then that I am not, nor ever have been in favor of
> bringing about in any way the social and political equality of
> the white and black races,—that I am not or ever have been
> in favor of making voters or jurors of negroes, nor of qualifing
> them to hold office, nor to intermarry with white people, and
> I will say in addition to this that there is a physical difference
> between the white and black races which I believe will for ever
> forbid the two races living together on terms of social and
> political equality.*[39]

The bulk of the Charleston debate was an exchange between
two candidates of their respective conspiracy charges: Lincoln accused Douglas of being part of a conspiracy to extend slavery, and
Douglas accused Lincoln of being part of a conspiracy to abolish it.

By the time of the fifth debate, at Galesburg on October 7,
the summer weather had ended, and the crowd—the largest at any
debate thus far, numbering well over fifteen thousand—stood shiver-
ing in what one reporter described as "an Arctic frost, accompanied
by a sour northwest wind" as they listened to the candidates speak
from a platform on the campus of Knox College.[40] Douglas complained that the Buchanan administration was using all its power in
the state to defeat him, and—in a passage that was more prophetic
than he could have known—called the Republican party a dangerously sectional organization, whose leaders hoped "that they will be
able to unite the northern states in one great sectional party, and
inasmuch as the North is the strongest section, that they will thus
be enabled to out vote, conquer, govern and control the South. Is
there," he asked, "a Republican residing in Galesburg who can
travel into Kentucky and carry his principles with him?" [41]

38 *Chicago Press and Tribune,* Sept. 21, 1858, quoted *in ibid.,* p. 234.
39 *Ibid.,* p. 235.
40 *Ibid.,* p. 285.
41 *Ibid.,* p. 290.

Lincoln replied that the Republican party's platform was sound, and asked: "Is it the true test of the soundness of a doctrine, that in some places people won't let you proclaim it?" [42] He also predicted that the time was rapidly approaching for Douglas "when his pill of sectionalism, which he has been thrusting down the throats of Republicans for years past, will be crowded down his own throat." [43]

At Quincy, a week later, the two weary candidates came together again, and Lincoln attempted to reduce the whole difference of opinion to its simplest terms: "no other than the difference between the men who think slavery is a wrong and those who do not think it wrong." [44] The Republicans were the former group, the Democrats the latter. Douglas defended his concept of popular sovereignty, and what the people of Quincy heard, in essence, were new approaches to the same arguments about Dred Scott and conspiracies.

The final debate, at Alton, took place two days later. Douglas had complained before that the Buchanan administration was trying to sabotage his campaign, and now he charged that "in this state, every postmaster, every route holder, forfeits his head the moment he expresses a preference for the Democratic candidates against Lincoln and his Abolition associates." [45] Lincoln expressed his approval of Douglas' war with the administration, and noted that it seemed to be improving in quality:

> *At Quincy, day before yesterday, he was a little more severe upon the administration than I had heard him upon any former occasion, and I took pains to compliment him for it. I then told him to "Give it to them with all the power he had;" and as some of them were present I told them I would be very much obliged if they would* give it to him *in about the same way.*[46]

When the debates had ended the candidates continued to make individual appearances during the last two weeks of the campaign. Their respective supporters continued to argue over who had come off the better in the competition; but one consequence of the debates was already evident, and the *Press and Tribune* said it clearly in an editorial a few days before the election:

[42] *Ibid.*, p. 300.
[43] *Ibid.*, pp. 301–2.
[44] *Ibid.*, p. 332.
[45] *Ibid.*, p. 370.
[46] *Ibid.*, p. 376.

*Mr. Lincoln's efforts in this canvass have . . . made for him
a splendid national reputation. Identified all his life long with
the old Whig party, always in a minority in Illinois, his fine
abilities and attainments have necessarily been confined to a
very limited sphere. He entered upon the canvass with a reputation confined to his own state—he closes it with his name a
household word wherever the principles he holds are honored,
and with the respect of his opponents in all sections of the
country.*[47]

On November 2, 1858, the voters of Illinois went to the polls
to elect their state legislators. The result, in terms of total votes cast,
was almost an exact tie between Republicans and Democrats: Republicans 125,275; Douglas Democrats 121,900; Buchanan Democrats 5,071.[48] If the apportionment of seats had been more favorable
to the Republican northern counties, Lincoln might well have been
elected. As it stood, the Democrats retained control of both branches
of the legislature; when that body met on January 6, 1859, there were
54 Democrats and 41 Republicans and, in a strict party ballot, Stephen
Douglas was reelected United States Senator from Illinois.

Elsewhere in the North the 1858 elections were a disaster for
Democrats, and Douglas' reelection was undoubtedly a great personal triumph. In that moment of victory, Douglas could hardly have
suspected that the man he had just defeated would be the next
President of the United States. But one of the things Douglas had
done in the debates was to elevate Lincoln to his own level, giving
him stature and fame as a major spokesman of Republicanism. And
another thing the debates did was to force Douglas, competing for
election in Illinois, to make statements that would forever alienate him
from the South.

By 1860, as Lincoln had predicted, Douglas found the pill of
sectionalism crowded down his own throat. In that year the Democratic party split—the northern wing nominating Douglas for President and the southern wing nominating John C. Breckenridge of
Kentucky. At the Republican national convention Lincoln was nominated, after overcoming the early lead of Senator William Seward of
New York. In the presidential election there were four candidates—
Lincoln, Douglas, Breckenridge, and Senator John Bell of Tennessee,

---

[47] *Chicago Press and Tribune*, Oct. 29, 1858, quoted in *ibid.*, p. 405.
[48] Nevins, *op. cit.*, pp. 397–98.

representing the Constitutional Unionist party. Lincoln won easily, and his victory triggered a secession movement which picked up support and momentum with unexpected speed throughout the South.

The Republicans in victory were almost as confused as the Democrats in defeat. The Union was disintegrating, and the party leaders, including Lincoln, were uncertain about how to deal with the crisis. The party's ideology, mildly idealistic and moderately anti-slavery, had never really confronted the possibility of a war over slavery. The course of events forced Lincoln into a historic role which, left alone, he would never have sought. A recent analysis of the party's history says of Lincoln: "It is probable that he was at least a step ahead of the Republican party generally in his sympathy for the Negro as a human being. But on one point he was in firm accord with the Republican position. Lincoln would by no means risk war to free the slaves." [49] But war came, and "the shells which fell on Fort Sumter ended the equivocation. The South had given a new mission to the Republican party." [50]

The Lincoln-Douglas debates may not have been great distillations of political wisdom. The two candidates occasionally rose to eloquence, but more often their speeches were windy, repetitive, and full of distortions of one another's previous remarks. But whatever the merits of the dialogue, the debates were historically important: They made Lincoln a national figure and helped to polarize national opinion over slavery. The candidates were forced by the challenge of winning in Illinois into statements of position which made them both unacceptable to the South. The 1858 campaign was a major event in the sequence which led to the Civil War and the abolition of slavery, and it helped to bring about an alignment of political parties which would endure for over a hundred years.

[49] Milton Viorst, *Fall from Grace: The Republican Party and the Puritan Ethic* (New York: New American Library, 1968), p. 43.
[50] *Ibid.*, p. 47.

RECONSTRUCTION
AND
WHITE SUPREMACY

2

1876
South Carolina
Daniel H. Chamberlain vs. *Wade Hampton*

Reconstruction in the American South died state by state, and in nearly every case the sign of its death was the return of control of state government to loyal Southerners who had supported the Confederate cause and who now supported the cause of white supremacy. In some states, conservative governments were back in office within a few years after the end of the Civil War: In Tennessee, Virginia, Georgia, and North Carolina the coalition of freed Negroes, northern carpetbaggers, and cooperative southern scalawags remembered by southerners as the threefold villain of the Reconstruction era was never fully in control. In other states the struggle of the southerners to regain "home rule"—meaning white supremacy—took a longer time, but in the end was no less successful.

In South Carolina, the state where the war had begun with the firing on Fort Sumter, radical Reconstruction elements were still in power in 1875, ten years after Lee's surrender to Grant at Appomattox. The governor was Massachusetts-born Daniel H. Chamberlain. The majority of the members of the state legislature were blacks, and in the state population as a whole the whites were a minority of about 40 per cent.[1]

The government included many men who were honestly trying to build the new South—in one image or another—and others who

[1] Population according to the 1870 census was: white 289,667; Negro 415,814. *Handbook of South Carolina* (Columbus, S.C.: The State Company, 1908), p. 524.

were mainly trying to build their own bank accounts. It was the latter group who set the tone of the state capital. One northerner who spent some time there recalled later:

> *The body as a whole was in a legislative atmosphere so saturated with corruption that the honest and honorable members of either race had no more influence on it than an orchid might have on a mustard patch. . . . The capital atmosphere seemed to produce a peculiar intoxicating effect. Just to breathe it made one feel like going out and picking a pocket.*[2]

Chamberlain, an abolitionist before the war, had come to South Carolina in 1866 to plant cotton. He drifted into politics, served as attorney general for four years, and during his term was involved in a few of the profit-making operations—such as the sale of the state-owned Greenville and Columbia Railroad—by which Governor R. K. Scott, Senator "Honest John" Patterson, and others were enriching themselves at public expense. But when he ran for governor in 1874 it was as a reform candidate, and when he was elected he began to show a serious concern for the future of the South.

"The evils which surround us . . ." he promised in his inaugural address, "will be transitory. The great permanent influences which rule in civilized society are constantly at work and will slowly lift us into a better life." [3] Southern historians usually talk of him with grudging respect: Hampton M. Jarrell, for example, calls him "one of the most able, and, in some respects, most admirable men produced in the South by Radical Republicanism." [4] Chamberlain's attempts at reform won him some friends among conservative South Carolinians during his two-year term, and as the 1876 election approached he hoped to be returned to office with a wide basis of support—from Democrats as well as Republicans—which would give him strength to deal with the less responsible elements in his own party.

But the position of those Democrats who believed in supporting Chamberlain was shaken late in 1875 when, on a day the governor was absent from the capital, the legislature, defying him, elected as

---

[2] Reprinted from *Wade Hampton and the Negro*, by Hampton M. Jarrell, p. 32, by permission of the University of South Carolina Press. Copyright 1949 by the University of South Carolina Press.

[3] David Duncan Wallace, *South Carolina: A Short History* (Chapel Hill: University of North Carolina Press, 1951), p. 593.

[4] Jarrell, *op. cit.*, p. 41.

circuit judges a pair of men who were in southern eyes the worst possible kind of Reconstructionists. One was W. J. Whipper, a Negro, and the other was Franklin J. Moses, Jr., a former governor who had been indicted for theft during his term of office. Chamberlain's statement to the press that he considered their election "a horrible disaster" [5] probably helped him hold onto his support among the South Carolina whites, as did his refusal to sign the commissions of the two judges-elect. But there was in the state an increasingly large and active group of militant whites who believed that it might be possible to win control of the government away from the Reconstructionists entirely and elect an administration of true southern Democrats, "from governor to coroner." As the factions divided, the Democrats who favored supporting Chamberlain became known as Fusionists, those who favored trying to elect an all-Democratic administration as Straightouts. Among the Straightouts there was much interest in what was called the "Mississippi Plan," a systematic campaign of intimidation of Negro voters which had enabled whites in that state to win control from a black majority.

Both Fusionists and Straightouts were trying, in their opposing ways, to gain a greater voice for whites in the state government when, on a hot and humid day in June of 1876, the governor went to Charleston to attend the celebration of the centennial of the Revolutionary battle of Fort Moultrie. Chamberlain rode in a carriage in the parade and delivered the opening address from a decorated stand in the city park. The grand marshal, leading the parade on horseback, was Wade Hampton, the large (six foot, 240 pounds) and imposing South Carolinian who had been before the war one of the richest landowners in the South and a state senator, during the war a famous general and chief of cavalry of the Confederate Army, and since the war—according to a correspondent to *The Nation*—one of the "most popular and best-loved men in the South today." [6] The people of Charleston cheered both the Confederate hero and the Reconstructionist governor, and at a banquet that evening Hampton sat on one side of the toastmaster and Chamberlain on the other. Everything was cordial between the two, but they were about to become opponents in one of the bitterest election contests in the history of the South.

[5] *Ibid.,* p. 46.
[6] *The Nation,* I, (1865), 524, quoted in Manly Wade Wellman, *Giant in Gray* (New York: Charles Scribner's Sons, 1949), p. 200.

Hampton had been promoted for the governorship by various groups from time to time, but at the time he came to Charleston he was not planning to run for the office. However, on the train returning home from the celebration, he happened to meet General Martin Witherspoon Gary, who had served under him during the war. Gary, sometimes called the "bald eagle," was a small, goateed, hot-tempered man, a leader of the Straightouts and also a Democratic leader in Edgefield County—an area with a large Negro population and a tradition of Ku Klux Klan activity. Gary urged Hampton to seek the Democratic nomination for the governorship, and Hampton agreed to consider it.

While Hampton was considering, an incident took place which undoubtedly helped the Straightout cause. The site of the incident, which became known as the Hamburg Massacre, was a little town in Aiken County, which adjoined and had once been a part of Edgefield County, in the southwestern part of the state where advocacy of the Mississippi Plan was so strong that the idea was already being referred to as the Edgefield Plan. The trouble began on the Fourth of July, 1876, when some Negro militiamen, parading in the street, got into a scuffle with some young whites who were passing through Hamburg. The two whites complained that the blacks had been obstructing the highway, and a few days later the militiamen were to appear before a trial justice. Several hundred armed white men came to Hamburg on the day of the trial and the attorney for the whites—General M. C. Butler, who was also a Straightout leader and father of one of the young men—demanded that the militiamen turn in their weapons. They refused and took refuge in an abandoned warehouse used as their armory, where they were beseiged by the whites. One of the white men was killed in that battle and so was a Negro town marshal who happened to be in the building. The whites began firing on the armory with a small cannon, and the militiamen fled from the building. They were rounded up and taken to a place near the railroad, where a large group of armed whites stood guard over them. At about two o'clock the next morning, five of the Negroes were taken from the group, one by one, and shot.

What angered white Democrats was not the incident itself but Chamberlain's subsequent handling of it, which they considered to be unfairly pro-Negro: he called for federal troops, used an all-black coroner's jury to investigate the killings, and had 61 white men— many of them prominent citizens—bound over. It made it easier for

Straightouts to argue that Reconstructionist rule inevitably meant Negro rule and that the only choice for the whites lay between political victory for the Democrats or armed revolt that would result in military government.

On August 12, Chamberlain ventured into Edgefield County to make a campaign address. He found the town of Edgefield packed with people; armed white riders gave the rebel yell as they galloped through the streets, and part of the reviewing stand had already collapsed from the weight of the crowds surging across it. At the same moment that Chamberlain walked onto the stand, so did Generals Butler and Gary, who demanded a "division of time" so they could make speeches also. Gary and Butler proceeded to make bitter denunciations of Chamberlain as the crowd yelled its approval, and after some three hours of chaos the governor left, "amid a torrent of jeers and yells which continued to reach my ears without cessation until I had passed beyond the limits of the town." [7]

A few days later, when the Democrats held their state convention at Columbia, Wade Hampton attended as a delegate from Richland County. Butler made the speech nominating Hampton for governor, and Hampton, after asking the convention to consider other candidates, was nominated by acclamation. In accepting the nomination, he made a speech that was far more moderate in tone than those of the Straightout leaders who had been backing him.

> *I shall be Governor of the whole people, knowing no party, making no vindictive discriminations, holding the scales of justice with firm and impartial hand, seeing, as far as in me lies, that the laws are enforced in justice tempered with mercy, protecting all classes alike. . . .*[8]

The Straightouts had found themselves a strong candidate, and Hampton's emergence as the Democratic nominee was a final blow to the Fusionist movement. And, although many northerners saw him as an example of the most dangerous kind of unrepentant rebel— mainly because he had taken a stand against the constitutionality of Reconstruction at the 1868 Democratic convention—Hampton's views were in fact relatively moderate. Before the war he had defended the Union and opposed the reopening of the slave trade. After the war he had advocated "conferring the elective franchise on the negro, on

[7] Walter Allen, *Governor Chamberlain's Administration in South Carolina* (New York: G.P. Putnam's Sons, 1883), p. 376.

[8] Jarrell, *op. cit.,* p. 52.

precisely the same terms as it is to be exercised by the white man
. . . a slight educational and property qualification *for all classes*." [9]

Thus on the surface the election was a contest between moderate
men: a carpetbagger who wanted to be a respected statesman in his
adopted home, and a Southern aristocrat who promised the freed
Negro a voice in government. But just below the surface, it was
another kind of contest entirely. The situation in South Carolina,
General Gary had said, "is a question of race, and not of politics." [10]
For the Democrats to win it was necessary to unite the whites and
divide the blacks—and while Hampton tried to use talk to persuade
Negroes to vote for him, Gary used terror.

"The only way to bring about prosperity in this state," said
Hampton in the speech which formally opened his campaign, "is to
bring the two races in friendly relations together." [11] Throughout his
campaign he appealed, in his aristocratic way, for black votes. One
reporter who traveled with him wrote:

> *When he addressed the negroes, as he invariably did, whether*
> *many or few of them were at his meetings, he talked as if he*
> *had been on the steps of his plantation house reasoning with*
> *the people on his place seeking information and advice, kindly,*
> *friendly, and frankly, without offensive condescension, with no*
> *wheedling, no sentimental appeals, except in reference to the*
> *past glories of the state and hopes for her future.*[12]

While Hampton went about speaking for peace and cooperation,
the Straightouts mobilized as if for war. "Rifle clubs" and "sabre
clubs" were organized throughout the state, and under the leadership of Generals Gary and Butler they became famous as the "Red
Shirts." The uniform was adopted in reference to the Republican
tactic of "waving the bloody shirt" to prove anti-Reconstructionist
violence, and it became—together with the cry of "Hurrah for
Hampton"—a suitably romantic symbol of white unity and determination.

> *Unexpectedly, and without apparent reason, mounted Red*
> *Shirts would appear on the streets of a town, or on the roads,*
> *firing pistols in the air, and making the welkin ring with their*
> *clamor. The noise and tumult was well calculated greatly to*

9 *Ibid.*, p. 19.
10 *Ibid.*, p. 57.
11 Wellman, *op. cit.*, p. 260.
12 Jarrell, *op. cit.*, p. 63.

*exaggerate in the negro's mind the numbers of the mounted
Red Shirts and to strike terror into his heart.*[13]

No political gathering in the campaign of 1876 was complete
without a body of Red Shirts. If the meeting was for Hampton, they
paraded through the streets like a military honor guard. If the meeting was for Chamberlain they would either stand silently—sometimes
on foot, sometimes on horseback—on the outskirts of the crowd, or
they would advance to the platform, as they had during the chaotic
rally at Edgefield, and ask for a division of time so that one of their
number could also address the crowd.

The Red Shirts were not the only armed men in South Carolina.
There were federal troops, armed Negro and white militia, and Negro
secret societies with such names as the Live Oaks and the Hunkidoris.

In such a climate, it was inevitable that there would be outbreaks of violence, and before the campaign was over there were
many of them. One of the worst was in Ellenton, about 20 miles from
Hamburg. As is usually the case with such incidents, accounts of
the causes and course of the slaughter differ enormously. Southern
partisans say two Negroes attempted to rob a white woman, and
whites formed a legal posse to capture the fugitives. The governor's
account says that white rifle clubs organized as cavalry units and
moved out, first against Negro Republican clubs and then against
Negroes in general, in a deliberate campaign to frighten them into
submission. Whatever the initial cause of the fighting, it went on for
several days, and before it was over, at least one white man and
thirty to forty blacks had been killed. One of the blacks killed was
Simon P. Coker, a member of the state legislature and a delegate to
the Republican convention which only a few days before had renominated Chamberlain for the governorship.

Chamberlain claimed that the Straightout leaders had put the
Mississippi Plan into effect, and were conducting a massive and well-
organized campaign to intimidate Negro voters. In a letter to the
New York Tribune he said:

> *In the county of Aiken and the adjoining counties of Edgefield
> and Barnwell the white Democrats began as early as last July
> systematically to inform the colored Republicans that the
> Democrats had resolved to carry the coming election, and that
> the colored Republicans would have to vote with them. In*

[13] Henry T. Thompson, *Ousting the Carpetbagger from South Carolina*
(Columbia, S.C.: The R. L. Bryan Company, 1927), p. 117.

August and the early part of September these threats took a more definite form. The colored Republicans were told far and wide that if they did not vote the Democratic ticket they would be killed. Scarcely a colored man can now be found to whom these threats were not personally made. They were ordered to discontinue their political meetings, and were told that a list of all their leaders had been made out, and that these leaders would be killed.[14]

The governor also claimed that economic pressure was being applied. He had a considerable amount of documentary support for this charge, since many Democratic clubs had publicly adopted sets of resolutions such as the following:

1. *Resolved,* that we will not rent land to any Radical leader, or any member of his family, or furnish a home, or give employment to any such leader or his family.

2. That we will not furnish any such leader, or any member of his family, any supplies, such as provisions, farm implements, stock, etc., except so far as contracts for the present year are concerned.

3. That we will not purchase any thing any Radical leader or any member of his family may offer for sale, or sell any such leader or any member of his family any thing whatever.

4. That the names of such persons, who may be considered leaders, be furnished to this Club at the earliest date, and that a list of the same be furnished each member of the Club.

5. That whenever any person or persons who shall be denominated Radical leaders by a vote of this Club shall cease as such, these resolutions shall become null and void so far as such leader or leaders, or any member of his or their families, are concerned.

6. That we will protect all persons in the right to vote for the candidates of their choice.

7. That these resolutions be published, and that all the Democratic clubs in the county and throughout the State are hereby requested to adopt them.[15]

On October 17, mainly as a result of the Ellenton riots, President Grant issued a proclamation declaring the rifle clubs unlawful and ordering them to disband. On the same day, all available federal troops in the military division of the Atlantic were ordered transferred to South Carolina.

[14] *New York Tribune,* October 25, 1876, quoted in Allen, *op. cit.,* pp. 411–12.
[15] *Ibid.,* p. 381.

Newspapers in New York and politicians in Washington were most interested in what was going on in South Carolina—not only because of Hampton's national reputation as one of the leading generals of the Confederacy, but because 1876 was also a presidential year, and the state's vote would be important in determining the outcome of the national election. The Republican candidate, Rutherford B. Hayes, was counting on the Republican majority in the state to deliver its seven electoral votes to him, but the Democrats hoped that the Hampton ticket might carry the slate of Democratic electors in the state and thus—with similar victories throughout the rest of the "solid South"—would bring the victory to their candidate, Samuel Tilden.

The reaction to Grant's proclamation was characteristic of the campaign—moderation from the candidate, resistance from his backers. Hampton's statement said:

We cannot disperse because we are not gathered together. We cannot "retire peacably to our abodes" because we are in our homes in peace, disturbed only by the political agitations created by the governor and his minions. But we resignedly— and cheerfully, in the performance of our duty—suspend the exercise of our individual and private rights in order to prevent evil to the whole people.[16]

The Red Shirts were not so forbearing. According to one Hampton biographer, Manly Wade Wellman:

As for the Democratic rifle clubs, they obeyed Grant's order to disperse by going more or less underground. Some of them openly mocked the President and his power. An armed group in Columbia, which possessed four field pieces and was trained to operate as a battery of horse artillery, cheerfully announced that it was reorganized as "the Hampton and Tilden Musical Club, with twelve four-pounder flutes." Others renamed themselves 'Tilden's mounted baseball clubs." Rifles and ammunition continued to arrive in shipments from outside, disguised in dry-goods boxes and provision barrels. . . .[17]

Militant Straightouts still massed in large numbers at political rallies, and their resentment of federal power grew as arrests were made for disturbing Republican meetings. *The Nation* protested the use of the troops, calling them "really an armed force in the service,

[16] Wellman, *op. cit.*, pp. 263–64.
[17] *Ibid.*, p. 265.

and acting under the orders of one of the parties to a political contest." [18]

At Republican meetings the power of the federal troops restrained the Red Shirts from their practice of demanding a division
of time, and at the Democratic meetings Hampton backers planned
displays of southern pageantry and white solidarity in a similar
atmosphere of barely restrained violence. At Hampton's final campaign appearance, in Columbia, the white ladies of the city staged a
pageant which featured a fire truck with 32 little girls on it, represent-
South Carolina's 32 counties. According to one woman's account
of the ceremony, "as the truck with the 32 little silver-winged girls
was entering the gates the Negroes, women and men, threatened
and insulted them, and a soldier (from Edgefield) cried: 'Have we
got to take this?' 'Keep the peace,' was the General's order, and he
obeyed." [19]

The white population was overwhelmingly pro-Hampton, and the
sending in of additional federal troops only strengthened their resolve
to regain control of the state government. It has been estimated that
by election time there were less than five hundred white men in the
whole state—not counting officeholders—who supported Chamberlain.

On November 7, the day South Carolinians went to vote for
state and national offices, the polls were officially guarded by federal
troops and unofficially guarded by Red Shirts. Violence had been
expected, but, except for a confrontation in Edgefield between
General Gary and a federal officer, there were no serious outbreaks.
How much went on behind the scenes, in the way of bribery, intimidation, or ballot-tampering, is a subject that will be eternally
disputed by the partisans of Southern history.

As the returns began to come in and be tabulated in the following days, there were early indications of a Hampton victory, although
Chamberlain was leading by large majorities in the districts with
the heaviest Negro registrations. It was not until three days after the
election that the result appeared definite: Hampton had won, by a
vote of 92,261 to Chamberlain's 91,127, and the Democrats had also
gained a narrow majority in the legislature; but in the presidential
contest, Republican electors had carried the state for Hayes. Although

[18] *The Nation*, XXIII (October 1876), 237, quoted in Jarrell, *op. cit.*,
p. 82.
[19] *South Carolina Women in the Confederacy* (Columbia, 1903–7), I,
383ff., quoted in *ibid.*, p. 85.

that ended the campaign, it was only the beginning of another dispute which would leave the country for months without a President-elect, and South Carolina with two governors.

The State Board of Canvassers—a body composed of five Republican officeholders, three of whom were candidates for re-election—had the authority of tabulating the vote, and voided the elections in Edgefield and Laurens Counties on the basis of "intimidation and fraud." This left the two counties without representation in the legislature and—since the eight representatives and two senators not certified were all Democrats—held the majority for the Republicans. It also made it possible—since the legislature would have to approve the returns in the gubernatorial contest—for Chamberlain to be declared reelected.

At the end of November, as the time came for the legislature to convene, all the bitterness and conflict and confusion of the Reconstruction focused on the state capital, Columbia. The town filled with federal troops, armed members of Negro Republican clubs, and —as the word went out to General Gary's followers around the state —some three to five thousand Red Shirts. There was a company of federal troops assigned to the Statehouse, with orders to admit only those legislators whose election had been certified by the Board of Canvassers. When the representatives from Edgefield and Laurens Counties were not admitted, the other Democrats also refused to enter and take their seats. The Republican legislators, almost all of whom were Negroes, assembled inside and elected their speaker of house, E. W. M. Mackey, a white man from Charleston.

While the legislature met, it seemed as though the Civil War was about to begin again. One southern historian wrote:

The hour of noon, November 28, 1876, was the most critical time for South Carolina in all that critical year. Peace trembled in the balance. An immense crowd of outraged Democrats from all parts of the state packed the plaza in front of the State Capitol. It looked as if these fiercely determined men would at any moment storm the building, brush aside the United States soldiers and take forcible possession of the Hall of the House of Representatives. Had they done so the State House would have been red with blood. Chamberlain and General Ruger sat in the Governor's private office in the west wing of the State House, where they could see from the window the surging mass. Upon the request of Chamberlain, General Ruger sent an officer to find Hampton, who was still

*in the State House, to ask him to quiet the angry crowd out-
side. Hampton promptly complied. He appeared at the front
entrance to the State House. Immediately the tumult ceased.
Every Democrat stood in silence to hear what the revered
leader might say. Had he said "Let it be war!" there would
have been war; but in a clear, calm voice he pleaded with his
followers for peace:*

*"My friends: I am truly doing what I have done earnestly
during this whole exciting contest, pouring oil on the troubled
waters. It is of the greatest importance to us all, as citizens of
South Carolina, that peace should be preserved. I appeal to
you all, white men and colored, as Carolinians, to use every
effort to keep down violence or turbulence. One act of violence
may precipitate bloodshed and desolation. I implore you, then,
to preserve the peace. I beg all of my friends to disperse, to
leave the grounds of the State House, and I advise all the
colored men to do the same. Keep perfectly quiet, leave the
streets, and do nothing to provoke a riot. We trust to the law
and the Constitution, and we have perfect faith in the justice
of our cause."*

*No sooner had Hampton ended his plea when the crowd, only
a few minutes before turbulent and rebellious, dispersed
promptly and quietly. In three minutes' time there was scarcely
a man to be seen on the State House grounds.*[20]

But Red Shirts from all over the state were still converging on
Columbia, and the danger that there would be a military conflict
to supplement the political battle was still present. The political situation itself became increasingly complicated: While the Republican
lawmakers met in the Statehouse and elected a Republican speaker—
Mackey—the Democrats retired to the meeting hall of the local rifle
company, declared themselves to be the legally elected legislature of
South Carolina, and elected their own speaker, W. H. Wallace, a
former Confederate general. From then on the two opposing bodies
were known as the Mackey House and the Wallace House. On
November 30 the latter group, using those Democrats who had
official certifications of election as an advance guard, stormed the
hall of the House of Representatives and installed Wallace in the
Speaker's chair. For five days and four nights the two groups stayed
in the same room, each trying to conduct the business of state and
ignore the other. There were continuing rumors that the Statehouse
was about to be invaded by Hunkidoris or Red Shirts, or both, and
finally the Wallace House withdrew. The Mackey House, meeting in

[20] Thompson, *op. cit.*, pp. 142–43.

joint session with the Senate and not counting the returns from Edge-field and Laurens Counties, then declared Chamberlain reelected by a vote of 86,216 to Hampton's 83,071.[21]

Again the Red Shirts were ready to do battle:

> *They surged through the capitol, crying for vengeance upon the political usurpers. Climbing upon a box, Gary called down maledictions upon Chamberlain and his crew. He advocated purging the state of men who dragged its Government through the slime. This was music to the ears of those who recognized the battle-cry of a warrior. . . .*[22]

And again Hampton persuaded his followers to avoid any con-flict with the federal troops. If Hampton had given in to Gary and the others who wanted to take over by force, the Red Shirts could undoubtedly have succeeded. They far outnumbered the federal forces, they were in every sense a fully armed and organized military body, and they were eager for the conflict. But in the long run, as Hampton well knew, there would be reinforcements from the North and the chances of regaining home rule would be lost.

Instead, he carried his argument to the State Supreme Court. That body—whose chief justice was Franklin J. Moses, Sr., father of the man whom Chamberlain had refused to certify as a circuit judge—handed down a decision that the Edgefield and Laurens re-turns were legal and that Wallace, not Mackey, was consequently the "legal speaker of the lawfully-constituted House of Representa-tives of the State of South Carolina." [23] Wallace then asked the com-mander of the federal troops to support him in another move on the Statehouse—but the general, who was under orders from President Grant to support Chamberlain, refused to do so. The Wallace House assembled again in their own meeting-hall and proceeded to declare Wade Hampton the legally elected governor of South Carolina.

On December 10, Chamberlain was inaugurated as governor. In his inaugural speech he said:

> *It is written in blood on the pages of our recent national history, that no government can rest with safety upon the en-forced slavery or degradation of a race. . . . I denounce the conduct of the recent election on the part of our political op-*

[21] Allen, *op. cit.*, p. 444.
[22] William A. Sheppard, *Red Shirts Remembered* (Spartanburg, S.C., 1940), pp. 180ff., quoted in Jarrell, *op. cit.*, p. 111.
[23] Thompson, *op. cit.*, p. 151.

ponents in this State as a vast brutal outrage. Fraud, proscription, intimidation in all forms, violence—ranging through all its degrees up to wanton murder—were its effective methods. The circumstances under which we have assembled today show us how nearly successful has been this great conspiracy.[24]

On December 14, Hampton was inaugurated as governor in a similar ceremony a few blocks away. He said:

We owe much of our late success to colored voters, who were brave enough to rise above the prejudice of race and honest enough to throw off the shackles of party in their determination to save the State. To those, who, misled by their fears, their ignorance, or by evil counsellors, turned a deaf ear to our appeals, we should not be vindictive, but magnanimous. Let us show to all of them that the true interest of both races can best be secured by cultivating peace and promoting prosperity among all classes of our fellow citizens.[25]

There was a victorious parade through the streets after Hampton delivered his address and that night, although Reconstructionists still held the Statehouse, Hampton's supporters gave an inaugural ball and celebrated the recovery of home rule for the South.

And while South Carolinians disputed the question of who had legally been elected governor, the rest of the country tried to decide who had been elected President. At first it appeared that Tilden, the Democrat, had won. The morning of November 8 the *New York Tribune* was sure enough of the outcome to run a story headlined "Tilden Elected." The Democrats had clearly carried New York, New Jersey, Connecticut, Indiana, and most of the South except Florida, South Carolina, and Louisiana—three states where returns were being disputed. They had 184 undisputed electoral votes, and Tilden needed 185 to be elected. Democrats felt certain that they would win at least one of the doubtful states; Hayes, on the other hand, had 165 undisputed votes—to win, he would need *all* of the states in question. To settle the matter, a special bipartisan commission was formed; it was composed of five Representatives, five Senators, and five Supreme Court justices.[26]

In Columbia, Hampton set up offices in the Democratic state headquarters and began to do business as governor. He immediately

[24] Allen, *op. cit.*, p. 446.
[25] Wellman, *op. cit.*, p. 286.
[26] John Hope Franklin, *Reconstruction After the Civil War* (Chicago: University of Chicago Press, 1961), pp. 212–13.

obtained the support of important elements in the state, who passed resolutions making it clear that they would pay their taxes to him, and not to Chamberlain. In view of the condition of the state treasury, this was an important consideration. Hampton levied a voluntary tax and began to collect funds; as state agencies began to apply to him instead of to Chamberlain for money, his power steadily increased.

The question of who was to be the next President of the United States was not resolved until March 2, two days before the date of the inauguration. The commissioners decided to accept the returns from the states and not "go behind" them—which would have required investigating local election procedures. Since all of the disputed returns were Republican, all of the disputed returns went to Hayes, who was accordingly declared elected. Democratic leaders had accepted this decision before it was formally announced, but had demanded as the price of their acceptance that all remaining federal troops be withdrawn from the South.

Rutherford B. Hayes was duly inaugurated as the nineteenth President of the United States, and soon after he had taken office he called the two governors of South Carolina to meet with him in Washington. After meeting separately with Hampton and Chamberlain, Hayes took up the matter with his cabinet and decided on April 10 as the date for withdrawing troops.

Chamberlain knew that his administration could not endure without support from Washington. Hampton was consolidating his power throughout the state, and was also reorganizing the state militia to include the rifle clubs. A few days after Hayes made his announcement, Chamberlain published a statement saying: "By the recent decision and action of the President of the United States, I find myself unable longer to maintain my official rights, and I hereby announce . . . that I am unwilling to prolong a struggle which can only bring further suffering upon those who engage in it." [27]

The era of Reconstruction came to a quiet close on April 11, 1877. The company of infantrymen who had been guarding the Statehouse had departed the day before, and that morning Chamberlain cleared out his personal possessions from his office and was driven in a carriage through the crowded streets to his home. At exactly noon, his secretary handed over the seal and keys of the office to Hampton's representative.

Hampton always maintained after the election that his policy

[27] Allen, *op. cit.*, p. 480.

of asking Negroes to support his cause was what had made it successful, that he had carried the state with the help of some 17,000 Negro votes, but Ben Tillman of Edgefield County said "every active worker in the cause knew that in this he was woefully mistaken. . . . Gary preached the only effective doctrine for the times: that 'one ounce of fear was worth a pound of persuasion.' . . ."[28]

If there were significant numbers of blacks who voted for Hampton, they made a bad bargain for their race. Hampton was probably sincere in his aristocratic ideal of allowing qualified Negroes to participate in government, and some did hold office in his administration. But techniques of disenfranchising Negroes through complicated election laws developed rapidly, and within a few years the threat of any black voting majority had been eliminated. The real victory was Gary's, not Hampton's, and the man who finally did the most to shape the kind of political society which developed in South Carolina was Gary's young follower from Edgefield County, "Pitchfork Ben" Tillman.

3

1890
South Carolina
Ben Tillman vs. *Alexander C. Haskell*

When Wade Hampton won his victory in 1876, Ben Tillman was a 29-year-old farmer in Edgefield County and an energetic worker for the Democratic cause. He was a leading member of the local Sweetwater Sabre Club, an active participant in the Hamburg mas-

[28] Jarrell, *op. cit.,* p. 61.

sacre, and, according to some historical accounts, the originator of the idea of uniforming whites in red shirts as a defiant reference to Reconstructionist "waving the bloody shirt."

Next to Generals Butler and Gary he was probably the most active Straightout leader in the county, but he was not of their class and would not normally have been expected to aspire to any political office himself. They had both served prominently in the war, but Tillman, having lost one eye at the age of 17, had not served at all. They were both lawyers; he had no college education. They were both members of prominent plantation families; the Tillmans, although prosperous and respectable enough, never had any social pretensions. Furthermore, Tillman's manner hardly marked him to rise beyond his class, and when he was elected to the captaincy of his sabre club it was more in spite of his personality than because of it. As Tillman's biographer, Francis Butler Simkins, puts it: "Although he was rough in manner and appearance, ungenerous in disposition, and not capable of inspiring intimate personal devotion, he was given this recognition because of his long and zealous service in the interest of white supremacy, his personal integrity, and his commanding manners." [1]

Ben Tillman was the youngest of a family of ten—three girls and seven boys—and the males in his family had not been lucky. His father died of typhoid at the age of 46, his oldest brother was killed in the Mexican war, another was killed by two brothers in a family feud, another was killed in a fight in Florida, another died of a fever, and one died as a result of wounds received in the Civil War. The only other surviving brother, George, had studied at Harvard and served in the state legislature—but he also killed a man in a fight over a faro game, ran away to join the filibustering expedition of William Walker in Nicaragua, and returned to a manslaughter charge for which he served two years in jail. Ben himself had barely survived an eye infection. The eye was removed by a surgeon under primitive conditions, and Ben was left with an empty left eye socket which added to his rather menacing appearance.

After the 1876 election Tillman remained moderately active in the Democratic party. He became chairman of the Edgefield County organization in 1880 and supported General Gary's unsuccessful

[1] Francis Butler Simkins, *The Tillman Movement in South Carolina* (Durham, N.C.: Duke University Press, 1926), p. 46.

attempt to win the Democratic nomination for governor.[2] In 1882, he was a delegate to the Democratic state convention. But there is no indication that he had any personal political ambitions. He was, first of all, a farmer.

His experiences were not so different from those of other farmers during this period: he worked hard, overinvested, got into debt, and never quite succeeded in getting out of it again. In his frustration he developed a strong resentment for the creditors who were able, he said, "to pick a large crop of cotton whether they grew it or not." [3]

In South Carolina a new class of postwar rulers had emerged. The rule of the carpetbaggers and scalawags had ended, at least politically, but the antebellum plantation economy had been destroyed for good and the population of the towns had grown. And it was in the towns that the new merchant class grew up, profiting on high-interest loans to the farmers, investing in trade and manufacturing, and naturally exerting influence on the state's political life. Although the men who held office were usually aristocrats like Wade Hampton, the newly wealthy financiers in the cities were at least as powerful a group, and in fact the two elements easily accommodated each other in the formation of a new conservative establishment. Most farmers, politically unsophisticated and accounting themselves lucky that the government was at least back in the hands of white southerners, regarded this establishment as a fact of life, unchangeable. But there were some who wanted change and intended to get it, and they were not only southern farmers. The agrarian myth was turning sour for farmers all over the country who saw themselves as hard-working, debt-ridden, and exploited, and their discontents were beginning to take political form in the uncertain upheaval known as the agrarian revolt.[4]

Tillman's first activities on behalf of the farm problem were of merely local scope. He became interested in the subject of education for farmers, and in 1884 he started a group called the Edgefield Agricultural Club. When this foundered he launched another organi-

---

[2] Gary's political aspirations were repeatedly frustrated. In 1877 he sought a vacant U. S. Senate seat, which went instead to General Butler; the next Senate vacancy went to Hampton; Gary died not long after his 1880 defeat for the gubernatorial nomination.

[3] Francis Butler Simkins, *Pitchfork Ben Tillman* (Baton Rouge, La.: Louisiana State University Press, 1944), p. 89. Used with permission.

[4] For an analysis of this movement see Richard Hofstadter, *The Age of Reform* (New York: Vintage Books, 1955).

zation, called the Edgefield County Agricultural Society, and became its president. The membership of the society was small, somewhere between thirty and sixty, but it gave him an opportunity to make some speeches and gain enough of a reputation as a farm leader to be elected one of the county's three delegates to the joint convention in 1885 of the State Grange and the State Agricultural and Mechanical Society—and it was at that meeting, held in the little town of Bennetsville, that Tillman and his political style began to win statewide attention.

The speech he made was rousing and direct, phrased in biting straightforward language unlike the prevailing oratorical style of the times. He spoke of the difficulty of the position farmers were in, the unfairness of the credit system, and the inadequacy of the type of leader they usually elected from among themselves:

> *He enters the State House a farmer; he emerges from it in one session a politician. He went there to do something for the people. After breathing the polluted atmosphere for thirty days he returned home intent on doing something for himself. The contact with General This and Judge That and Colonel Something Else, who have shaken him by the hand and made much of him, has debauched him. He likes this being a somebody; and his first resolution, offered and passed in his own mind, is that he will remain something if he can.*[5]

The *Columbia Daily Register* reported that Tillman's speech was "the sensation of the meeting," and that "almost every sentence was responded to with prolonged applause, showing that the farmers were *en rapport* with the scathing irony which he dealt out to the political close corporation." [6] When the convention was over, Tillman returned to his farm and began to write a series of letters to the conservative *Charleston News and Courier*.

In the letters he charged again that the politicians and the state department of agriculture were doing the farmers more harm than good, and that there was an urgent need for a better center of agricultural education than the "pitiful, contemptible, so-called agricultural annex to South Carolina College" which then existed. The letters were widely quoted and discussed in other newspapers, most of which ridiculed the ideas and dismissed the writer with such de-

[5] Simkins, *Pitchfork Ben Tillman*, p. 94.
[6] *Ibid.*

scriptions as "Farmer Tillman" and "the agricultural Moses." [7] (It was some years before Tillman acquired the nickname that finally stayed with him: Pitchfork Ben.) But one newspaper said Tillman had "no conception of his popularity among a certain class of political farmers," and might someday become governor.[8]

Actually Tillman was well aware of the following he had won, and was proceeding to mobilize it. He organized a statewide convention of farmers who assembled in Columbia on April 29, 1886, and passed a batch of Tillman-drafted resolutions which advocated, among other things, a new agricultural annex to the state college, a repeal of the lien law which had been responsible for much of the mortgaging of agricultural property, and the calling of a convention to make a new state constitution. The main reason Tillman wanted a new constitution was to alter the voting laws so as to prevent any possibility that the Negro majority might regain political control of the state. In response to those delegates who urged him to run for governor, Tillman said, "I commenced this fight pure and honest, and only a farmer. I will end it as I began, and for a reward I ask only your good opinion and confidence." [9] But although Tillman chose not to run for office, he had already become one of the most powerful men in the state. The farmers were turning into an articulate political force, and he was its dictator.

Tillman and his disciples were much in evidence at the Democratic state convention in 1886, but not particularly effective. Tillman did not find a candidate for governor to whom he could give his wholehearted support, and the convention voted down three of his proposals: the constitutional convention plan, a system for reapportioning representation to future Democratic conventions according to white population only, and an idea that was becoming popular with reform movements across the country—nomination of candidates to state office by direct primary instead of by vote at a convention.

Essentially the same proposals were introduced as bills by Tillman followers—actively prodded by Tillman himself, who was present as a lobbyist—when the state legislature convened later that year; but only one minor Tillman-inspired bill—providing for the establishment of state agricultural experiment stations—was passed into law. Tillman denounced the "oligarchy of lawyers" [10] for failing to respond to the

---

[7] Simkins, *Tillman Movement*, p. 64.
[8] *Charleston News and Courier*, March 5, 1886, quoted in *ibid.*
[9] *Ibid.*, p. 67.
[10] *Ibid.*, p. 78.

farmers' expressed needs, and waited out the year. In the next legislative session the constitutional convention bill failed to get the required two-thirds majority, and Tillman wrote a bitter "farewell
letter" to the *News and Courier,* denouncing the "imbecile statesmen"
for their failure to "draw the fangs of the negro monster," [11] and
announcing that he personally intended to retire to his farm.

The retirement lasted about three months, until the death of
one Thomas C. Clemson, a son-in-law of South Carolina's most
famous statesman, John C. Calhoun. Clemson left to the state the
814-acre Calhoun estate and a cash endowment of $80,000, specifying
that it be used to establish a separate agricultural college. This, of
course, had been one of Tillman's favorite ideals, and his part in
the project was made official by the will, which named him as one
of the college's lifetime trustees.

The college bequest would have to be accepted by the state
legislature, but there was an election coming up and Tillman hoped
the 1888 legislature might be composed of representatives more
favorable to his ideas.

When the state Democratic convention met in 1888, Tillman
was back in action and in his best form, denouncing the delegates
as representatives, not of the people, but of "rings and cliques."
Looking around the hall of the House of Representatives, he said,
"When I think of the crimes which have been committed in this hall,
I shudder to enumerate them—financial extravagance, tricky practices. . . . The members have been bamboozled or affected in some
way by Columbia water or whisky, or by Charleston brains." [12]

This speech, like many of Tillman's addresses to such bodies,
was regarded as less than scintillating by most of the immediate
audience, but it was not the immediate audience he cared about:
it was the farmers around the state who would read their local papers
and chuckle over the news of how he had taken on the politicians
in their own hall.

The delegates turned down a primary election proposal by a
large majority, but they did approve of another proposal for opening
up the political dialogue—a series of public debates to be held between political candidates.

At the first of these debates Tillman himself—although still
not a candidate for any office—appeared as the opponent of the

[11] *Ibid.,* p. 83.
[12] *Ibid.,* pp. 87–88.

governor, J. P. Richardson, and the lieutenant governor, William Mauldin. Tillman was there because the incumbents had nobody running against them and he was the closest thing to an organized opposition available. The debate was held in the small community of Hodges, and the rural audiences cheered Tillman's remarks about the politicians and his denunciation of one of his archenemies, editor F. W. Dawson. He described Dawson as "a buzzard who had escaped from the market house of Charleston and gone into the *News and Courier* office where it is spewing its slime on me." [13]

At the debates that followed, Tillman was either the main speaker or the main subject. Finally he appeared in Charleston to oppose Dawson himself before a hostile audience of city-dwellers.

Tillman started out by calling the people of Charleston "the most arrant set of cowards that ever drew the fresh air of heaven," for continuing to put up with their elected leaders, and called Dawson "the old man of the seas clinging around the neck of South Carolina, oppressing the people and stifling reform." [14]

Dawson could not quite equal Tillman in face-to-face namecalling, but an editorial which came out in the *News and Courier* after the debate called Tillman the leader of "people who carry pistols in their hip pockets, who expectorate upon the floor, who have no tooth brushes and comb their hair with their fingers." [15]

After the debates and the conventions of the various county Democratic organizations, there was another state convention for the purpose of selecting nominees. The Tillman faction, larger this time than at any previous state gathering, selected the state attorney general, Joseph H. Earle, as their candidate for governor. But Earle, choosing not to oppose the incumbent candidate, declined the offered support and Richardson was renominated. And again the party rejected the primary proposal by an overwhelming vote.

These failures were more an indication of a lack of political finesse than of political power. Actually, the Tillman forces were well within the gates by this time, and their numbers were growing. The elections that year gave them a majority in the House of Representatives and almost half of the Senate. The lack of a majority in the upper house prevented the passage of the entire farm program—during the 1888–89 session the constitutional convention move failed

[13] *Ibid.*, p. 90.
[14] *Ibid.*, p. 93.
[15] *Charleston News and Courier*, August 30, 1888, quoted in *ibid.*, p. 94.

again—but the Tillmanites did get a primary election law (which would still leave the final decision on whether to have primaries up to the individual parties), acceptance of the Clemson bequest, and a law making it possible for the state railroad commission to fix freight and passenger rates.

The 1888 elections had given the Tillmanites partial control of the state government; in the 1890 elections they planned to make the victory complete. This meant they would have to find a candidate for governor, and by this time it was obvious that there could be only one real spokesman for the Tillman forces: Tillman. He had dominated the movement from the beginning, and it must have been apparent to such men as Attorney General Earle—whom the farmers had offered to support in 1888—that accepting such support would mean becoming a follower of Tillman, not a leader of a movement. Tillman was simply not the kind of man who would content himself with discreet behind-the-scenes politicking.

Early in 1890 Tillman and two of his closest advisers—G. W. Shell and John Irby of neighboring Laurens County—called a statewide convention of the Farmer's Association. The call to the convention denounced the incompetence and corruption of the "aristocratic oligarcy" that ruled the state, and concluded:

> *Fellow Democrats, do not these things cry out for a change? Is it not opportune, when there is no national election, for the common people, who redeemed South Carolina from radical rule, to take charge of it? Can we afford to leave it longer in the hands of those who, wedded to ante-bellum ideas, but with little of the ante-bellum patriotism and honor, are running it for the benefit of a few families and for the benefit of a ring of selfish politicians?* [16]

The convention that assembled in Columbia in March of 1890 was described by one newspaperman as "one of the queerest deliberative bodies that has ever assembled in the State House." [17] But what the conservatives feared most about the convention was not its lack of elegance but the possibility that it would so deeply divide the Democratic party as to lead to a revival of Republican—and black —power.

The group clearly regarded itself as a political body, and its main item of business was endorsing a candidate for governor. There

[16] *Ibid.*, p. 105.
[17] N. G. Gonzales, quoted in *ibid.*, pp. 106–7.

was a considerable amount of opposition to Tillman's endorsement
from delegates who saw him as a fine agitator but an unthinkable
governor; but in the end, thanks to some parliamentary maneuvering
by Irby and the convention chairman, State Senator Jasper Talbert,
Tillman was nominated by acclamation. In addressing the convention
Tillman described himself as "the only man who has the brains,
the nerve and the ability to organize the common people against the
aristocracy." [18]

Eugene B. Gary, the nephew of Tillman's early mentor in
Edgefield County, became the candidate for lieutenant-governor. The
farm movement, at this point, was beginning to take on the appearance
of a formidable political machine. It had candidates for every office,
either farmer-politicians like Tillman or lawyers who saw it as a
promising side to be on, and it had the support of one influential daily
newspaper, the *Charleston World*.

The conservative elements held a preconvention meeting of their
own and selected Joseph Earle as their candidate, partly as a reward
to him for having refused to side with the farmers in 1888. Earle,
although not of aristocratic family background, was a dignified and
handsome gentleman who had served patiently in the Democratic
ranks and in the office of attorney general; his running mate was John
Bratton, a planter and former Confederate general.

The preconvention campaign was conducted mainly through
another series of debates, which were even rowdier than those of
1888. In the rural communities the farmers applauded and cheered
"the one-eyed plowboy" and in some cases refused to allow Earle
and Bratton to be heard at all. At Columbia Tillman faced a hostile
crowd and a platform of dignitaries which included the graying Wade
Hampton, now a United States Senator. "Shoulder to shoulder,"
Hampton said, "I implore you men of South Carolina, not to forget
the past." After Hampton's exercise in traditional southern oratory,
the meeting quickly got down to an exchange of personal insults.

Tillman accused the present government of being composed of
"men who seek positions for money," [19] and was himself accused of
having shirked his duty to the South by avoiding duty in the Civil
War. One of the other speakers present vindicated the honor of the

---

[18] There is some doubt about the exact words used by Tillman in this
speech. This is his own version, as published in a letter to the *News and
Courier*, Nov. 5, 1890. *Ibid.*, p. 108.
[19] *Ibid.*, p. 120.

Tillman family by testifying to the heroism in action of Tillman's brother Jim, and Tillman himself replied: "When any man comes here and talks about my record, I simply spew him out at the mouth. The Democratic party is full of leprosy." [20]

A few days later, Hampton went to the town of Aiken, in Tillman's home county, to speak on behalf of Earle, and was booed so loudly by the crowd that he was unable to speak and sat down. The conservatives denounced this as an unpardonable show of discourtesy against the state's most revered leader, but no apology came from the Tillman side. The incident, however, was a significant indication of the deep changes that were taking place in the state, and to some extent in the entire South: Evocation of the glory and gallantry of the Confederacy—or a personification of those qualities, such as Wade Hampton—were no longer enough for the farmers. Pressured from above by the politicians and moneylenders, threatened from below by the ever-present black masses, they were interested in leaders who would address themselves more directly, if less eloquently, to their needs.

As it became increasingly obvious that Tillman would be the victor in the September nominating convention, his conservative opponents came up with the idea of having the delegates to the convention elected by primary instead of by the county committees. In view of the fact that it was Tillman who had been the strongest advocate of primaries, this would have been a most ironic development, but it did not take place. The delegates were selected in the usual manner, and in the preconvention maneuvering Irby emerged as the new chairman of the state executive committee—which, for the first time, put the official machinery of the party itself under Tillman's control.

It also moved the party into a breakdown of structure comparable, in a small way, to the breakdown of government which had led to the competing legislatures fourteen years before. This time there were two state executive committees—the one led by Irby, which had the strongest claim to legitimacy, and the one led by the conservatives, who had in effect seceded from the party. The conservatives claimed that the nominating convention would not be legal. But the convention, dominated by the farmers, took place as scheduled and the entire Tillman ticket was nominated. The anti-Tillman forces, led

[20] *Ibid.*, p. 121.

by A. C. Haskell, proceeded to call their own nominating convention.

Haskell, who now emerged as the most determined foe of the Tillman movement, was the embodiment of everything Tillman was not: a lawyer, a bank president, and a former colonel in the Confederate Army. He was also the man who, at the meeting in Columbia, had attacked Tillman for his failure to serve in the Civil War, and was one of Wade Hampton's closest friends and most loyal supporters.

The anti-Tillman Democratic convention met in October, calling itself the party of Straight-Out Democracy and evoking wherever possible the tradition of the victory of 1876. Haskell himself accepted the party's nomination for the office of governor, and a statement issued by the convention charged Tillman and his followers with having "done more harm and brought greater sorrow on the State than the sword or the hand of man in any other shape has effected." [21]

The efforts which Haskell's group made to claim a direct heritage from Wade Hampton, the Red Shirts, and the glory of 1876 were in reality symptomatic of the fact that Haskell did not have the full support of the conservative establishment. There were many people who could not stand Tillman, but Tillman did at this point base his claim to the nomination on the support of legitimate party delegates. And, worst of all, Haskell had indicated that he would be willing to seek the support of Negro voters. "When the white race divides," he had said, "it is a question with the colored race which party will govern the state." [22] This possibility—a break in white unity that might lead to black control—was to most South Carolinians a far worse prospect than that of Tillman in the Statehouse.

Most of the conservative newspapers, including the *News and Courier,* decided to support Tillman. "Captain Tillman," said the *Lancaster Ledger,* dignifying Tillman with the title of his office in the Sabre Club, "was not our choice for Governor, but he was the choice of a large majority of the Democratic Party. . . . Every Democrat is pledged in honor to vote for him." [23]

Hampton himself indicated that he would vote for Tillman, but he would not go so far as to make any statement against Haskell. "I shall not," the Senator said, "denounce the man who was my comrade in war . . . and my trusted friend in 1876." [24]

[21] *Ibid.,* p. 131.
[22] *Ibid.,* p. 129.
[23] *Lancaster Ledger,* Oct. 8, 1890, quoted in *ibid.,* p. 131.
[24] *Ibid.,* p. 132.

Haskell did, as he had hoped, get some support from the few Negroes who were still active in state politics—Tillman's well-publicized intention of calling a new constitutional convention to disenfranchise black voters by law helped Haskell there—but they lacked the numbers or the organization to make a real difference. In the 14 years since the Democrats had taken over, the overwhelming majority of blacks had ceased to consider themselves to have any part in government. The executive committee of the Republican party did endorse Haskell, which mainly served to strengthen Tillman's position among the active and voting white Democrats.

Thus, Haskell's support came from a curious coalition of voters: conservative Democrats who regarded Tillman as an upstart and an affront to the state's traditions, and black Republicans who knew well that a Tillman victory would lead to a firm and final exclusion of their race from the democratic process.

The vote went overwhelmingly for Tillman—59,159 to Haskell's 14,828—and it also gave his supporters a majority of one hundred seats in the state legislature.[25] And so the post-Reconstruction era in South Carolina moved into a new phase: the legislature that had once been dominated by recently freed slaves, and then for nearly 14 years by the aristocrats of the old Confederacy, was now composed mostly of farmers.

In Tillman's inaugural address he stated with his customary straightforwardness his intention to do something about the threat posed by the existence in the state of a large—if inactive—body of black citizens:

> *The whites have absolute control of the government and we intend, at any hazard, to retain it. The intelligent exercise of the right of suffrage is as yet beyond the capacity of the vast majority of colored men. We deny, without regard to color, that all men are created equal, it is not true now and was not true when Jefferson wrote it.*[26]

But it took time—even with his farmer majority and with Irby installed as Speaker of the House—for Tillman to pass his programs into law; the conservative forces were still well organized and articulate, particularly in the upper house, and Tillman's first two-year term was a combination of defeats and minor victories. His proposal

25 *Ibid.*, p. 134n.
26 *Ibid.*, p. 137.

for a constitutional convention failed to get the required two-thirds majority, but he did succeed in getting a reapportionment of the legislature which favored rural areas, a reorganization of the state university system, and a shift of the tax burden from landowners to corporations. Probably the most dramatic evidence of Tillman's power was the defeat of Wade Hampton for reelection to the United States Senate; Irby, then 36, was sent to Washington in his place, and the aging hero's political career was ended.

Tillman was not at all satisfied with the performance of the 1890–91 legislature. He called them "driftwood which the tidal wave of Tillmanism has swept into the Capitol," [27] and went to the voters in 1892 to ask for a second term for himself and a more cooperative legislature to back up his programs. The electorate responded handsomely; Tillman was reelected by a large majority and the new legislature was dominated by men who had pledged him their support and received his blessing: 24 out of 36 in the Senate, and 102 out of 124 in the House. The new legislature promptly passed the constitutional convention bill.

The convention proposal had to be approved by the voters in a referendum, and the convention itself did not take place until 1895. In the meantime, Tillman completed his second term and moved on to the United States Senate, turning over the governorship to another of General Gary's nephews, John Gary Evans.

Senator Tillman was the central figure at the convention and personally took the chairmanship of its suffrage committee. The plan that he devised and incorporated into the new state constitution is described by his biographer as follows:

> In general it was like a provision of the Mississippi constitution of 1890. It gave the suffrage to every male adult in South Carolina if he fulfilled the following qualifications: he must have lived in the state for two years, the county for one year, and the voting precinct for four months; he must have paid his poll tax six months before election and must not have been guilty of any one of a specified list of crimes. Up to January 1, 1898, a man who fulfilled these requirements, and who could read any section of the constitution, or could "understand and explain it when read" to him, was to be a lifetime voter. After that date the person who fulfilled the aforementioned residence, tax, and court qualifications, and could read and write any section of the constitution submitted to

[27] *Ibid.*, p. 157.

*him by the registration officer, or who had paid taxes the pre-
vious year on property assessed at $300, could become a voter.
The board of registration in each county should be composed
of "three discreet persons;" no provision was made for bipartisan management. . . . It was assumed that the "three discreet persons" would apply the "understanding" and the
"reading and writing tests" with "discretion" sufficient to
exclude the great mass of Negro illiterates from the polls while
allowing this privilege to the corresponding class of whites. In
other words, a strong barrier had a gate and its key was given
to friendly white men "who will know what is expected of
them."* [28]

Tillman defended the suffrage restriction as the only way of
insuring against the return of Reconstructionist corruption; this, he
said, "must be our justification, our vindication and our excuse to
the world that we are met in Convention openly, boldly, without
any pretense of secrecy . . . to so restrict the suffrage . . . that this
infamy can never come about again." [29] The new constitution went
into effect on New Year's Day of 1896.

By this time Tillman had become a national figure, and he went
to the 1896 Democratic national convention as a possible nominee
for the presidency. He was widely admired as a champion of the
agrarian cause and famous as "Pitchfork Ben" after a speech in
which he called President Cleveland "an old bag of beef" and promised
that he was "going to Washington with a pitchfork and prod him in
his old fat ribs." [30]

Tillman made an impressive speech at the 1896 convention, but
he was overshadowed by an even greater crowd-pleaser: William
Jennings Bryan. Bryan became the presidential nominee after he had
swept the convention off its feet with the famous "Cross of Gold"
speech, and Tillman returned to Washington. For many years he
kept the Senate in a more or less continual state of uproar with
speeches which caused northern newspapers to denounce him as
"a filthy baboon," [31] "a slang-whanging buffoon and demagogue," [32]
and a supreme example of the "ignorance, intolerance and violence
of the State's mean white trash." [33] In 1902 he was censured by the

[28] Simkins, *Pitchfork Ben Tillman*, pp. 296–98.
[29] *Ibid.*, p. 298.
[30] *Ibid.*, p. 315.
[31] *The New York Times*, quoted in *ibid.*, p. 323.
[32] *Springfield Republican, ibid.*
[33] *Philadelphia Record, ibid.*, p. 324.

Senate after getting into a fist fight with his state's junior senator, John L. McLaurin, on the Senate floor.

Eventually the agrarian movement, in South Carolina and elsewhere, lost its revolutionary impetus as the farmers found their way to the sources of power. And Tillman himself, as the years wore on, began to sound more like a contented politician than a leader of rural rebellion. The time finally came when he could call the Senate "the most august deliberative assembly in the world," and "the only bulwark against revolution." [34] He remained in the Senate until his death in 1918.

On the grounds of the statehouse in Columbia there is a statue of Wade Hampton, and, not far away, a statue of Ben Tillman. Hampton holds a position of greater reverence in the state's history, but of the two it was undoubtedly Tillman who had the deeper and more lasting effect on the course of politics. And it was Tillman who served as the prototype of future southern leaders of the common man, from Huey Long to George Wallace.

[34] *Ibid.,* p. 20.

PROGRESSIVISM
AND
PRIMARIES

4

1912
The Republican Presidential Primaries
William H. Taft vs. *Theodore Roosevelt*

Tammany Hall Boss William M. Tweed's classic and much-quoted remark that he didn't care who did the electing so long as he could do the nominating was a practical man's recognition of the fact that the first step in the business of getting elected to office is at least as important as the second, and sometimes more important. The nomination process is a basic component of our democratic system, but unfortunately it is not always democratic—and this is most true at the highest level, the nomination of candidates for the office of President of the United States.

Since the early years of the Republic there has existed a persistent if not always coherent sentiment that the public ought somehow to have a voice in the nomination of candidates for the Presidency, and not be restricted to merely expressing a preference between candidates picked by party elites. Twice in American history the nominating procedure has undergone major reform, each designed to bring it nearer the ideal of representative democracy. The first reform was the national party convention, instituted in the 1830's as a change from the older system of nominating presidential candidates in congressional caucus. The convention system was a considerable improvement: it was more representative in character; it enhanced the independence of the President by removing his nomination from Congress; and it provided a means for preparing an authoritative party platform.[1]

[1] Eugene H. Roseboom, *A History of Presidential Elections* (New York: The Macmillan Company, 1957), p. 106.

But the convention system also had some undemocratic aspects. The delegates were usually politicians, party work horses, and political job-holders—and consequently more attuned to the shifting centers of power than to grass-roots public sentiment. The conventions were ridden with factionalism, sectionalism, and special-interest influence, and cynical manipulations and deals were a customary part of the business transacted. There was public pressure for still another reform, and in the early 1900's that pressure became part of a political movement—progressivism.

The people who called themselves Progressives were in some cases western and midwestern heirs of the Populist movement, in some cases eastern businessmen interested in good government, in some cases Republicans, in some cases Democrats. The most precise use of the term would be to describe the liberal wing of the Republican party, but the term was not always used precisely: Progressive sometimes seemed to be synonymous with patriotic, and even conservative Republicans liked to style themselves as "true Progressives."

Most Progressives were concerned about reform, and as the Progressive movement grew and its ideals became defined, Progressives advocated new ideas such as the recall, the referendum, and the initiative as ways to protect the voters against special interests and political machines. One of the favorite ideas for improving the democratic system was the primary election. Throwing the party's decision-making procedures open to the voters, the Progressives argued, was one way to reduce the power of the bosses. Primaries came into wide use at the state and local level, and the Progressives turned their attention to the machinery of selecting presidential candidates. They envisioned a nationwide system of primaries in which the presidential candidates would in effect be nominated by the people. And so began the second reform of the presidential nominating procedure.

In 1901 Florida passed a law allowing party leaders—if they chose to do so—to call primary elections to choose delegates to national conventions. In 1905 Wisconsin, led by its arch-Progressive governor, Robert M. LaFollette, Sr., passed a stronger law which made popular election of delegates mandatory. But so far the laws only made it possible for the voters to elect delegates; they provided no way for the voter to tell the delegates whom to vote for at the convention. In 1906, Pennsylvania passed a primary law making it possible for delegate-candidates to have printed on the ballot along-side their names the name of the presidential candidate they intended to vote for at the convention—but in the next election, in 1908, not a single delegate-candidate in either party chose to commit himself in this fashion. In 1910, a true presidential preference primary law was passed in Oregon: it allowed the voters to (*a*) elect delegates and (*b*) vote for presidential candidates. The delegates would then be bound to vote for the winner of the presidential popularity poll.[2]

By February of 1912, six more states had passed presidential primary laws on the Oregon model, and five others had optional or partial primaries.[3] So far they had not had any noticeable effect on the decisions made at any national conventions, and most Progressives thought it would take several more years and several more states before they would begin to do so—but it came about that the word's best-known Progressive, Theodore Roosevelt, put the presidential primaries to work sooner than anyone had expected.

When Theodore Roosevelt succeeded to the Presidency in September of 1901 upon the assassination of President McKinley, he was the youngest President in American history and possibly the most energetic. In the remaining years of McKinley's term he established a reputation as a trust-buster by fighting to dissolve the Northern Securities Company, and pugnaciously extended United States influence abroad in such adventures as the American-supported revolution which separated Panama from Columbia and cleared the way for the building of the Panama Canal. In 1904 he became the first succession President in history to win his party's nomination for another term. When he decided to retire in 1908 he chose his secretary of war—William Howard Taft of Ohio, a 350-pound former judge and onetime governor-general of the Philippines—to be the next President. After Taft had been duly nominated and elected, Roosevelt went off to hunt wild animals in Africa.

The man he had selected for President was not, whatever Roosevelt may have expected, the same kind of executive. Taft was politically conservative, personally lethargic and easy going; although he had been a fine judge and administrator he was not skilled in high-level political strategy, and he had a way of saying the wrong thing in public. His first major challenge in office was calling a special session

---

[2] James W. Davis, *Springboard to the White House* (New York: Thomas Y. Crowell Company, 1967), pp. 25–26, 40.

[3] Louise Overacker, *The Presidential Primary* (New York: The Macmillan Company, 1926), p. 13.

of Congress to pass a new downward-revised tariff bill, which had been one of his key campaign pledges. The Payne-Aldrich Tariff Bill, which finally emerged from Congress after much wrangling and logrolling, contained as many upward revisions as downward ones. Taft had not only failed to get the kind of bill he had promised the voters; he had alienated many Congressmen—particularly Progressive ones—in the process. Taft signed the bill, and, instead of denouncing it—as Roosevelt probably would have—as a sellout to the special interests, he went on a speaking tour to defend it and told a crowd at Winona, Kansas, that the bill was the best ever passed by the Republican party.

Another unforgivably un-Rooseveltian act of Taft's was his decision to fire Gifford Pinchot, the head of the U.S. Forest Service. Pinchot, a close friend of Roosevelt's and a holdover from the Roosevelt administration, had gotten into a dispute with his superior, Secretary of Interior Richard A. Ballinger, whom he claimed had been too cooperative with special interests in matters involving public water-power sites and Alaskan coal claims. This was a rousing issue to progressives; special interests were involved; conservation was involved. And Roosevelt had been a strong conservationist.

Pinchot's agitations led to a series of articles about the Interior Department by various muckraking journalists, and also launched a congressional investigation. After Senator Jonathan Dolliver of Iowa made public a letter which Pinchot had written him, Taft decided to fire Pinchot. Unknown to Taft, Pinchot had already written another letter, to Roosevelt, telling the ex-President that Taft had lost the confidence of Progressives and was proving unable to prevent the reactionaries from dominating his administration.[4] Roosevelt received the letter when he had finished his safari and sent for Pinchot, who came to meet him on the Riviera. So at least as early as the spring of 1910, Roosevelt was listening to advisers who told him that Taft was not carrying on the Progressive cause.

Roosevelt spent some weeks touring Europe and then returned to his home at Sagamore Hill. Throughout that summer he was often visited by politicians, especially from his party's Progressive wing, who came to talk to him about affairs in Washington. He managed for a very short while to restrain himself from actively taking part in politics; but soon he was in the middle of the New York State

[4] William Draper Lewis, *The Life of Theodore Roosevelt* (The United Publishers, 1919), p. 328.

Republican convention, making speeches around the country about his philosophies of government, and arguing the same philosophies— conservation, the "new nationalism," control of big business—in the magazine *Outlook,* of which he had become a contributing editor.

The conflict between the liberals and conservatives in the Republican party took a new turn in January of 1911, when the liberals organized the National Progressive Republican League. The league's intention was to back someone against Taft at the 1912 convention, and the man who appeared to be the most likely candidate was LaFollette of Wisconsin. LaFollette was one of the country's leading Progressives, but he had his shortcomings as a presidential candidate. One was his personality: He was uncompromising and humorless, given to long-winded speech making, and he managed to be a complete autocrat in his own relationships at the same time that he went about the country crusading for democracy and the rule of the common man. Also, his following was mostly in the Midwest and many of the more respectable—and eastern—members of the Progressive movement regarded him as a dangerous radical, "a twentieth-century Cromwell who would march on Washington some day with a fanatical army of wheat and dairy farmers." [5] LaFollette formally declared his candidacy in June of 1911, but he was never a serious threat to Taft's renomination.

While LaFollette's campaign got off to its unpromising start and Taft's policies continued to irritate Progressives, Roosevelt was naturally asked many times if he would consider running again for the Presidency. He parried the questions, avoided comment—and, sometime in the latter months of 1911, began to believe that it might actually be necessary and possible for him to resume the country's leadership.

Early in February LaFollette appeared at a banquet of a publishers' convention in Philadelphia and made a speech which was so rambling and erratic that some people believed he was having a nervous breakdown. LaFollette was upset at the time over the illness of his daughter and angered by hecklers in his audience—but, whatever the cause of his behavior at the banquet, reports of it convinced many people that he was emotionally unstable.

A week later, seven Republican governors—from Wyoming, Kansas, Michigan, Missouri, Nebraska, New Hampshire, and West

[5] George H. Mayer, *The Republican Party 1854–1966* (New York: Oxford University Press, 1967), p. 322.

Virginia—met in Chicago and drafted a petition requesting Roosevelt to run. The open letter sent to Roosevelt from the Chicago meeting concluded:

> *In submitting this request, we are not considering your personal interests. We do not regard it as proper to consider either the interests or the preference of any man as regards the nomination for the Presidency. We are expressing our sincere belief and best judgment as to what is demanded of you in the interests of the people as a whole. And we feel that you would be unresponsive to a plain public duty if you should decline to accept the nomination, coming as the voluntary expression of the wishes of a majority of the Republican voters of the United States, through the action of their delegates in the next National Convention.*[6]

On February 21, a reporter in Cleveland asked Roosevelt if he intended to run; Roosevelt's answer was, "My hat is in the ring." He went on that day to make a speech in Columbus, advocating proposals which put him a step or two ahead of the most advanced Progressives: He backed the recall, the referendum and the initiative, and a scheme for popular recall of judicial decisions. A few days later he made his official announcement of candidacy in a reply to the governors' letter:

> *I deeply appreciate your letter and I realize to the full the heavy responsibility it puts upon me, expressing as it does the carefully considered convictions of the men elected by popular vote to stand as the heads of government in their several states.*
>
> *I absolutely agree with you that this matter is not to be decided with any reference to the personal preferences of any man, but purely from the standpoint of the interests of the people as a whole. I will accept the nomination for President if it is tendered to me, and I will adhere to this decision until the Convention has expressed its preference. One of the chief principles for which I have stood and for which I now stand, and which I have always endeavored and always shall endeavor to reduce to action, is the genuine rule of the people; and therefore I hope that so far as possible the people may be given the chance, through direct primaries, to express their preference as to who shall be the nominee of the Republican Presidential Convention.*[7]

If Roosevelt had remained in office he would, as President, have had control of the patronage and the party machinery, and he probably

---

[6] Lewis, *op. cit.,* p. 335.

[7] Lawrence F. Abbott, "The Roosevelt Campaign: A Review," *The Outlook,* June 8, 1912, p. 338.

would have been less eager to bring about an immediate change in the system. As it was, the primaries were his best opportunity to go directly to the people and show convention delegates he was the stronger candidate; his strategy, then, became one of using the primaries and at the same time advocating them as the more democratic means of choosing a presidential nominee.

Taft's best hopes lay with the older system: He could be sure of the delegations from the South—where skeleton Republican organizations existed for little else but to distribute government jobs and send delegates to national conventions—and he had the support of party leaders in some of the heavily populated eastern states. Taft did not welcome the battle with Roosevelt, and feared he would lose it. He told an aide:

> *I have a strong presentiment that the colonel is going to beat me in the Convention. It is almost a conviction with me. I shall continue to fight to the last moment, but when you see me claiming victory or my friends claiming victory for me, remember that I feel I am losing. . . .*[8]

But in spite of Taft's pessimism about the coming fight, the odds were good that the routine workings of party machinery and party loyalty would win it for him.

Early in March Roosevelt's campaign manager—Senator Joseph M. Dixon of Montana—challenged Taft to a nationwide primary contest, which Taft's campaign manager—Congressman William McKinley, the late President's son—naturally did not accept. Roosevelt prepared to fight Taft in eight states (California, Nebraska, New Jersey, New York, North Dakota, South Dakota, Wisconsin, and Oregon) which already had presidential primary laws, and the Progressives mobilized to widen the battle. A round of struggles between Taft and Roosevelt forces rocked state capitals around the country, and when it was over five more states (Massachusetts, Pennsylvania, Illinois, Maryland, and Ohio) had presidential primaries.[9]

The first primary was scheduled to take place on March 19 in North Dakota. LaFollette, Roosevelt, and Taft were on the ballot. LaFollette was actively campaigning in North Dakota, but Taft stayed in Washington and Roosevelt decided to stay home also and launch

---

[8] Archie Butt, *Taft and Roosevelt* (Garden City, N.Y.: Doubleday, 1930) II, 846.

[9] Davis, *op. cit.,* p. 46.

his campaign with a speech at Carnegie Hall. The speech, which was rather clouded and oratorical, talked about America's task "to strive for social and industrial justice, achieved through the genuine rule of the people"—possibly an indirect reference to primaries—and the need for "leaders of inspired idealism, leaders to whom are granted great visions, who dream greatly and strive to make their dreams come true; who can kindle the people with the fire from their own burning souls"—undoubtedly an indirect reference to himself.[10]

When the returns came in from North Dakota, they showed that the first statewide presidential preference primary in the history of the United States had been won by LaFollette, with 34,123 votes to Roosevelt's 23,669.[11] President Taft came in a weak third with 1,659 votes, which happened to be just 16 more than the number of federal officeholders in the state.[12] Roosevelt's supporters called it a defeat for Taft, Taft's supporters called it a defeat for Roosevelt, and LaFollette's supporters called it a victory for LaFollette—and all of them were right. For Taft it was worse than defeat; it was a humiliation—but Taft had not been expecting a victory. For Roosevelt it was a hard blow to take at the beginning of his campaign, while he was still trying to raise money, instill some optimism into his followers, and represent himself as riding on a wave of popular support. For LaFollette it was a remarkable comeback after having been written off by the experts.

Late in March Roosevelt received another defeat—this time from Taft—in the New York primary. Roosevelt charged—and the charge was probably true—that the pro-Taft state officials had run a dishonest election. "They are stealing the primary elections from us," he said. "I cannot and will not stand quietly by while the opinion of the people is being suppressed and their will thwarted." Roosevelt did not stand quietly by, but he was unable to prevent Taft from getting 83 of the state's 90 delegates. The next primary, in LaFollette's home state of Wisconsin, was another victory for LaFollette—and his last; in April the primaries began to go for Roosevelt.

His first big win was in Illinois, and it was a solid victory throughout the state, in every county. Roosevelt's campaign manager promptly announced that the Illinois primary ended the movement for Taft's nomination. "Wherever the voters themselves have had a

[10] Lewis, *op. cit.*, pp. 344–45.
[11] Overacker, *op. cit.*, p. 236.
[12] Mayer, *op. cit.*, p. 326.

chance to measure him with their own yardstick the result has been one unanimous repudiation," he said, offering the North Dakota, Wisconsin, and Illinois primaries as evidence. "This makes it impossible for any sane Republican leader to longer consider Taft as a possible candidate. . . . Roosevelt will be nominated on the first ballot."

Although this was nothing but campaign rhetoric, there is evidence that the Taft people were somewhat inclined to see things the same way. McKinley publicly admitted that his side had expected to be beaten, but not that badly, and conservatives began to talk about finding a new candidate, possibly Chief Justice Charles Evans Hughes. Still, Taft was picking up large numbers of delegates in the caucuses and conventions of states which did not have presidential primaries —a survey published in *The New York Times* after the Illinois primary gave Taft 337 votes, Roosevelt 113, and LaFollette 36. (The same poll showed that on the Democratic side Champ Clark, Speaker of the House of Representatives, had 137 votes to New Jersey Governor Woodrow Wilson's 35.) There were struggles going on all over the country in local and state party conventions, and most—but not all—of the struggles were being won by loyal party workers who would vote for Taft. In some states where progressivism was strong, however, pro-Roosevelt delegates were being elected; and in other states the Roosevelt forces, refusing to recognize the legitimacy of the existing pro-Taft party organizations, were holding rival conventions and selecting their own delegates. Sometimes the conflict in party meetings became physically violent—there was a riot at a Republican convention in Michigan early in April, and at about the same time three Roosevelt men were charged with assault in Missouri after beating up the pro-Taft chairman of a county caucus.

Meanwhile their leader declared: "We knocked them over the ropes in Illinois. And I want to see them take the count in Pennsylvania." He went on a whistle-stop speaking tour across the state which ended with a rally at the Philadelphia Opera House. In his speech at Philadelphia he took on the newly formed legal association which had criticized his proposals about the courts—his critics, he said, were all corporation lawyers who represented the trusts and special interests. In spite of their selfish opposition, he proposed to make "legislature and court alike responsible to the sober and deliberative judgment of the people, who are masters of both legislature and courts."

The Pennsylvania primary was another victory for Roosevelt and a defeat for both Taft and the party machine—headed by Boies Penrose, a ponderous Senator who was almost as heavy as the President. Bossism itself had become a campaign issue, part of T.R.'s whole thesis that he represented a politics of true and open democracy while Taft stood for special interests, corruption, and oligarchical control. He had flayed Taft for accepting the support of such men as Penrose of Pennsylvania, William Barnes and Samuel Koenig of New York, and George Cox of Ohio. The charge was true, but it still left Taft somewhat bewildered. "It is true that I have had the bosses with me," he wrote his brother, and complained: "Association with them when it is by and for Roosevelt has nothing of evil in it. It is only when they support me that the bosses are wicked." [13] A few weeks later, after he had decided to begin attacking Roosevelt, Taft said, "I don't recollect in the seven years that Theodore Roosevelt was President that his path was strewn with the bodies of dead bosses that he had killed."

Actually, the conflict in Pennsylvania had been one boss against another. William Flinn of Pittsburgh had tied his power aspirations to Roosevelt's campaign, and in the state convention which followed the election his followers took over control of the party machinery from Penrose.

Within a week after the Pennsylvania victory, Roosevelt won two more primaries, in Oregon and Nebraska. These were both states with long traditions of populism and progressivism, and in both of them Roosevelt came in first, LaFollette second, Taft third. These were not important to Taft—but the Massachusetts primary, coming up on April 30, was. That populous state would send 27 delegates to the convention, and it had a stalwart Republican organization which would do its best to deliver the votes for Taft. Late in April, it became public knowledge that Taft had decided to change his campaign tactics: So far he had talked about the issues and about his own programs and had avoided any personalized conflict. But now, it was announced, he would go into Massachusetts and attack Roosevelt's record.

"This wrenches my soul," he told an audience from the rear of

[13] Letter to Horace D. Taft, April 14, 1912, quoted in Henry F. Pringle, *The Life and Times of William Howard Taft* (New York: Farrar & Rinehart, Inc., 1939) II, 773.

his train. . . . I do not want to fight Theodore Roosevelt, but sometimes a man in a corner fights. I am going to fight."

Part of Taft's fight had to do with an antitrust suit which his
administration was bringing against International Harvester. As the
suit was being filed a Massachusetts Congressman claimed that
Roosevelt, when President, had deliberately stalled a suit against
International Harvester. A White House–inspired Senate resolution
called for the records of the earlier International Harvester investigation to be made public; and, although there was never any clear
proof that there had been corruption in Roosevelt's administration,
the whole affair was damaging to his reputation as a trust-buster.

While the International Harvester issue was breaking in the
newspapers, Taft made a speech in Boston in which he attacked
Roosevelt for violating the tradition against running for a third
term:

> *Mr. Roosevelt would accept a nomination for a third term on
> what ground? Not because he wishes it for himself. He has
> disclaimed any such desire. He is convinced that the American
> people think he is the only one to do the job (as he terms it),
> and for this he is ready to sacrifice his personal comfort. He
> does not define exactly what "the job" is which he is to do,
> but if we may infer from his Columbus platform it is to bring
> about a change of the social institutions of this country by
> legislation and other means which he may be able to secure as
> President. . . . I need hardly say that such an ambitious plan
> could not be carried out in one short four years. . . . We are
> left to infer, therefore, that "the job" which Mr. Roosevelt is
> to perform is one that may take a long time, perhaps the rest
> of his natural life. There is not the slightest reason why, if he
> secures a third term, and the limitation of the Washington,
> Jefferson, and Jackson tradition is broken down, he should not
> have as many terms as his natural life will permit. If he is
> necessary now to the government, why not later?* [14]

Roosevelt's reply to the Boston speech was: "I do not think
that Mr. Taft means ill; I think he means well, but he means well
feebly." Taft's attacks were, admittedly, not exactly hard-hitting,
but for the kindly President it was a great change to be attacking at
all. "I was a man of straw," he told another Massachusetts audience,
"but I have been a man of straw long enough. Every man who has

[14] Pringle, *op. cit.*, pp. 780–81.

blood in his body, and who has been misrepresented as I have been is forced to fight." Unfortunately for Taft, his statement that he had been a man of straw got more attention than his promise that he was going to stop being one.

While Taft was overcoming his reluctance to attack his former chief, his campaign manager called Roosevelt a traitor to the party for running ads in Massachusetts newspapers telling voters they did not have to be Republicans to vote for him. Registration of voters by party affiliation was still rare, and Roosevelt was taking advantage of the fact. "It means," said McKinley, "that Theodore Roosevelt is making a paid bid for the votes of Democrats, Socialists, and Prohibitionists to defeat President Taft, who is asking for Republican votes." [15]

The Massachusetts primary was a victory for Taft, but not a clear one. One of the shortcomings of presidential primaries was— and is—that they are sometimes confusing to the voters. In Massachusetts each ballot had eight columns and each voter was required to make 22 cross marks—voting for delegates from his district and state delegates-at-large. In the lists of delegates-at-large there were competing delegates pledged to Taft and the voter could choose any eight of them; however, if he voted for more than eight, his ballot was invalidated. There was also a place on the ballot to express a preference for Roosevelt, Taft, or LaFollette. The results of the election showed that Taft had won the preference vote, by 86,722 to Roosevelt's 83,099 [16]—but somehow Roosevelt had won the 8 delegates-at-large, by a plurality of about 8,000, and 10 of the 28 district delegates.[17]

Taft's only comment on the outcome was that he found it "satisfactory." Roosevelt magnanimously announced that, in view of Taft's win in the preference vote, he would expect the delegates-at-large to support Taft:

> If any one of them hesitates to do so I shall immediately write him and urge him with all the emphasis and insistence in my power to take the course indicated and support Mr. Taft at the Convention. In this fight I am standing for certain great principles, which I regard as vital to the present and future welfare of this Nation. . . . Foremost among these principles

[15] The New York Times, April 25, 1912.
[16] Overacker, op. cit., p. 236.
[17] Lewis, op. cit., p. 348.

> *is the right of the people to rule. . . . If the majority of the*
> *rank and file of the Republican party do not wish me nomi-*
> *nated, then most certainly I do not wish to be nominated.*[18]

This gesture won a good deal of favorable attention: *The New
York Times* called it "a manly and honorable thing." [19] A Democratic newspaper, the *Brooklyn Eagle,* was one of the many publications which, although not particularly impressed by the show of
generosity, felt that Roosevelt had emerged as the real winner in
Massachusetts:

> *Colonel Roosevelt's surrender of the eight delegates at large*
> *from the State of Massachusetts may deceive some people, but*
> *apparently the delegates themselves are not among the num-*
> *ber. . . . As usual, the Colonel is playing shrewd politics. . . .*
> *This achievement the Roosevelt men are entitled to regard as*
> *a victory, considering that every member of the Massa-*
> *chusetts Congressional delegation except Senator Lodge . . .*
> *was more or less actively arraigned against the Colonel's*
> *candidacy. To divide a State delegation in the face of this*
> *massed opposition is no small triumph. . . .*[20]

The next primary, in Maryland, also had a complicated ballot
arrangement, with a presidential preference vote and election of
delegates—not to the national convention, but to a state convention
which would in turn elect the national delegates. The chances of
confusion were increased by the high rate of illiteracy among the
voters. The outcome was another win for Roosevelt, 29,124 to Taft's
25,995.[21] The only problem this time was that a good number of the
delegates elected were actually Taft men, which meant that at the
state convention' they would undoubtedly elect like-minded delegates,
who would go to the national convention pledged to vote for Roosevelt in the first ballot and then most likely switch to Taft.

From the beginning of the campaign there had been persistent
rumors that if Roosevelt were not nominated by the Republicans he
would bolt the party and run as an independent candidate. These had
always been denied, but the increasing charges from the Roosevelt
camp that Taft's supporters were using illegal tactics kept them alive.
Campaigning in Maryland Roosevelt charged: "In Kentucky and

[18] "The Massachusetts Primary," *The Outlook*, May 11, 1912, pp. 62–63.
[19] *The New York Times,* quoted in *ibid.,* p. 64.
[20] *Brooklyn Eagle,* quoted in *ibid.*
[21] Overacker, *op. cit.,* p. 236.

Indiana, in New York City and elsewhere Mr. Taft knows well that the delegates elected for him represent barefaced frauds. . . ." But when a reporter asked him about the rumors that he would bolt, Roosevelt's answer was, "Not a word, not a word."

On May 14 Roosevelt won in California, where he had been supported by Governor Hiram Johnson and one of the strongest progressive state organizations in the country; then the contest shifted to Ohio.

The Ohio primary was the hardest-fought of the entire campaign. Ohio had 48 delegate votes in the convention; more importantly, it was Taft's home state, where a Roosevelt victory would seem to be undeniable proof of his greater popularity. Ohio had no presidential preference vote, only an election of delegates with nothing on the ballot to show whom any delegate supported. "As it stands in Ohio," Roosevelt said, "many of the voters may not know whether they are casting their ballots for me or not, and I will have to go there and teach them which delegates to vote for."

Both Taft and Roosevelt campaigned through Ohio by train; in the first part of the campaign as Taft's train moved through the river counties Roosevelt's train pursued it. Taft was making a point of talking to farmers who were concerned about his reciprocal trade agreement with Canada, which they feared might lower the prices of American farm products. Roosevelt had favored reciprocity, but in the Ohio farm country he changed his mind and began to criticize it. Taft was attacking Roosevelt for his "wild and ridiculous notions about Constitution and constitutional law," and then LaFollette began his campaign in the state and attacked Roosevelt for posing as the enemy of big business when he was receiving the backing of three powerful industrialists—George W. Perkins, Judge E. H. Gary, and Dan Hanna, son of the late Marcus Hanna. The three, LaFollette charged, had set up a million-dollar campaign fund for Roosevelt, and Hanna had furnished the train in which Roosevelt was now touring the state.

Taft also made an issue of Roosevelt's support from Hanna and from Toledo boss Walter Brown, a brewery and public utilities lobbyist whom Roosevelt had called a patriot and a Progressive. Taft said:

> *My friends, Mr. Roosevelt has introduced the issue of the bosses. He says that I am the candidate of the bosses and he is against them all and they are all against him. You have right*

> *here, in Northern Ohio, the only man who is in full commis-*
> *sion as a boss, Walter Brown of Toledo, and he is backed by*
> *Dan Hanna, who is associated with all the great interests in*
> *Northern Ohio, and they own three newspapers. . . . I am*
> *not attacking Mr. Roosevelt because Mr. Brown supports him.*
> *He is just like me and just like any other person in politics.*
> *He takes the support of any man who comes to him, without*
> *asking for a certificate of character.*[22]

This was in part an understandable personal attempt of Taft's to keep sharing the guilt in the matter of bossism; it was also a reaction to one aspect of Roosevelt's campaign strategy. By campaigning as the popular hero, the trust-busting Progressive, Roosevelt was winning substantial support among people who did not normally vote Republican.

In Ohio, as in Massachusetts, there was no registration of voters by party, but the election code did say that in order to vote in a party's primary one had to have been "in the past affiliated with the party." On that basis, Taft workers were preparing to try to challenge crossover voters at the polls; meanwhile, Taft tried to reduce Roosevelt's popularity among the working classes by pointing out the colonel's strong connections with party bosses and Wall Street multimillionaires.

Ohio was another triumph for Roosevelt, and the hardest blow of all for Taft. Roosevelt delegates won 165,809 votes; Taft men a total of 118,363.[23] The actual number of delegates elected was 31 for Roosevelt, 11 for Taft; Taft's control of the party machinery would give him the 6 delegates-at-large who would be elected at the state convention. But those were minor consolations—the main fact about the Ohio primary was that Taft had been decisively beaten in his own home state.

After Ohio there was a noticeable change in the tone of the campaign: as it moved on to New Jersey, Taft seemed to become strident. "I am here to warn you," he told one audience, "that in this preliminary contest before the Chicago Convention there is a crisis in your country's history that ought to nerve you to activity to prevent the dangers that threaten us as a constitutional Government." Roosevelt's campaign was like a victory parade—his crowds were large and noisy and enthusiastic, and he joked with them and elatedly

[22] *The New York Times,* May 18, 1912.
[23] Davis, *op. cit.,* p. 278.

predicted a first ballot triumph in Chicago and a new era of social betterment. The odd fact about this is that—while Taft was acting more and more like a defeated candidate and Roosevelt was acting more and more like a winner—every realistic estimated showed that Taft would be renominated. *The New York Times*'s running score of delegates showed that as of May 23, after the Ohio primary, Taft had 555 delegates, Roosevelt 377, LaFollette 37.[24] And Taft needed only 540 to be nominated.

Roosevelt won in New Jersey—61,297 to Taft's 44,034—and won again in South Dakota on June 4, the last primary before the convention.[25] It increased his delegate strength, but his only chance of being nominated lay in challenging the credentials of large numbers of Taft delegates chosen by party conventions, mostly in the southern states. Before the convention opened the Taft-Roosevelt contest was focused in the national committee hearings on contested delegates. The committee hearings were the real crisis of the convention. Outside the building where the committee was meeting went on all the preparations for convention showmanship and, if it came to it, convention violence—Roosevelt men dressed in Rough Rider uniforms were galloping through the streets of Chicago to remind the public of the colonel's heroism at San Juan Hill; inside the convention hall a barbed-wire fence festooned with red, white, and blue bunting was being rigged around the speaker's platform and a police committee under the direction of former Yale football star Pudge Heffelfinger was preparing to meet any disturbance. But whatever happened in the hall would be anticlimax—the real battle was the Roosevelt group's hopeless fight to challenge the credentials of 254 Taft delegates and have their own men seated instead. But Taft men were in control of the committee and when all the claimants had been heard, Taft men got 235 of the contested seats.

After this defeat—which the more realistic politicians in the Roosevelt forces had fully expected—the talk of a coming party bolt swept through Chicago. Then, dramatically, Roosevelt himself arrived. This was not done in 1912—declared candidates were expected to maintain a dignified distance from the convention city and let their followers fight it out. But Roosevelt stormed into Chicago, told reporters who asked how he felt, "I'm feeling like a bull moose!"

---

[24] *The New York Times,* May 23, 1912.
[25] Overacker, *op. cit.,* p. 236.

and proceeded to tell 20,000 of his faithful who filled an auditorium: "We fight in honorable fashion for the good of mankind; fearless of the future; unheeding of our individual fates; with unflinching hearts and undimmed eyes; we stand at Armageddon, and we battle for the Lord." The religious note inspired the opposition to get out a handbill announcing that Mr. Roosevelt planned to walk on the waters of Lake Michigan at 7:30 the following evening.[26]

There was more parliamentary maneuvering after the convention opened, as the Roosevelt men carried the argument over contested delegates onto the convention floor. But at this point the battle was effective only to let Progressives observe the full strength of the Taft steam roller and strengthen their will to follow Roosevelt out of the party when the time came. Meanwhile, Roosevelt was busily lining up financial support for this third party—which was guaranteed by George W. Perkins, of International Harvester.[27] On the convention floor, Ohio publisher Warren G. Harding made the nominating speech for Taft, calling him "the greatest Progressive of the age," and Taft was nominated on the first ballot with 561 votes.

The Progressives left and reconvened at Orchestra Hall to launch their third party. A few weeks later the Progressive party, also commonly known as the Bull Moose party, held its first national convention and nominated Roosevelt for President and California's governor Hiram Johnson for Vice-President. The Democrats, meeting in Baltimore just after the Republican convention, had, after 46 ballots, nominated Woodrow Wilson. Wilson's nomination was a blow to Roosevelt's hopes, because Wilson was also a liberal and, unlike Roosevelt, he had a well-organized national party behind him. In the three-cornered election in November Wilson won 435 electoral votes, Roosevelt 88, and Taft 8.

After 1912 the drive for presidential primaries continued for a while, and by 1916 there were laws providing for them in 26 states. Then the number began to decline; the idealists were becoming disenchanted with the results, and the professional politicians had never liked them to begin with. There was another surge of popular interest in presidential primaries after World War II, paralleling the growth of mass communications media.

---

[26] Mayer, *op. cit.*, p. 328.
[27] *Ibid.*, p. 329.

Although primaries have become major news in recent years, their importance in the nominating procedure is more difficult to assess. One thing is certain: No candidate can win a nomination at the present time by winning primaries alone. The total number of delegates so chosen is not enough to constitute a majority in either party's convention. In 1912, when Theodore Roosevelt became the first candidate in American history to use the primaries in a try for a presidential nomination, he did so knowing the primaries could not win enough delegates, but might give him a way of demonstrating and at the same time building his popularity. It was an article of Progressive faith that the primaries would in time become the accepted national method of nominating presidential candidates—but the reform faltered and remains unfinished. Many politicians have tended to agree with Harry Truman's opinion that presidential primaries are "eyewash," and others have recognized, as Theodore Roosevelt did, that they were a powerful tool for manipulating public opinion. But in themselves presidential primaries still do not determine presidential nominations—any more than they did in 1912.

RADICALS AND
REFORMERS
IN THE 1930's

5

1930
Minnesota
Floyd B. Olson vs. *Ray P. Chase*

Although Floyd Björnsterne Olson is remembered as one of the leading radical politicians of the 1930's, he was actually a man who formed his opinions and guided his career with caution, prudence, and a good eye for the possibilities of success; he liked to think of himself as an opportunist. Another seemingly contradictory fact about him is that, although he occupies an important place in the history of midwestern agrarian politics, his own life was lived in the city: he was born and raised in a predominantly Jewish neighborhood in Minneapolis, studied law, and served for two years as county attorney in a heavily urbanized area. His farm background consisted of a few summer jobs during his young manhood. Yet farmers, especially midwestern farmers, regarded Olson as one of their great champions during the Depression years; and, as much as any man, he represents a bridge between the Populism of the 1890's and the New Deal of the 1930's. He is also one of the forefathers of a state party from which a later generation of politicians—including Hubert Humphrey and Eugene McCarthy—emerged to national prominence in the 1960's.

The wave of agrarian discontent that began to move across the United States in the years after the Civil War was not a brief uprising, a thing to occupy the public mind in an election or two and then subside. It was part of a slow and deep change in the way most Americans lived their lives and earned and spent their money. It was part of the country's long historical journey from the time when Andrew Jackson had said to Congress that "the agricultural

79

interest of our country is so essentially connected with every other and so superior in importance to them all, that it is scarcely necessary to invite it to your particular attention," to the time when another President would say, "The business of America is business." [1]

As the American economy became less agriculture-oriented and more business-oriented, farmers felt themselves victimized by the changing system. Although often their farms were mortgaged, they were forced to continue borrowing at high rates of interest in order to purchase the manufactured items they needed. In order to ship their crops to market they had to use the railroads, which, until federal regulation began, were free to fix their rates and cut deeply into the farmer's profits. They were equally at the mercy of the owners of mills and grain elevators. In the late nineteenth century these complaints began to be articulated into political aims, and farmers began to organize among themselves to make demands on the political system. For example, in 1873 an Illinois State Farmers' Association—which a year later would evolve into an Independent Reform party—met and issued a "Farmers' Declaration of Independence," which read in part:

> We . . . the producers of the state in our several counties assembled . . . do solemnly declare that we will use all lawful and peaceable means to free ourselves from the tyranny of monopoly. . . . That to this end we hereby declare ourselves absolutely free and independent of all past political connections, and that we will give our suffrage only to such men for office, as we have good reason to believe will use their best endeavors to the promotion of these ends. . . .[2]

In the Midwest and West there emerged many third parties, some of which became elements in the national Populist movement. In the South, agrarian reformers were generally kept within the Democratic party structure by the fear of what a breakdown of one-party rule might do to white supremacy. Tom Watson of Georgia, a Populist leader, said the argument against independent political movements in the South could "be boiled down to one word—nigger." [3]

The same industrialization process which was pushing agricul-

---

[1] Calvin Coolidge, Jan. 17, 1925.

[2] Anna Rochester, *The Populist Movement in the United States* (New York: International Publishers, 1943), pp. 19–20.

[3] John D. Hicks, *The Populist Revolt* (Minneapolis, 1931), p. 218, quoted in George H. Mayer, *The Republican Party 1854–1966* (New York: Oxford University Press, 1967), p. 237.

ture into a back-seat position in the American economy—and, in the process, bringing about the articulation of a new set of political interests—was at the same time creating yet another political force: labor. Farmers and workers often regarded one another with mistrust and doubted that they had political goals in common—but it was a favorite argument of radical theorists that the two were natural allies. They were both the true producers of wealth, who created America's goods out of their toil, and they were both exploited by the financial entrepreneurs. The 1892 convention which gave birth to the People's party was dominated by members of various farmers' organizations, but other groups which sent delegates included the Knights of Labor, the United Mine Workers of Ohio, and the Ancient Order of Anti-Monopolists.

The People's party, which attempted to mold the various elements of the Populist movement into a permanent third party, never managed to become a truly national organization. Its presidential candidate in 1892, James B. Weaver, won 22 electoral votes—all from the Midwest and West. The Populist movement failed to unseat the existing major parties, but many of its goals were eventually accepted—first by the Democrats and later, in the era of Theodore Roosevelt Progressivism, by the Republicans. As that happened, most of the state third parties which had arisen with the movement disappeared.

Then, in the 1920's, there were new signs of possible major realignments of party loyalties. Stuart Rice published a study in 1924 which suggested three reasons for the instability:

> *(1) Habits of independence created by the insurgent revolt of 1912. It is probable that many staunch Republicans, under the sway of Theodore Roosevelt's vigorous personality, broke loose for the first time from their habitual party ties. Having thereby ceased to be "regulars," it seems likely that many such individuals have never since felt themselves as definitely bound as before to a party organization. (2) A majority of the nation's women were enfranchised between 1916 and 1920. In most cases these new voters were without previous party allegiances or voting habits. (3) Situations growing out of the war have confronted many individuals and groups with a conflict between established political habits and the drive of new emotional sympathies or antagonisms.*[4]

[4] Stuart A. Rice, *Farmers and Workers in American Politics* (New York: Columbia University Press, 1924), pp. 26–27. Reprinted by permission.

One aspect of this instability was a renewed move to unite the farmers and the workers into a single political force. The Farmer-Labor movement was strongest in the Midwest. It emerged as a political party in Minnesota in 1918, when David H. Evans, endorsed by both the farmers' Nonpartisan League and the State Federation of Labor, ran for governor—unsuccessfully—as the candidate of the "Farmer-Labor party." [5]

The party was at first only a temporary coalition, created mainly because the Nonpartisan League candidate for the Republican nomination had been defeated in the primary. The coalition was dominated by the Nonpartisan League, whose leader, an ex-farmer named A. C. Townley, felt that in general it was best for the league and the unions to work within the existing parties. But in 1919 some union leaders organized a Working People's Nonpartisan League, with definite intentions of building it into a third party. As the third-party movement grew there was disagreement between the two leagues; Townley resigned from the movement in 1922, and later the two leagues were merged into the new Farmer-Labor Federation. In 1922 a Farmer-Labor candidate, Henrik Shipstead, was elected to the United States Senate, and there was new speculation around the country that a national third party might be in the making. "The discontented farmer and the aspiring laborer have got together," William Allen White wrote in the *New York Sunday Tribune*.[6] *The New York Times,* however, said, "Farmer-Labor is a contradiction and an absurdity in terms." [7]

The state in which the new party was trying to function was solidly Republican. It had cast its electoral votes for Lincoln in 1860 and had gone Republican in every presidential election since then with the one exception of 1912, when the state had been carried by Theodore Roosevelt.

Wheat had been Minnesota's main crop in its first years of settlement, but gradually there had been an increase in other crops, and a boom in dairy farming. Parts of the state were covered by thick forests, which were logged and the logs milled and processed into building material and paper products.

[5] Theodore C. Blegen, *Minnesota: A History of the State* (Minneapolis: University of Minnesota Press, 1963), p. 479.

[6] *New York Sunday Tribune,* Nov. 12, 1922, quoted in Rice, *op. cit.,* p. 31.

[7] *The New York Times,* Aug. 6, 1923. © 1923 by The New York Times Company. Reprinted by permission.

Another major source of Minnesota's wealth was the iron mines, the fantastically rich Mesabi and Vermillion ranges in the northern part of the state which were producing nearly half of the iron ore for American industry. The mines had brought new workers into Minnesota, and they had also attracted the attention of John D. Rockefeller, Andrew Carnegie, and J. Pierpont Morgan, whose tradings and mergers gave birth eventually to the United States Steel Corporation. So as Minnesota's agricultural patterns changed, the whole state developed from an exclusively agricultural area to a state of iron mines and railroads and factories. In addition to farms and farm towns it contained densely populated areas, such as St. Paul–Minneapolis and the port city of Duluth on Lake Superior. One of these urban areas, Hennepin County—which includes Minneapolis—was the home and political base of the most successful politician to emerge from the Farmer-Labor movement, Floyd B. Olson.

In his early years Olson, after completing a night school law course, flirted with both the existing major parties in Hennepin County. He tried for the Democratic nomination for Congress in 1918 and 1920, and in between managed to win an appointment as assistant county attorney from the county's Republican government. Late in 1920, when the incumbent county attorney was dismissed for misconduct, Olson was moved up to fill the vacancy. It seems entirely possible that, if there had been room at the top, Olson might have run for state office as a Republican. His biographer says that in these early days "His political convictions seemed to have a chameleonlike quality difficult to square with his later professions of left-wing orthodoxy." [8]

Olson was reelected twice as county attorney—a nonpartisan office—and during his terms he developed useful political contacts and political experience without having to tie himself to any party or faction. He had no statewide reputation, but his position in Hennepin county was sufficient to make him a valuable addition to the still-struggling Farmer-Labor party.

Olson began to be noticed by the Farmer-Labor leadership in 1922 and 1923 as a result of this activities in the county attorney's office. In a highly publicized dynamiting case, Olson's investigation revealed that the president of the Citizens' Alliance, an antiunion

[8] George H. Mayer, *The Political Career of Floyd B. Olson* (Minneapolis: University of Minnesota Press, 1951), p. 14.

businessmen's organization, had hired a private detective to try to frame a union official. No conviction resulted from the affair, but liberals were impressed by Olson's criticism of the Citizens' Alliance. He said:

> If private organizations—no matter what kind they may be— which undertake to enforce the law without cooperating with the duly constituted authorities, and in disregard of the police, are not wiped out, this country will soon reach a condition where faction and class violence will be the rule and not the exception.[9]

It was not the strongest possible denunciation, but any kind of opposition to the powerful Citizens' Alliance by a Hennepin County officeholder was, to union men, a welcome change.

Soon after that, Olson started a grand jury investigation into the reasons behind the rapid rise in coal prices—which in turn stimulated the Interstate Commerce Commission to investigate and to rescind an increase in the freight rate for coal shipments. Olson's battle against the price of coal, in the middle of a Minneapolis winter, also helped develop his new image as a defender of the working classes.

It was at about this time that Olson began to be mentioned as a possible candidate for governor in 1924. He campaigned actively, making speeches to labor groups and becoming acquainted with local Farmer-Labor leaders. His strategy was based on becoming the candidate of the urban and labor segment of the party, who would be heavily represented in the party's forthcoming state convention at St. Cloud. But, although leadership in the party was gradually passing from the farmers to labor, the union men were afraid that any attempt to exercise too strong a control over the party's decisions at this point would break the fragile alliance that held it together. The farmers wanted the St. Cloud convention to forgo endorsing a candidate for governor and leave it to be decided by an open primary in June; and the labor wing agreed. Olson was forced to compete for the nomination against seven other candidates. It would be a difficult contest: most of the candidates were old-timers who were well known to the Farmer-Labor movement, but Olson was 33 and had only recently joined the party.

Olson's leading opponent in the primary was Tom Davis, a

---

[9] *Minneapolis Labor Review,* Jan. 12, 1923, quoted in Mayer, *Political Career,* p. 26.

veteran of the Nonpartisan League and the first Farmer-Labor campaign, a native of rural western Minnesota, a grizzled, frock-coated country lawyer whose specialty was representing farmers in suits against the railroads. Davis naturally tried to characterize Olson as an ambitious politician who was trying to climb abroad the Farmer-Labor bandwagon. Olson won the endorsement of the Hennepin County Farmer-Labor central committee, which helped him consolidate his strength in Minneapolis, and he also won the personal endorsement of the dying Charles A. Lindbergh, an ex-Congressman and father of a young pilot who a few years later would become one of America's greatest celebrities. Lindbergh's personal prestige and background as a Nonpartisan League campaigner helped Olson in the rural areas. In the end, Olson's slim primary victory—he led Davis by a few hundred votes—was probably due to a splitting-up of the farm vote.

The Farmer-Labor party was better organized in 1924 than it had ever been, and after the June primary it had a young, attractive and articulate candidate. But the Republicans still had a far greater registration in Minnesota; they had a strong candidate of their own in Theodore Christianson, former speaker of the state House of Representatives; and, before the campaign was over, they had a chance to identify Olson with communism.

In 1924, at the same time that Olson was running for the governorship of Minnesota, Senator Robert M. LaFollette of Wisconsin launched his third-party campaign for the presidency of the United States. LaFollette's Progressive party, like the Farmer-Labor party of which Olson was now a leader, had roots in the old Populist movement, and it was inevitable that there would be some link between the two campaigns. The possibilities of close cooperation were badly damaged, however, by a convention of radicals in St. Paul in June.

The organizers of the convention, who included some Farmer-Labor activists and some Communists, were meeting to form a national organization to support LaFollette. LaFollette himself would have nothing to do with the convention because of the Communists involved; he boycotted it, refused to accept its support, and urged his followers to do likewise. But Olson took no stand against the convention; some of his party's leaders were involved in it, and the official Farmer-Labor policy was to accept any man's vote, Communist or not. Olson's failure to repudiate the St. Paul convention made it easier for the Republican opposition and press to accuse him of seeking Communist support, and it also led to friction within the state between the LaFollette organization and the Farmer-Labor party. There were completely separate campaign organizations where there might have been close cooperation, and there were serious conflicts over the collection of campaign funds.

When the votes had been counted in November, Minnesota was still a strong Republican state. Christianson defeated Olson by a margin of some 43,000 votes out of a total of 865,000; and, by an even wider margin, Calvin Coolidge defeated LaFollette.[10]

After 1924 the growth of the Farmer-Labor party lost some of its impetus, and Olson went into a long period of maintaining a certain distance from Farmer-Labor politics. He was of course well known around the state after the campaign, and he was a young man to have been a candidate for governor; according to his biographer, he told a friend that he intended to devote six years to building statewide support before he would try for the office again.[11]

In 1925, the Farmer-Labor movement underwent a major reorganization, primarily to avoid charges of procommunism in future elections. In order to bring about the change and dramatize it for the public, the Farmer-Labor Federation was dissolved and a new group, the Farmer-Labor Association, was formed to take its place. The constitution of a new association prohibited Communists from becoming members.

Olson became a member of the executive board of the association, but he showed no eagerness to be its candidate again. In 1926 he did not seek the gubernatorial nomination and instead occupied himself with running for reelection in the nonpartisan office of county attorney. His victory, at the same time that Magnus Johnson, the Farmer-Labor candidate for governor, was defeated, helped maintain the conviction of many of the party's leaders that he was a strong votegetter, possibly more needed by the party than the party was needed by him. In 1928 he declined the nomination again, and another candidate, Ernest Lundeen, was defeated by Christianson.

As the 1930 election approached there were indications that it might be a good year for a Farmer-Labor candidate. One major turning point was the New York stock-market crash of October 29, 1929. In retrospect that day marks the end of the prosperous, Republican-dominated era of the 1920's and the beginning of the Depression; at the time, however, the portents were not so easy to read. On the day

[10] Mayer, *Political Career*, p. 35.
[11] *Ibid.*, p. 37.

after the crash, an article in a Minneapolis newspaper had these headings: LEADERS FIND BUSINESS GOOD IN NORTHWEST. GENERAL SITUATION FUNDAMENTALLY SOUND, BANKERS AND OTHERS REPORT. FARMERS ARE OPTIMISTIC. LIVESTOCK INDUSTRY SATISFACTORY. MORE EMPLOYMENT THAN A YEAR AGO.[12]

A factor much easier to assess was Governor Christianson's decision, after his six years in office, to run for the United States Senate. It meant that the Farmer-Labor candidate, whoever he might be, would probably not have to face quite so formidable an opponent.

The 1930 Farmer-Labor convention was scheduled to begin on March 27 at St. Paul. As the time approached, Olson had frequent meetings with various party leaders but refused to say whether he definitely wanted the nomination. As late as February 10, he was still hinting that he might decide to run for Senator instead of governor. It was not until March 23 that he definitely announced he would seek the gubernatorial endorsement. In the following two days his urban supporters assured that he would get it: A caucus of Hennepin County delegates voted to back Olson on the 24th, and on the 25th the caucus of Ramsey County delegates, in neighboring St. Paul, voted likewise. Since those two delegations combined made up more than half the total, the convention opened with Olson already in control.

He sat in with the platform committee, and saw to it that the document which emerged was far less radical than the platform he had had to campaign with in 1924. Committee members were persuaded to delete items calling for a forty-hour work week, unemployment insurance, a state income tax, recognition of Soviet Russia, and government ownership of key industries. Where Socialist proposals remained, the term "public ownership" was not used. In his message to the convention Olson stressed reform over economics. He said:

> *The people of Minnesota are desirous of promoting efficiency in, and returning integrity to, the government of Minnesota. They realize that the Republican Party has been and is in politics for securing patronage and special privilege. You know and I know that the Farmer-Labor Party is in politics for securing efficiency and integrity in government and for securing economic justice and equality of opportunity for the citizens of the state.*[13]

[12] Blegen, *op. cit.,* p. 521.
[13] John S. McGrath and James J. Delmont, *Floyd Björnsterne Olson* (St. Paul: The Authors, 1937), p. 41.

Clearly, Olson was shifting the entire Farmer-Labor party to the right. After the convention a conservative St. Paul newspaper said "the body of radicalism goes marching on, but the soul lies mouldering in the grave of forgotten political philosophies." [14]

Although Olson's belief that it was "not up to the Farmer-Labor party to introduce new and unique ideas of government" did not sit well with old-line radicals, it gave the party new political respectability and a much better chance of overthrowing the Republican establishment. The Republicans had been in power for a long time; there was no secret about their use of patronage in filling public jobs, and there had been occasional scandals regarding misuse of public money. It seemed unlikely that even in 1930 the majority of Minnesotans would vote in a party of agrarian radicals, union men, and Socialists; but, Olson calculated, the chances were good that they might vote in an administration pledged to nonpartisanship, economy, and honest government.

In the June primary there was much more interest in the Republican contest than in Farmer-Labor. Olson was unopposed and running with the convention's preprimary endorsement, but the Republicans had several candidates competing for the gubernatorial nomination, as well as a contest for the senatorial nomination between Governor Christianson and the incumbent, Thomas D. Schall, the nation's only blind senator. Many Farmer-Laborites crossed over in the open primary to vote Republican; the total showed 477,816 Republican ballots cast, 75,050 Farmer-Labor.[15] Olson won the Farmer-Labor nomination, former state auditor Ray P. Chase won the Republican nomination, and Ed Indrehus won the Democratic nomination. The surprises of the primary were the senatorial nominations: The aging Schall defeated Christianson—which may have been a result of the crossover vote—and the convention-endorsed Farmer-Labor candidate lost the nomination to Ernest Lundeen.

The latter upset was embarrassing to Olson, who had made a behind-the-scenes deal for cooperation with the Democrats. The understanding was that the Democratic candidate for governor, Indrehus, would make only a token campaign against Olson, and the Farmer-Labor candidate for senator would return the favor in *his* campaign.[16] Lundeen, however, had not been a party to the bargain.

[14] *St. Paul Pioneer Press,* March 31, 1930.
[15] Mayer, *Political Career,* p. 49.
[16] *Ibid.*

Later in the campaign, Chase charged that Olson had also intrigued with certain factions in the Republican party. Olson did openly seek support of both Republicans and Democrats, and an independent Olson-for-Governor committee was set up to work outside of the Farmer-Labor movement. At the same time, the Farmer-Labor party was recruiting new members and establishing new clubs throughout the state; contrary to the evidence of the primary vote, Farmer-Labor was more of a genuine political party and better organized than it had ever been.

Through the summer of 1930, as the candidates moved out across Minnesota in search of votes, Chase came up with a campaign technique new to the rural Midwest. He traveled in an automobile trailer with a loudspeaker system on top. Using this, he was able to cover the country rapidly, making speeches from rural crossroads and village main streets with a minimum amount of advance preparation; by mid-September, according to his campaign committee, he had made 225 speeches.

Olson stuck to more traditional methods. A newspaper dispatch from his campaign read:

> *If there is a political meeting in town, and a tall, slightly smiling gentleman of easy gait and thoughtful stoop approaches from the direction of the grain elevator, the depot or the implement shop, look again. It may be Floyd B. Olson, Farmer-Labor candidate for Governor. If it is, that will be the first warning that you have that he has arrived. For Mr. Olson has shunned all the modern and scientific campaign aids adopted in the novel vote drive of his Republican opponent and sticks to old-fashioned campaigning.*[17]

The report did not mention that Olson, who, according to contemporaries had a voice that could be heard a block away, had less use for a loudspeaker system.

As the Olson campaign progressed it won new followers among women's organizations, civic groups, attorneys, businessmen. By campaigning as a reformer, Olson was putting together a new political coalition. Chase criticized Olson for playing down his party's traditional Socialist doctrine. "The Farmer-Labor party," he claimed, "is dead. Its soul fled when its principles were abandoned." [18] But before

[17] *St. Paul Dispatch*, Oct. 10, 1930, quoted in McGrath and Delmont, *op. cit.*, p. 44.
[18] *Minnesota Union Advocate*, Aug. 7, 1930, quoted in Mayer, *Political Career*, p. 52.

the campaign was over, Chase was discovering the possibilities of non-partisanship also: He was the first candidate in the history of Minnesota Republicanism to publish campaign material without the party designation.

Olson's campaign promises included guarantees that he would build his administration with qualified men, regardless of their party affiliations; reorganization of the state's crime-fighting agencies; support of relief and price stabilization laws for farmers; and a tax on chain stores (a new and fast-growing business in Minnesota) to protect small-town merchants. The only major welfare state proposal which he continued to advocate strongly throughout his campaign was an old-age pension. On October 15 he told a St. Paul audience: "We are engaged in mass production and machines are fast taking the place of men. In this mad machine period when a man or woman reaches the age of forty-five, he or she is a candidate for the scrap heap. Provision must be made into law for the protection of the aged." [19]

National politics were reflected in Olson's attempts to identify Chase with Herbert Hoover. Hoover had carried Minnesota in 1928, but he was unpopular with farmers because of his opposition to the McNary-Haugen Bill for stabilizing farm prices, and he was becoming unpopular with businessmen for his failure to deal with the country's economic problems. Speaking in the little town of Waterville, Olson criticized Hoover for his "do-nothing" policy and criticized Chase for praising Hoover.

While many small businessmen were being persuaded by Olson, big business tended to stick with Chase. Minnesota's powerful and controversial lumber king, E. W. Backus, in a statement that probably did Chase more harm than good, declared: "I have been a Republican in Minnesota for forty years and I have quite an investment in the Republican party." [20]

In the last days of the campaign there were charges that the leading elder statesman of the Farmer-Labor party, Senator Henrik Shipstead, did not endorse Olson. The white-haired ex-dentist was, at that time, the only member of the United States Senate from a minor party. He was, in such a position, hardly capable of putting many Farmer-Labor principles into action, but he was a highly respected leader of the party and his refusal to approve of Olson might persuade many of the members that Olson had, as the Republicans

[19] McGrath and Delmont, *op. cit.,* p. 46.
[20] *Ibid.,* p. 46.

claimed, abandoned the party's principles. He claimed to have fears of Olson's possible connections with the Minneapolis underworld, but actually his coolness toward Olson was probably only jealousy toward a rival for the party's leadership.[21] At any rate, after an Olson representative followed him to Los Angeles and then returned with him to Minneapolis, Shipstead issued a restrained endorsement of Olson's candidacy.

Olson had challenged Chase to a series of debates, which Chase declined, but near the end of the campaign there was one joint appearance in Minneapolis. It was a three-way debate, although Indrehus, the Democratic candidate, who was conducting a rather relaxed campaign, described himself as more of a referee between two real fighters. It was not much of a debate in any case. Both Chase and Olson delivered prepared speeches; Olson's was another attack on the inefficiencies of the administration, including its policy of finding jobs for party old-timers who had been voted out of elective offices. "The present administration," he said, "is an administration of lame ducks. The state blue book shows the appointive officers of thirteen state commissions to be lame ducks, men who have been defeated by the people and then appointed to office by the machine." [22]

The real significance of Olson's campaign lay not so much in what he said as in what he did not say. What he said was for the most part the rhetoric of reform, which as he expressed it sounded more like the campaign of a nonpartisan fusion candidate than the campaign of a Farmer-Labor leader. The platform of 1930 had relieved him of the burden of most of the party's traditional Socialist doctrine, and, as the campaign progressed, Olson had quietly dropped even some of the measures of the platform of 1930—such as abolishing injunctions against labor unions. The returns showed the effectiveness of his strategy: he won by a margin of nearly two hundred thousand votes, far more than his most optimistic backers had expected. The vote was Olson, 473,154; Chase, 289,528; Indrehus, 29,108.[23]

During the six years Olson served as governor the Minnesota Farmer-Labor party, although always seething with conflict between its urban and rural segments, its militant radicals and its pragmatic politicians, was unquestionably the strongest third-party organization

[21] Mayer, *Political Career,* p. 55.
[22] *Ibid.,* p. 47.
[23] *Ibid.*

in the United States; in Minnesota, the Democrats were the real third party. Olson himself moved gradually to the left and emerged as one of the country's leading radicals, although his tendency to modify his doctrines to suit the occasion continued to disappoint many of the party's activists.

Olson's first legislature was dominated by conservatives, and he was unable to pass any of his major programs. As the depression increased the need for relief for needy families, he was criticized by party leftists for organizing a statewide campaign for contributions from private donors before trying any kind of government program consistent with welfare-state philosophy.

Olson became a close friend of New York's Democratic governor, Franklin D. Roosevelt, and in the 1932 campaign there was again behind-the-scenes cooperation between Democrats and Farmer-Labor. Olson was reelected and for the first time in its history Minnesota cast its presidential electoral votes for a Democrat.

During his second term Olson became more militant; depression conditions were increasing the public demand for government action and conservatives were on the defensive. Olson fought hard for welfare legislation and made fiery speeches over the radio and on the steps of the state capitol to let his constituents know he was fighting. In 1933 he won a state income tax law, the beginnings of an old-age pension system, and a law banning the use of injunctions in labor disputes. By executive order he called a temporary halt to the mortgage sales by which destitute farmers and homeowners were being evicted throughout the state. The cost of relief programs rose to $9,000,000 in 1933 and to more than $33,000,000 in 1934—85 per cent of which was absorbed by the federal government.[24]

As his national reputation grew he became the spokesman for a plan for a system of federal price supports for farmers, and an enthusiastic backer of the National Recovery Act with its fair trade practice codes and protection of organized labor. He was considered by Roosevelt for the post of first ambassador to Soviet Russia and was considered by left-wingers as a possible third-party presidential candidate for 1936.

In 1934 when Olson began his campaign for his third term the cautiousness of 1930 seemed for a while to have been abandoned. He told the 1934 convention that the party's mission was:

24 Blegen, *op. cit.*, p. 526.

> . . . *not to make more secure the position of those who rule the economic world but to bring more security and comfort to the masses who create our wealth and receive little of what they create and no thanks for their toil as a reward.* . . . *Our ultimate goal is a co-operative commonwealth wherein government will stifle as much as possible, the greed and avarice of the private profit system and will bring about a more equitable distribution of the wealth produced by the hands and minds of the people.*[25]

And he also said, in an unprepared addition to the written text of his speech: "I am frank to say I am what I want to be. I am a radical." [26] Olson left the convention after that rousing speech, and the inspired delegates proceeded to write a platform that he would be busy trying to live down for the rest of the campaign. It demanded "a complete reorganization of the social structure into a cooperative commonwealth" and contained a public ownership section calling for state control of mines, public utilities, transportation, banks, and factories. The platform was a good source of material for Olson's opponents. One said that "for the first time . . . the Farmer-Labor party goes before the voters stripped of camouflage and expediency, revealed as the menace it is, supporting principles of government un-American and unwise to experiment with." [27]

Olson had to make a statewide radio speech interpreting the platform, and finally managed to have the party central committee issue a revised platform which separated the public-ownership items as "ultimate aims," and clearly stated that "The Farmer-Labor party is opposed to state ownership and operation of small businesses such as grocery stores, meat shops, department stores, millinery establishments, drug stores, and similar enterprises." [28] But the charges of Communist influence continued, and throughout the campaign Olson was forced to deny them. He was reelected to a third term, but only by a plurality of 72,453.[29]

His final term of office was marred by a deadlock with the legislature and by physical illness. He had suffered from ulcers for years; then, in late 1935 and the first weeks of 1936, a series of examinations at the Mayo Clinic revealed that he had an advanced

[25] McGrath and Delmont, *op. cit.*, pp. 247–48.
[26] Mayer, *Political Career*, p. 171.
[27] *Ibid.*, p. 173.
[28] *Ibid.*, p. 179.
[29] McGrath and Delmont, *op. cit.*, p. 112.

pancreatic cancer. He planned to run for the Senate in 1936 and, although he was steadily losing strength and weight and the cancer was spreading into his esophagus, he continued to campaign. On March 27, he appeared at the party's state convention and made a two-hour speech. In the June primary he won the senatorial nomination and Elmer A. Benson was nominated as the Farmer-Labor candidate for governor. He made a few more speeches and public appearances and for a while seemed to be recovering. In July he underwent another operation. He still planned to carry on the campaign and assured the Farmer-Labor central committee that he would "be physically well in ample time." [30] He was in the hospital again in August; President Roosevelt planned to visit him on August 31, but the last meeting did not take place. Olson died on August 22, at the age of 45.

Benson was elected in 1936, but he was the last Farmer-Labor governor of Minnesota. The party was deteriorating from within because of factionalism; it had lost its reform impetus in eight years of incumbency; and a revived Republican party led by young St. Paul attorney Harold Stassen was on the rise. In 1938 Stassen defeated Benson and Minnesota entered another long period of Republican ascendancy. That ended after the two opposition parties merged into the Democratic-Farmer-Labor party in 1944—a fusion brought about by another new group of political leaders, including Hubert Humphrey, Orville Freeman, and Eugene McCarthy.

The election of Floyd B. Olson to the governorship of Minnesota in 1930 and the resultant eight years of Farmer-Labor control of the state's executive branch was the most significant political accomplishment of any American radical party in the twentieth century; it is most unlikely that it would have come about at all if Olson had been a more consistent radical. He summed up his own philosophy in a speech to a youth conference when he said

> *I am an opportunist, and I hasten to call myself one. . . . I do not speak facetiously . . . an opportunist is one who will use any agency he finds at hand—whether he believes in the entire program—to translate into action such part of his own program as is possible. . . . I am an individualist in that I will go down the line with any organization that is going my way until I reach the crossroad.*[31]

30 *Ibid.*, p. 133.
31 Olson papers, memo of speech (undated), quoted in Mayer, *Political Career*, p. 255.

6

1933
New York City
John P. O'Brien–Joseph McKee–Fiorello LaGuardia

The urban political machine has come down through American history as a curious combination of big business, secret society, crime syndicate, political alliance, and self-contained welfare state. The oldest and best-known—and once the most powerful—of all the machines is Manhattan's Tammany Hall, which began its existence as the Society of St. Tammany on May 12, 1789, some two months after George Washington had begun his first term of office. Tammany was already a political force by the time of Thomas Jefferson's presidency, and by the late 1860's it had evolved into the prototype of the machine, complete with the first "boss," William M. Tweed. The Tweed Ring, during its few years of control, is estimated to have made some 30 to 200 million dollars through various kinds of kickbacks, embezzlements, and bribes.[1]

Tammany was an efficient and well-diversified business organization, delivering many kinds of goods and services. At its higher levels it exchanged public contracts for political contributions and personal payments to officials; in the middle ranges it provided jobs and business opportunities—many of the kind described as "honest graft," which meant simply making good use of inside information— to its members in exchange for years of faithful service in the organization. At its lower levels it was a center of community life, a benevolent big brother to the masses of new immigrants who came to New York with no skills for survival in a society they did not

[1] Charles Garrett, *The LaGuardia Years* (New Brunswick, N.J.: Rutgers University Press, 1961), p. 10. Used with permission.

understand; to them, in exchange for votes, it provided loans, help, advice, and more jobs.

Since votes were the fuel that kept the machine operating, there were ways of insuring the supply: Ballot-boxes were stuffed; votes were bought outright or voters were intimidated by physical force or threats; unqualified voters—sometimes illegally naturalized citizens, sometimes illegally registered "floaters"—were used; returns were sometimes falsified. Usually returns were falsified only when it became absolutely necessary—a common strategy in close elections was to wait until all the votes had been counted and then, if the other side appeared to have won, doctor the returns just enough to change the result. This required, of course, control of the machinery of city government, which Tammany had: in the era of Boss Croker, around the turn of the century, policemen were not only members of the organization but were expected to pay for their jobs and promotions. The courts—especially the lower courts—also were usually cooperative with Tammany.

Election-tampering became a more difficult process as time went on. In the 1890's New York began to use the secret ballot, which reduced outright intimidation to some extent. Another change was the adoption of voting machines, which, as D. W. Brogan put it, had some of the effects that the coming of cash registers had in the bookkeeping of saloons. It did not prevent fraud, but it did make fraud more difficult and risky.[2]

Naturally there were protests against Tammany's power. There were exposés of municipal corruption such as Lincoln Steffens' classic muckraking book, *The Shame of the Cities,* and there were crusading newspapers such as young William Randolph Hearst's *New York American* and *New York Evening Journal.* There were also citizens' groups such as the good-government organizations—generally known as the Goo-Goos—the League of Women Voters, and various reform clubs.

It was not unusual for a group of civic reformers to put together an organization of sufficient power to defeat Tammany and its associated machines in a city election, and as a matter of fact victorious reform movements were as familiar a part of the New York political picture as was Tammany itself. But the reform groups came and went, whereas Tammany seemed to go on forever. Reform administrations were elected in 1844, 1853, 1857, 1861, 1863, 1872, 1894, 1901, 1909, and 1913, but never once were they reelected.[3] Invariably, there would be a weakening of unity among the elements of the reform movement, a failure to build a comprehensive and permanent political organization; and in the next election Tammany would be back. Some reformers would become discouraged at this backsliding tendency, but others patiently accepted reform as something that had to be done again and again. Rabbi Stephen S. Wise, who worked for many reform movements, said: "I hope we will never take the position that because filth comes back to a city after cleaning, no cleaning is to be attempted. It may as well be said that the city sewage system is not worthwhile because it must constantly be renewed." [4]

Actually, no reform administration was ever entirely successful in cleaning out the entire Tammany network of utilities and franchises, extortion operations, corporations depending on public contracts, and unqualified officeholders; and no city government was ever quite the same when Tammany returned to power. Over the years, partly because of reform victories and partly because of the continuing pressure of reformers, there were gradual improvements in city government.

Tammany was Democratic, and the successful reform movements usually had some sort of alliance with the city's Republican organization. The Republican party occupied a strange position in New York City. Since the state government was usually in Republican hands, there were enough crumbs of patronage drifting down from Albany to keep alive some semblance of a machine, although it seldom won elections. At another level, many of the city's most prominent businessmen and wealthy families were Republicans.

Tammany and the Democratic machines of Brooklyn and the Bronx were, among other things, academies of practical politics, providing training and advancement for new leaders. But few young politicians of any consequence found their way up through the ranks of the city's Republican organizations. One of the few who did, to the surprise and occasional embarrassment of his own party, was Fiorello LaGuardia. LaGuardia, born in New York of an Italian father and

---

[3] Garrett, *op. cit.,* p. 45.
[4] Stephen Wise, *Challenging Years: The Autobiography of Stephen Wise* (New York: G. P. Putman's Sons, 1949), pp. 21–22, quoted in *ibid.,* p. 46.

an Italian-Jewish mother,[5] was an excitable little man—five foot
two—with a high-pitched voice and a great appetite and enthusiasm
for politics. He won his first election in 1916, defeating Congressman Michael Farley—who was a Tammany man, a saloon owner,
and president of the National Liquor Dealers' Association. LaGuardia
had been defeated in the same Lower East Side district by Farley
two years before but he had continued to campaign tirelessly, speaking to voters in both Yiddish and Italian. The unprecedented Republican victory in the strong Tammany district won LaGuardia an
immediate statewide notoriety. His political career after that had
many ups and downs, and although he was sometimes unpopular and
sometimes defeated, he was never obscure; he had a natural talent
for getting publicity.

He was commissioned in the Army during World War I and
became nationally famous as the "Flying Congressman," although his
greatest service was not flying but talking—he made speeches on
behalf of the Allied cause throughout Italy. He was reelected in
1918 when Tammany, in a sudden burst of patriotism, decided not
to oppose him. In 1919 he ran for the office of president of the
Board of Aldermen of the City of New York—the second-highest
office in the city—and was elected. Expecting that his next move
would be into the mayor's office, he resigned from Congress. But
his two-year term was a long feud with Tammany on one side and the
Republican Old Guard on the other, and he was defeated for reelection. In 1922 he threatened to run as an independent candidate
against the Republican governor, and to keep him out of that election
the party leaders offered him the congressional nomination in an
Upper East Side district with a fairly strong Republican registration.
He accepted the nomination, but in his campaign he advocated a
minimum wage law, old age pensions, modification of Prohibition,
direct primaries, recall, referendum, and United States leadership in a
move for world-wide outlawing of war—all contrary to the positions
of the eastern Republican establishment.

LaGuardia called himself a Progressive, and said, "I am a
Republican, but I am not running on the Republican platform. I
stand for the republicanism of Abraham Lincoln; and let me tell
you now that the average Republican leader East of the Mississippi

[5] See Jay Franklin, *LaGuardia: A Biography* (New York: Modern Age
Books, 1937), pp. 9–10, for a discussion of LaGuardia's Jewish ancestry.

doesn't know any more about Abraham Lincoln than Henry Ford knows about the Talmud." [6] He was elected by a margin of 254 votes and returned to Washington, where he allied himself with the Progressive bloc of Republicans led by Senator Robert LaFollette of Wisconsin. In 1924 he bolted the Republican party to support LaFollette's third-party campaign for the Presidency, and in his own district he found himself opposed by the Republican party but endorsed by the Socialists. LaFollette was defeated, but LaGuardia was reelected; and in 1926 and 1928 he was reelected again, after a reconciliation of sorts with New York's Republican leadership. He was not their idea of a Republican, but he was the only man in New York City who seemed able to beat Tammany with any regularity. In 1929 he made a try for mayor, against incumbent Jimmy Walker. But with feeble support from the Republicans and running against one of the most popular politicians Tammany had ever produced, LaGuardia was badly beaten, with 367,675 votes to Walker's 867,522.[7] He was elected to another congressional term in 1930, but in 1932 the Democratic election sweep that made Franklin D. Roosevelt President also helped a Tammany candidate win LaGuardia's seat in Congress. LaGuardia, a private citizen again, took a job as arbitrator for a labor union.

Meanwhile, the administration of Mayor Walker was running into trouble. "Beau James," the embodiment of New York in the 1920's, was an easygoing leader who let the city's business take care of itself while he vacationed in Palm Beach and Europe, carried on a well-publicized extramarital affair with an English actress, and had his picture taken with celebrities at night clubs and Broadway plays. He was the son of a Tammany politician, but had started out to become a songwriter: One of his compositions, "Will You Love Me in December As You Do in May," was a hit in the early 1900's. Then he entered politics himself. He was never much of a statesman— as a member of the state legislature his main achievements were bills on behalf of legalized boxing and Sunday baseball games—but Tammany's leaders liked him and he advanced rapidly. When he became mayor he was immensely popular, and throughout his first term few New Yorkers seemed to blame him for not taking his civic responsibilities more seriously. But in his second term, as the 20's

[6] Lowell M. Limpus and Burr W. Leyson, *This Man LaGuardia* (New York: E.P. Dutton & Co., 1938), pp. 135–36.
[7] Garrett, *op. cit.*, p. 63.

ended and America moved into the Depression years, the love affair ended. It began to come out that Walker's glamorous reign was the front for a city government as corrupt as anything since the days of Boss Tweed.

One scandal was the investigation of Magistrate Albert H. Vitale, which brought out his close association with gangster Arnold Rothstein and revealed that Vitale, in his four years on the bench, had managed to save $165,000 although during that period his total earnings were only $48,000.[8] Another judge was convicted of helping to defraud thousands of small investors through a fraudulent bank, and indicted for taking $190,000 in fees from a shipping line in return for helping to obtain desirable pier leases.[9] Another was tried for mail fraud and office-purchasing—specifically, paying $10,000 to the sheriff of New York County each time he was reappointed to the bench.[10]

These were serious charges, but nothing unusual for a Tammany administration and not enough to do Walker real harm. They were enough, however, to bring public pressure for a full investigation of the courts. Franklin D. Roosevelt, then governor of New York, requested it, and a commission headed by Samuel Seabury, a prominent New York attorney, was appointed. The Seabury investigations, first of the courts and then of the entire city government, continued through 1932.

The first general court investigation uncovered a profitable ring in which policemen, an assistant district attorney, lawyers, and bail bondsmen worked together to extort money from prostitutes. As described by Charles Garrett, it operated this way:

> Policemen, members of the Vice Squad, often with the aid of stool pigeons who acted as agents provocateurs, would inveigle a prostitute into compromising herself by accepting marked money. Then the police would arrest her and charge her with prostitution. If the arrested prostitute had no money or decided to accept punishment, the police would at worst get credit for another arrest. If she had money and did not want to go to jail, she would accept the help of a bondsman and a lawyer in the ring, who would bleed her plenty for their services. The bondsman was the pay-off man who would collect from the victims and divide the proceeds among the lawyers

8 *Ibid.*, p. 65.
9 *Ibid.*, p. 65.
10 *Ibid.*, p. 66.

*and the police. The lawyers and bondsmen would take care
of the prosecutor. When the case would come to court, the
defendant would plead not guilty, the policeman who made
the arrest would change his testimony on an essential point, the
prosecutor would weaken his case, and the defendant would be
discharged.*[11]

The investigations moved up through the levels of city government, and eventually turned on the mayor himself. Walker, it appeared, had in 1927 helped the Equitable Coach Company in its efforts to obtain a city-wide bus franchise, and soon afterward went on vacation to Europe with a $10,000 letter of credit bought for him by Equitable's New York representative. He had accepted $26,000 in bonds from an investment banker involved in a taxi company at a time when a Taxicab Control Board was being set up. Ten of the above bonds—valued at $10,000—were bonds of the Reliance Bronze and Steel Corporation, which in 1931 was awarded a $43,000 contract for construction of traffic light standards. Russell Sherwood, Walker's financial agent, left for Mexico, but it came out that he had deposited nearly a million dollars, mostly in cash, in various accounts.[12]

None of the revelations added up to firm proof that Walker had accepted bribes, but they were enough for Seabury to forward to Roosevelt an impressive statement of charges, together with an accusation that Walker's misconduct rendered him "unfit to continue in the office of Mayor." [13] While Roosevelt was trying to decide what to do, Walker resigned, on September 1, 1932.

Upon Walker's resignation, Joseph V. McKee, president of the Board of Aldermen, became acting mayor. McKee, who belonged to the Bronx machine headed by Boss Flynn, had often fought with Tammany and had some supporters among the city's reform elements and anti-Tammany newspapers. He was 44, a young-looking man who had taught at Fordham University and had picked up the nickname of "Holy Joe" as a result of his practice of opening meetings of the Board of Aldermen with a prayer.

McKee hoped to be able to stay in office for the remainder of Walker's term, but the court ruled that a special election would be necessary. In the special election, Tammany leaders overruled the

11 *Ibid.,* pp. 68–69.
12 *Ibid.,* p. 76.
13 *Ibid.,* p. 77.

Bronx boss, who wanted McKee to be the Democratic nominee, and instead gave the nomination to one of their own men, Surrogate John P. O'Brien. The reformers could not agree on a candidate; the Republicans nominated an elderly politician named Lewis H. Pounds, and O'Brien was elected. Jimmy Walker was gone, but Tammany Hall still ruled New York City. O'Brien, a veteran of 30 years of machine politics, was a man who took his orders from the Hall. After his election reporters asked him whom he planned to appoint as police commissioner, and his answer was "I don't know. I haven't heard yet." [14]

The strongest sign of anti-Tammany sentiment in the city was the 260,000 write-in votes won by McKee.[15] A write-in vote of that size was unprecedented, and it indicated what a well-organized reform group might have been able to accomplish. It also gave Boss Flynn the idea that he might try to challenge Tammany by running McKee as a reform candidate in the next regular mayoral election. There was just a year remaining in the term of office that would now be completed by O'Brien, and McKee began an active campaign to become leader of a reform movement. He won the approval of several good-government groups and also of Republican organizations in Manhattan, Brooklyn, and Queens. Then in May of 1933, while the reform movement was growing stronger and he looked like its probable candidate, McKee suddenly decided to accept the position of president of the Title Guarantee and Trust Company, and announced that he was retiring from politics for good. A few days later, Fiorello LaGuardia reentered the scene.

LaGuardia issued a public statement proposing a fusion ticket, to be made up of candidates representing various political elements in the city. Fusion tickets were a common part of New York politics: A union of Republicans with Independent Democrats and various other groups was usually the only kind of organization that could successfully compete with Tammany. But the fusion ticket LaGuardia came up with was incredible. It proposed former governor and 1928 presidential candidate Alfred E. Smith as mayor, Socialist Norman Thomas as president of the Board of Aldermen, Republican Robert

[14] Bella Rodman and Philip Sterling, *Fiorello LaGuardia* (New York: Hill and Wang, 1962), p. 144.

[15] The chief backing for the write-ins came from the *New York World-Telegram*. Garrett, op. cit., p. 93.

Moses for comptroller, and Mayor O'Brien for surrogate.[16] The kicker to LaGuardia's announcement was his statement that, if Smith did not agree to run for mayor, he would seek the nomination himself. It was, of course, most unlikely that Smith, a product of Tammany, would lend his name to an anti-Tammany ticket, and it was even less likely that O'Brien would want to run for the office he had held before he became mayor. LaGuardia's announcement was in reality a challenge to the reformers. He wanted to be their candidate for mayor, and he was strong enough—with his anti-Tammany reputation, his Italian and Jewish following, and the union support he had won with his co-authorship of the prolabor Norris-LaGuardia bill in Congress—so that he could undoubtedly upset their plans if he decided to launch his own campaign. Many of the leading reformers were conservatives who favored such possible candidates as General John F. O'Ryan, a World War I division commander. But while other possible candidates could not quite seem to make up their minds, LaGuardia remained vociferously available. Maurice P. Davidson, head of the City Fusion party, said later:

> *LaGuardia . . . was dancing around and thundering in the index about what he was going to do. He wanted the nomination! He wanted it! God! Nobody else wanted it! They were afraid of it—afraid of being licked, afraid they couldn't carry it through. There were lots of reasons they always gave, sometimes personal. But here we had a man all the time who knew he wanted it. He wanted it!* [17]

There were two important reasons that the reformers had to pay attention to LaGuardia. One was the threat of what he might do if not chosen; the other was the fact that Samuel Seabury backed him. Seabury, the dignified, white-haired attorney whose investigations had brought out the corruption in the Walker administration, was the living symbol of reform to most New Yorkers. His opinion could not be ignored, and he was sold on LaGuardia.

Seabury had been won over to LaGuardia by another prominent civic leader, A. A. Berle, professor of corporation law at Columbia University and a member of President Roosevelt's much-publicized Brain Trust. Berle had become acquainted with LaGuardia in Wash-

---

[16] Limpus and Leyson, *op. cit.,* p. 358.
[17] From *LaGuardia Comes to Power: 1933,* by Arthur Mann, p. 80. Copyright © 1965, by Arthur Mann. Published by J. B. Lippincott Company.

ington and had great respect for his ability and honesty. The support of men such as Berle and Seabury was what LaGuardia needed most. One quality he definitely lacked was dignity, and reform leaders tended to come from the upper classes; he needed the help of such solid citizens to overcome the reservations of those who disliked either his flamboyant style or his liberal politics.

The reform groups which had been trying to get together behind a candidate included the City Fusion party, the Independent Fusion Committee, the Citizens Union, anti-Tammany Democrats, and Republicans. They had been meeting frequently to discuss possible candidates and finally, on August 4, Seabury persuaded them to accept LaGuardia. A complete Fusion ticket was then put together, with candidates for all major city offices, and representing both Republicans and independent Democrats. These candidates became the nominees of both the Republican party and the newly renamed City Fusion party.[18] The two parties cooperated closely throughout the campaign.

The Fusion ticket emerged as a strong and well organized challenge to Tammany, and from the moment its formation was announced its chances of victory appeared good. Mayor O'Brien was making conspicuous efforts to slow down the reform movement by improving city government himself, but somehow he was not coming across as a reformer. In the primary election on September 19 he was opposed for the Democratic nomination by several candidates, and although he won, the total vote of his opponents was over 130,000 [19]—an indication that Tammany might be unable to deliver the Democratic vote in November.

It appeared that the election would shape up as a contest between a vigorous Fusion movement and a slipping Tammany, but soon after the primary the situation changed: Joseph McKee changed his mind again, and came back into the race.

According to Bronx Boss Ed Flynn, the McKee reentry was at the request of President Roosevelt, who was "very much upset about what was happening in Tammany Hall," and "considerably distressed by the administration of O'Brien." [20] Flynn went to Washington to

[18] This had originally been formed as the City party. See Garrett, *op. cit.,* pp. 96–97.

[19] *Ibid.,* p. 105.

[20] Edward J. Flynn, *You're the Boss* (New York: The Viking Press, 1947), p. 133.

confer with Roosevelt, and upon his return began to round up support for McKee. Since the primaries were over there was no question of going for the Democratic nomination; it was necessary for a new party to be formed. The name chosen for the new group was the Recovery party, an attempt to borrow a bit of the Roosevelt magic. Roosevelt had made no public statement on behalf of McKee, but some of his advisers became active in the campaign, and, as Flynn notes, "the word 'recovery' was very popular at the time, since Roosevelt had been President for several months and economically the country was on the upgrade." [21] Among those who joined McKee's campaign were Averell Harriman, the railroad tycoon who later became governor of New York; Raymond Moley, another member of the Brain Trust; and Roosevelt's chief political adviser, James A. Farley, who was both postmaster-general and chairman of the Democratic party in New York.

McKee declared that he would tolerate "only fine, decent people" in the Recovery party, and that he was not merely Flynn's candidate. "As I stand before you," he said, "I owe allegiance to no political boss, nor am I hampered or fettered by any allegiance to leader or machine." As for LaGuardia: "No one can have any confidence in him because his whole record has been a record of opportunism, instability and explosiveness. . . ." [22]

LaGuardia and his backers recognized immediately the strength of the new McKee organization, and LaGuardia began to concentrate on McKee as his most dangerous opponent. Attention was directed to the existence within the Fusion campaign of such groups as the Roosevelt Democrats for LaGuardia and the New Deal Democratic League for LaGuardia, and McKee was called just another machine candidate. "They're making a primary out of an election," Seabury said. "Fusion nominated a ticket so good and so strong that its mere nominations caused the Curry machine to crumble and broke Tammany's back. What happened then? They changed the name of the Tammany candidate from O'Brien to McKee." [23]

This was a considerable oversimplification. Walter Lippmann, who was also for LaGuardia, wrote a more sophisticated analysis of the differences between reform McKee style and reform LaGuardia style:

21 *Ibid.*, p. 135.
22 *Time,* Oct. 23, 1933, p. 13.
23 *Ibid.*, p. 14.

*Can the machine be sufficiently reformed by men who, until
a month ago, were part of it? Or is it desirable to overthrow the
whole machine of misgovernment and install men who are entirely unentangled with it? Is New York to wipe the dust off
the furniture or sweep out the dirt that is under it? Is it going
to trust Mr. McKee to reform the district leaders or is it going
to separate those district leaders from treasury and the sources
of government power? Do the people wish a partial change of
control at the top or a radical change of control from top to
bottom? In the McKee faction they have men who have been
a part of the existing machine, have done business with it,
have acquiesced in it, have sustained it, still represent an important part of it, and, barring miracles, must continue to compromise with it. In Fusion they have a group of candidates who
are the sworn enemies of the machine, owe nothing to it, have
every interest in destroying it, and no interest in compromising
with it.*[24]

Before the entry of McKee and the Recovery party, the campaign had been one in which the difference between the candidates
and the choice to be made seemed fairly clear. As it turned into a
three-way contest everything became more complicated. Both La-
Guardia and McKee were campaigning as reformers, but LaGuardia
called McKee a machine candidate and McKee called LaGuardia an
irresponsible demagogue. Both of them were campaigning against
Tammany, but somehow the incumbent tended to be often ignored;
public attention focused on the conflict between the two challengers.
Among the newspapers, the *New York Times, Herald Tribune, World-
Telegram,* and *Evening Post* endorsed LaGuardia; the *Daily News*
and *Daily Mirror* tabloids, the Hearst *Evening Journal* and *American,*
and the conservative Republican *Sun* backed McKee; and O'Brien had
to be content with the support of Tammany's *New York Democrat.*[25]

There were still old Tammany hands who watched the public
commotion with scorn and believed that when election day came the
reform vote would split and the party faithful would go to the polls
as they always did, and O'Brien would be reelected. There were
facts to support this view: Of the approximately three and a half million eligible voters in New York City, only a million and a half
normally voted in municipal elections. In such a situation the
Tammany faithful constituted a solid block of votes that could usually

[24] *New York Enquirer,* Nov. 1, 1933, quoted in Mann, *op. cit.,* 106.
[25] *Ibid.*

carry an election; the machine's job was not to persuade anybody, but merely to "deliver the vote" of its dependable rank and file. But the LaGuardia organization was putting on a registration drive as well as an election campaign. By mid-October voter registration was up to 2,324,389.[26] McKee's forces did not join in the registration drive, but McKee's entry undoubtedly helped it by creating more public interest in the campaign. It also created new problems for O'Brien, as some party workers in Brooklyn, Queens, and Richmond who had cooperated with Tammany in the past now went with McKee, in the belief that the center of power was shifting from Manhattan to the Bronx.

McKee's organization was better financed than LaGuardia's— many of the wealthy conservatives who might have backed the Fusion campaign still found LaGuardia too far left for their taste—but the LaGuardia campaign was better organized, and reached into far more corners of New York politics. The Fusion ticket itself was a masterpiece of balancing. For mayor there was LaGuardia, who was a balanced ticket all by himself, being Italian, partly Jewish, an Episcopalian, and a left-wing Republican.[27] For president of the Board of Aldermen there was Bernard S. Deutsch, who was Jewish, from the Bronx, and a member of the City Fusion party. For comptroller there was W. Arthur Cunningham, Irish, from Queens, a Democrat. For district attorney there was Jacob Gould Schurman, of Dutch ancestry, from Manhattan, a Republican. At its lower levels the campaign organization had representatives in every ethnic, religious, professional, labor, and social group. Some of the young men who worked in the campaign were members of the East Harlem F. H. LaGuardia Political Club, commonly known as the *Gibboni* and led by LaGuardia's lieutenant Vito Marcantonio; others were Fusioneers, who came from the upper strata of New York society, and were led by Clendenin Ryan and Allan Stuyvesant.

LaGuardia himself was easily the most active member of the LaGuardia campaign. He went into every neighborhood in New York City, and made more speeches than both his opponents put together —usually about a dozen a day.[28] He promised an administration in

[26] *Ibid.,* p. 102.
[27] LaGuardia's Jewish ancestry was not well known at this time. He often made speeches in Yiddish, but he also made speeches in several other languages; he did not campaign as a member of the Jewish community.
[28] Mann, *op. cit.,* p. 103.

which jobs would be awarded for merit rather than political loyalty, improvement in the city's shaky finances, and extensive welfare and relief programs—public works, slum clearance, health centers, parks and playgrounds, free legal aid, tax-supported housing. He was in fact campaigning for public services which would remove the basis for Tammany paternalism, and at the same time out–New-Dealing McKee.

In mid-October, at the height of the campaign, an issue arose which seriously diminished whatever support McKee may have had among the city's largest ethnic voting group, the Jews. It arose because an attempt of McKee's to undercut LaGuardia's Jewish support backfired.

It started with a speech made by Seabury, who criticized New York's popular Jewish governor, Herbert Lehman. McKee sent LaGuardia a telegram demanding that he repudiate Seabury's remarks. LaGuardia sent back a telegram asking McKee: "ARE YOU TRYING TO DRAW A RED HERRING ACROSS THE COWARDLY, CONTEMPTIBLE AND UNJUST ATTACK THAT YOU HAVE MADE AND PUBLISHED AGAINST A GREAT RACE GLORIOUSLY REPRESENTED BY OUR GOVERNOR? ANSWER THAT, MR. MCKEE, AND THINK TWICE BEFORE YOU SEND ME ANOTHER TELEGRAM." [29]

The attack to which LaGuardia was referring—and which now came out, to McKee's embarrassment—was an article McKee had written for the *Catholic World* in 1915, while he was a high-school teacher. In the article McKee claimed that Jewish high-school students in the city outnumbered Christians three to one, that they were abandoning Judaism in favor of Socialism and materialism, and that "it is to such as these, that our [Catholic] children, who are without the benefits of education, must bow in later years." [30] Many of McKee's Jewish supporters issued statements denying that he was in any way anti-Semitic, but the damage had been done, and it probably contributed to another setback to the McKee campaign— Roosevelt's refusal to make an endorsement of him.

Ed Flynn said of the *Catholic World* incident:

> *There is really very little one can do in such situations. A purely emotional appeal, injected into the campaign near the close, completely obscured vital issues. There was one last*

29 Limpus and Leyson, *op. cit.*, pp. 368–69.
30 Joseph V. McKee, "A Serious Problem," *Catholic World*, May 1915, pp. 210–12, quoted in Mann, *op. cit.*, p. 114.

hope. Again I appealed to the President to come out with
some sort of statement, or in some way to show the people that
he was behind McKee. Being the politician he was, he was
quite aware of what was happening in New York, and ap-
parently had come to the conclusion that political expediency
dictated doing nothing. At any rate, nothing is what he did.[31]

The peak of the LaGuardia campaign was a gigantic rally in Madison Square Garden on the night of November 2. Airplane advertising during the day and torchlight parades converging on the Garden from all parts of the city after dark drew thousands of people, enough to fill the building and jam the streets outside. Inside, a band played the LaGuardia campaign song, and the crowd cheered wildly for both Seabury and LaGuardia.

Election day, November 7, was full of conflict and last-minute intrigue. The conflict was between Tammany toughs and LaGuardia's oddly assorted army of Ivy Leaguers and *Gibboni*. In Tammany's slum strongholds the toughs—many of them on loan from friendly organizations such as the Dutch Schultz mob—turned out by the hundreds, armed with brass knuckles and blackjacks, for the on-the-spot campaign work of allowing friendly voters to proceed to the polls and dissuading others. LaGuardia's squads moved into these dangerous neighborhoods, in even greater numbers, and took on the Tammany forces. The high vote in these precincts proved that the tactic was successful, but there were many casualties; one of them was Allan Stuyvesant, who ended election day in the hospital with a broken jaw.

That evening, early election returns showed LaGuardia well in the lead. He left Seabury's home, where he had been receiving the reports, and went downtown to appear at his victory celebration— then detoured to Police Headquarters in southern Manhattan to investigate a report that Tammany members of the Board of Elections were trying to hold up returns to prevent the election of Arthur Cunningham, the Fusion candidate for comptroller. The appearance of the mayor-elect in the tabulating room on the top floor of Police Headquarters was easily the most dramatic event in a dramatic day, and when LaGuardia gave orders that 400 policemen were to be sent out to see to it that the returns from the delayed precincts were properly brought in and counted, the order was obeyed. And Cunningham was elected.

[31] Flynn, *op cit.*, pp. 137–38.

In the final count, LaGuardia had 868,522 votes, McKee 609,053, and O'Brien 586,672.[32] It was not a complete victory for the Fusion forces, however. Fusion candidates for city-wide offices and the borough presidencies of Richmond, Brooklyn, and Queens were elected; but Tammany held its control of Manhattan, and the Flynn machine continued to rule the Bronx. The Board of Aldermen still had a Democratic majority, although that was weakened by its own internal factionalism.

LaGuardia, with characteristic energy and publicity-consciousness, reported for work on New Year's Day, January 1, 1934. One of his first official acts was to reduce his salary from Jimmy Walker's $40,000 to $22,500.[33] His first term in office had its failures, but on balance it was a model of what a reform administration should accomplish: It improved civil service, established sound fiscal policies, fought organized crime, completed public works projects, provided new and better parks and welfare services, and combated election fraud and violence. In 1937, LaGuardia did something no reform mayor of New York before him had been able to accomplish: He got reelected. The 1937 elections reduced Tammany's influence still further, and in that year LaGuardia decorated his office with the skin of a tiger.

Tammany politicians may have seen their defeat by LaGuardia and his Fusion allies in 1933 as just another reform cycle, which would pass in time and be replaced by machine politics as usual. But things were never the same again for Tammany after 1933.

The 1933 defeat was not an ordinary reform to begin with: Tammany was being attacked from many sides, and the traditional basis of its power had already weakened. Tammany was a Manhattan organization, and its domination of New York City politics arose from the island's importance as a population center. But Manhattan had been losing population to the other boroughs since 1920; furthermore, Tammany was led by the Irish—a group that by 1933 was outnumbered by the Italians, who were in turn outnumbered by the Jews.[34] The three-way contest in 1933 contained, among other things, a revolt of the Bronx machine against Tammany's domination; and

32 Garrett, op. cit., p. 113.
33 Limpus and Leyson, op. cit., p. 381.
34 Mann, op. cit., p. 92.

LaGuardia's victory was, among other things, a victory of an Italian over two Irishmen—one of whom had been tainted with the charge of anti-Semitism.

Other historical changes contributed to Tammany's demise: The flow of new immigrants from Europe slowed down; New Deal welfare legislation provided new sources of aid to needy individuals; and, at the same time that LaGuardia's election cut off one source of jobs for Tammany workers, Roosevelt began to use his own influence and patronage to build up new Democratic leadership at Tammany's expense. LaGuardia and President Roosevelt worked well together; federal aid helped New York City relief programs, and LaGuardia became a supporter of Roosevelt in his campaigns for reelection in 1936 and 1940. In 1941, LaGuardia was elected to a third term as mayor. He never managed to win the unqualified support of Republicans, but he had become America's most famous mayor, and possibly the most famous mayor of any city at any time. Those who had not heard of him for his reform programs and his war on Tammany Hall had heard of him as the little Italian who rode the fire engines and read the Sunday funnies to children over the radio. In the history and legend of New York City, the two best remembered mayors are Jimmy Walker and Fiorello LaGuardia.

7

1934
California
Frank F. Merriam vs. *Upton Sinclair*

In 1933 Upton Sinclair received a letter from Gilbert F. Stevenson, a member of the Los Angeles County Democratic Central Committee, proposing that he join the Democratic party and run for the Democratic nomination for governor of California.

Sinclair had been living in California since 1915, but he was not a Democrat and he had never held public office. He was a writer, a prolific writer who had published some 45 books, both fiction and nonfiction, of which the best-known was *The Jungle,* an exposé of the meat-packing industry. Politically he was a Socialist, and at various times he had campaigned as a Socialist candidate for Congressman from New Jersey, congressman from California, Senator from California, and governor of California. In each case he had conducted a token campaign, made a few speeches, and won a few votes.

Sinclair's life and personality were a curious blend of Puritanism and bohemianism, rebelliousness and *noblesse oblige.* Although a Socialist, he came from an aristocratic southern background. His own father had been an alcoholic, and one of the opinions he held most strongly—among his many strong opinions—had to do with the evils of drink.

Edmund Wilson, reviewing one of his books in 1932, said:

> *Sinclair's innocence, egoism, priggishness sometimes irritate us. . . . Yet he ends by inspiring us with respect. A fundamental earnestness and sweetness take the curse off his attitude*

> *of moral superiority; a devotion to values beyond his own interests outweighs his egotism. . . . Practically alone among American writers of his generation, he put to the American public the fundamental questions raised by capitalism in such a way that they could not escape them.*[1]

In 1934 Sinclair was 56 years old: In formal portraits taken at the time, with his thinning gray hair and rather severe expression, he resembled Woodrow Wilson; but he also had a boyish, toothy grin, and that, with his steel-rimmed spectacles, became the favorite device of the political cartoonists. His first marriage had ended in divorce, and he had been happily married to his second wife, Mary Craig Sinclair, for over 20 years. He had been crusading for one thing or another most of his life, and he has written that at this particular time he wanted only to live quietly, stroll about in the garden "with my mind full of my next chapter, and then presently bring a typewriter out into the sunshine, and sit there and pick away for three or four hours."[2]

At first he rejected the idea of becoming a Democrat and running for governor, but after a few meetings with Stevenson and some of his associates he changed his mind. In explaining his reasons for doing so, he struck an Armageddon note which was to become characteristic of the campaign. The issue, as he saw it, was between democracy and capitalist-dominated fascism: "One is going to destroy the other—the next two or three years will decide which. And if Big Business wins this fight, if Fascism comes to America as we have seen it come to Italy and Germany, what place will there be for an author?"[3]

He had broken with the Socialist party before, when he supported America's entry into World War I, and on September 1, 1933, he left the party again to register as a Democrat. This time his motives were admittedly more practical than ideological: "Fifty per cent of the people are going to vote a certain ticket because their grandfathers voted that ticket. In order to get anywhere it is necessary to have a party which has grandfathers."[4]

Once he had decided to run, he wrote a book outlining his pro-

[1] Edmund Wilson, *New Republic*, Sept. 28, 1932, p. 174.
[2] Upton Sinclair, *I, Governor of California and How I Ended Poverty* (Los Angeles: The Author, 1933), p. 3. Reprinted by permission.
[3] *Ibid.*, p. 5.
[4] Upton Sinclair, *I, Candidate for Governor and How I Got Licked* (Los Angeles: The Author, 1935), p. 6. Reprinted by permission.

gram for solving the state's economic problems. It was entitled *I, Governor of California and How I Ended Poverty,* subtitled *A True Story of the Future.* The cover of the small book announced:

This is not just a pamphlet.
This is the beginning of a Crusade.
A Two-Year Plan to make over a State.
To capture the Democratic primaries and
    use an old party for a new job.
The EPIC plan:
(E)nd (P)overty (I)n (C)alifornia!

The main element of the EPIC plan was production for use. Sinclair wrote:

I say that God created the natural sources of wealth for the use of all mankind, and not for the monopoly of a few. I say that the means of producing and distributing the necessities of life should be in the hands of the entire people, to be used for the people's equal benefit, and not for any privileged class.[5]

If the principles of EPIC fell somewhat short of Marxist Socialism, they went considerably beyond those of the New Deal, and Sinclair knew it: "I have watched with satisfaction a new birth of the Democratic principle under the leadership of Franklin D. Roosevelt. He has barely got started on his journey, but he is headed in the right direction, toward government control of business and industry—and I am shoving!" [6]

Actually, EPIC seems to have been much influenced by the co-op movement. Its intent was not a public takeover of the economy, but the establishment of an economy-within-an-economy which would be aimed at the immediate problems of poverty.

THE EPIC PLAN

1. A legislative enactment for the establishment of State land colonies, whereby the unemployed may become self-sustaining and cease to be a burden upon the taxpayers. A public body, the California Authority for Land (the CAL) will take the idle land, and land sold for taxes and at foreclosure sales, and erect dormitories, kitchens, cafeterias and social rooms, and cultivate the land using modern machinery under the guidance of experts.

2. A public body entitled the California Authority for Production (the CAP) will be authorized to acquire factories and production

[5] Sinclair, *I, Governor,* p. 2.
[6] *Ibid.*

plants whereby the unemployed may produce the basic necessities required for themselves and for the land colonies, and to operate these factories and house and feed and care for the workers. CAL and CAP will maintain a distribution system for the exchange of each other's products. The industries will include laundries, bakeries, canneries, clothing and shoe factories, cement-plants, brick-yards, lumber yards, thus constituting a complete industrial system, a new and self-sustaining world for those our present system cannot employ.

3. A public body entitled the California Authority for Money (the CAM) will handle the financing of CAL and CAP. This body will issue scrip to be paid to the workers and used in the exchanging of products within the system. It will also issue bonds to cover the purchase of land and factories, the erection of buildings and the purchase of machinery.

4. An act of the legislature repealing the present sales tax, and substituting a tax on stock transfers at the rate of 4 cents per share.

5. An act of the legislature providing for a State income tax, beginning with incomes of $5000 and steeply graduated until incomes of $50,000 would pay 30% tax.

6. An increase in the State inheritance tax, steeply graduated and applying to all property in the State regardless of where the owner may reside. This law would take 50% of sums above $50,000 bequeathed *to* any individual and 50% of sums above $250,000 bequeathed *by* any individual.

7. A law increasing the taxes on privately owned public utility corporations and banks.

8. A constitutional amendment revising the tax code of the State, providing that cities and counties shall exempt from taxation all homes occupied by the owners and ranches cultivated by the owners, wherever the assessed value of such homes and ranches is less than $3000. Upon properties assessed at more than $5000 there will be a tax increase of one-half of one per cent for each $5000 of additional assessed valuation.

9. A constitutional amendment providing for a State land tax upon unimproved building land and agricultural land which is not under cultivation. The first $1000 of assessed valuation to be exempt, and the tax to be graduated according to the value of land held by the individual. Provision to be made for a state building loan fund for those who wish to erect homes.

10. A law providing for the payment of a pension of $50 per month to every needy person over sixty years of age who has lived in the State of California three years prior to the date of the coming into effect of the law.

11. A law providing for the payment of $50 per month to all persons who are blind, or who by medical examination are proved to

be physically unable to earn a living; these persons also having been residents of the State for three years.

12. A pension of $50 per month to all widowed women who have dependent children; if the children are more than two in number, the pension to be increased by $25 per month for each additional child. These also to have been residents three years in the State.[7]

Another idea of Sinclair's, much ridiculed by his opponents, was to transact all public business completely in the open. In his "true story of the future" he described how this would work:

A reception room was fitted in the executive offices. The Governor sat at a large table, and on either side were seats for his attorneys and advisers when needed. Opposite to him sat the visitor. Tables were provided for the press and about a hundred seats for the public. The Governor explained briefly that this procedure was for the purpose of keeping the people of California informed as to how their affairs were being conducted. At the beginning, under the pressure of the emergency, it would be necessary to limit interviews to urgent business. Later there might be time to hear those who had anything of importance to say concerning the welfare of the State. Stenographers would take down the proceedings.

This unusual plan caught the attention of the public. It was the first time in history that a government had really dealt openly with the voters. The idea was so startling, and the clashes of personality were so entertaining, that the newspapers were obliged to report what went on in the Governor's Gold-fish bowl. Presently it occurred to one of the radio stations that this was an inexpensive form of public entertainment. They asked permission to install a microphone, and this was permitted, and it was not long before the national broadcasting companies heard of it, and important sessions in the Gold-fish bowl were listened to by the entire country.[8]

Sinclair optimistically declared: "I say, positively and without qualification, we can end poverty in California. I know exactly how to do it, and if you elect me Governor, with a Legislature to support me, I will put the job through—and I won't take more than one or two of my four years." [9]

Sinclair's uncomplicated proposals, his unshakable confidence that the state's problems could be solved by simple good will and good sense, won the support of thousands of Californians. The EPIC

[7] *Ibid.*, back cover.
[8] *Ibid.*, pp. 52–53.
[9] *Ibid.*, p. 7.

movement soon took the form of a loosely organized statewide league. Neighborhood EPIC clubs were formed throughout California, and continued to grow in number until there were nearly two thousand by the time of the general election. They raised funds, distributed campaign material, and performed precinct work; tireless and dedicated, they were Sinclair's greatest source of political strength and far more productive of results than the official party machinery of which he became the nominal leader after the primary.

The party which Sinclair joined when he changed his registration from Socialist to Democrat was, and had been for many years, a minority party. The Republicans had won every gubernatorial election since 1894, had won 13 out of 15 contests for United States Senate seats in the preceding 37 years, and had carried the state in every presidential election except two between 1884 and 1928.

But the state was growing, and the times were changing. Between 1930 and 1934 the population had increased by approximately 683,000, mostly as a result of immigration from other states. It was a time of depression, hardship, and unemployment: In June of 1934 there were 1,225,000 persons dependent to some extent on state charity, and the figures give no indication of how many newcomers were in need of help or out of work and ineligible for aid. As new residents came into the state and the depression grew more acute, Democratic prospects improved. Roosevelt carried California with a margin of over 500,000 votes in 1932, and since 1930 Democratic registration had doubled while Republican registration had declined: In 1932 there were 1,161,482 Democrats, an increase of 154.7 per cent since 1930; and there were 1,565,264 Republicans, a 4.5 per cent decrease over the same period.[10]

There was no lack of Democratic politicians eager to take over the leadership of this rapidly growing party, and serious intraparty conflicts had been developing long before Sinclair entered the picture.

Early in 1934 state party leaders met to choose an "official" Democratic candidate to oppose Sinclair; out of the meetings emerged not one but two candidates, each wanting to be identified with Roosevelt and the New Deal. One candidate was George Creel, World War I head of the Committee on Public Information and, since 1933, regional director of the National Relief Administration; Creel was a member of the faction led by Senator William Gibbs

[10] Eugene C. Lee, *California Votes: 1929–1960* (Berkeley: Institute of Governmental Studies, 1963), p. 38.

McAdoo. The other candidate was Justus Wardell, San Francisco businessman and regional director of the Public Works Administration, who had run against McAdoo for the senatorial nomination in 1932. The two factions were sufficiently preoccupied with the struggle for party control which the gubernatorial nomination represented that they failed to unite to combat the threat posed by Sinclair. Six other candidates—including Milton K. Young, who had been the nominee in 1930—also filed, which further helped to split up the vote among party regulars.

A contest for the Republican nomination began to take form behind the scenes as the incumbent governor, the colorful, cowboy-booted "Sunny Jim" Rolph, became seriously ill with a circulatory condition that, it became increasingly apparent, was terminal. After a long illness the governor died on June 2, 1934, and several candidates filed for the nomination: Among them were Lieutenant Governor Frank M. Merriam; former Governor C. C. Young of Burlingame; John R. Quinn, chairman of the Los Angeles County Board of Supervisors and former national commander of the American Legion; and Commissioner of Corporations Raymond C. Haight of Los Angeles. Haight also filed for the nomination of the small Commonwealth party.

Merriam, as acting governor, was the leading candidate. He had come to California from the Midwest in 1910 and had worked his way up through the Republican ranks with a career that, if something less than impressive, was solid and steady and had nothing in it to indicate that he was likely to make any drastic changes in the status quo. He had served in the Assembly for ten years, with two years as speaker. Elected to the State Senate in 1928, he had resigned in 1930 to run for lieutenant governor. He had also been active in the real estate business in Long Beach and was a vice-president of the Citizens State Bank of Long Beach. He was 70 years old, with a round face, bushy eyebrows, a bald head, and a benign smile.

Although Merriam had generally been identified with his party's more conservative elements, he began to move toward the political center early in his campaign, making speeches in favor of moderate public-welfare programs and indicating that he intended to cooperate with Roosevelt and the New Deal. His stance as a liberal was somewhat weakened, however, by his action during the San Francisco waterfront strike in July, when he sent National Guard troops into the city.

During the primary campaign most of the newspapers virtually
ignored Sinclair, but he was received by enthusiastic crowds of supporters everywhere he spoke, and in the August 28 primary he won
the Democratic nomination. The vote:

Democrat

Upton Sinclair	436,220
George Creel	288,106
Justus Wardell	48,965
Milton K. Young	41,609

Republican

Frank Merriam	346,329
C. C. Young	231,431
John Quinn	153,412
Raymond Haight	84,977

Commonwealth

Raymond Haight	3,421

Socialist

Milen C. Dempster	2,521

Communist

Sam Darcey	1,072 [11]

Sheridan Downey, the EPIC-endorsed candidate for lieutenant
governor, ran behind Sinclair but still won by a considerable
margin: He received 366,798 votes, over 200,000 more than his
nearest competitor, William Jennings Bryan, Jr.[12] EPIC candidates
for controller and attorney general were defeated, but a number of
EPIC endorsees for the State Senate and Assembly won their nominations, particularly in the southern California area where EPIC and
Sinclair had their greatest support.

Sinclair's victory was sufficiently strong to throw a scare into
everyone who had so far managed to dismiss his candidacy as a
harmless diversion on the political lunatic fringe. He had polled

[11] Frank Jordan, Statement of Vote at the Primary Election, Calif.
(State Printing Office, 1934) pp. 6–7. (Minor Democratic and Republican
candidates are not included.)
[12] *Ibid.*

some 90,000 more votes than Merriam, and the total Democratic vote was considerably larger than the total Republican vote. When all the primary votes had been tallied, it became obvious to everyone in California that Sinclair's chances of victory in November were very good indeed.

The nominee's first objectives were to consolidate his position of leadership over the party and, if possible, win the blessing of Roosevelt. Sinclair had already wired Roosevelt asking for a personal interview if he should be nominated, and a few days after the election he took a train to Washington. It had been understood before the meeting that Roosevelt would not make a personal endorsement, but it appears from several accounts that Sinclair was encouraged to believe Roosevelt agreed with the basic EPIC concept of production for use and planned to make a public statement in favor of it.

Sinclair emerged from the interview full of optimism, expecting Roosevelt to make a statement in a national radio address. On October 22, just before the broadcast, Sinclair told a group in San Francisco that if "President Roosevelt says what he told me he was going to say, I expect to be elected." [13] But the President's speech that evening made no reference to Sinclair or his ideas. "UPTON WAITS IN VAIN FOR F.D.R. BOOST," [14] headlined the *San Francisco News*.

The press also had predicted that there would be a conflict at the Democratic State Convention over the platform. Trying to avoid a major break with the Democratic regulars, Sinclair met with George Creel and Senator McAdoo before the convention and agreed to moderate the EPIC program for platform purposes.

When the convention assembled, EPIC supporters in the balcony unfurled a banner which read:

E   P   I   C

NO COMPROMISE   460,000 VOTES [15]

But there was compromise. The platform contained the essential EPIC proposals, in a much more moderate form than they had originally been stated by Sinclair. The word EPIC itself was not mentioned. After the platform had been adopted, Creel, McAdoo,

---

[13] Sinclair, *I, Candidate*, p. 182.
[14] *San Francisco News*, Oct. 23, 1934, George J. Hatfield Papers, Bancroft Library, University of California, Berkeley.
[15] *San Francisco Chronicle*, Sept. 1, 1934, *ibid.*

and Sinclair appeared together before the delegates and shook hands with one another. Only one day later, however, it became obvious that the break between the EPIC supporters and the regular party leadership had not been avoided after all. First, State Chairman Maurice Harrison announced that he would not support Sinclair. Then, after a Sinclair supporter, Culbert Olson, was elected as the new state chairman, Colonel William Neblett, a close associate of McAdoo who had aspired to the post, repudiated the platform and accused Sinclair of concealing "the Communistic wolf in the dried skin of the Democratic donkey." [16] Soon Justus Wardell, who had been the third-running gubernatorial candidate, and William Jennings Bryan, Jr., who had run for the lieutenant governorship, also joined the defectors. Each new defection was well publicized in California's newspapers.

The Republican candidate commanded considerably less enthusiasm from his supporters, but far better cooperation. He was not regarded by most observers as a particularly strong or impressive candidate. *Time* called him "a small-bore, Iowa-born politician." [17] George P. West, California political correspondent for *The New York Times,* said, "Governor Merriam is 70 years old, a prohibitionist, a Southern Californian out of Iowa, and it is not putting it too strongly to say that the dominant business men of San Francisco hold their noses as they throw all their resources into the campaign to elect him as a means of defeating Sinclair." [18]

It would be difficult to find a campaign in which a candidate with any wide support from the public was so totally opposed by the press as Sinclair. Not one newspaper in California, from the big-city dailies to the rural press, endorsed him. According to a survey made by the *Los Angeles Times* in September of 1934, 92 per cent of the daily, weekly, and semiweekly newspapers in the state had endorsed Merriam. Sinclair's only journalistic support came from his campaign's own publication, the *Epic News,* which was by no means an insignificant newspaper. It was published with an outer section edited by a former Scripps-Howard newspaperman, Reuben Borough, and largely written by Sinclair. Inner sections of the newspaper were edited and inserted by local EPIC groups throughout the state. The *Epic News* reached a circulation of 1,450,000 issues two

[16] *The New York Times,* Sept. 20, 1934, *ibid.* © 1934 by the New York Times Company. Reprinted by permission.
[17] Quoted in *Sacramento Bee,* Oct. 22, 1934, *ibid.*
[18] Quoted in *ibid.*

weeks before the primary, and during the high point of the general election campaign two of its issues had circulations of nearly two million each.[19]

Sinclair continued to turn out books throughout the campaign; printed in inexpensive editions, they sold widely. *I, Governor,* had sold 255,000 copies by election day. Other books written during the campaign were *EPIC Answers,* in which he described the effect of the EPIC program on various groups, such as farmers, businessmen and labor; it sold 65,000 copies. *The Lie Factory Starts,* Sinclair's reply to various charges made against him in the press, sold 50,000 copies; and a fourth book, *Immediate EPIC,* issued just after the primary, sold 65,000. In all, some 435,000 copies of the four books were sold, and Sinclair estimated that they brought in some 10 to 20 thousand dollars in campaign funds.[20]

The Republican campaign's use of the press was not simply a matter of passively accepting newspaper endorsements. It was, in fact, probably the most sophisticated, intense, and expensive use that any campaign thus far had made of advertising and public-relations techniques. The Republican State Central Committee hired Lord and Thomas, a leading national advertising agency; and the campaign organization of George Hatfield, Republican candidate for lieutenant governor, hired the new political public-relations team of Clem Whitaker and Leone Baxter.

Hatfield was Whitaker and Baxter's first candidate-client, and their performance on his behalf was both a major factor in their later success and a proving ground for some of the techniques which would become characteristic of later Whitaker and Baxter campaigns —and imitated by other professional campaign-management firms.

One noticeable element in a Whitaker and Baxter campaign was a tendency for it to be simplified, focused, dramatized. "Most every American," Whitaker once said, "loves *contest.* He likes a good hot battle with no punches pulled. He likes the clash of arms! So *you can interest him if you put on a fight.*" [21]

What Whitaker and Baxter put on in 1934 was not so much a fight as a crusade against the "menace of Sinclairism." They rather ignored their client's actual opponent, Sheridan Downey, and concentrated on Sinclair.

[19] Sinclair, *I, Candidate,* p. 20.
[20] *Ibid.*
[21] Stanley Kelley, Jr., *Professional Public Relations and Political Power* (Baltimore: The Johns Hopkins Press, 1956), p. 50. Reprinted by permission.

Sinclair's writings became the main ammunition in the campaign against him. Whitaker and Baxter and others read all of his books and selected quotations which seemed particularly radical or which would offend a significant body of voters. Various media were then used to disseminate the quotations. Irwin Ross describes one:

> *Clem and Leone . . . hired an artist named Bill LeNoire who did a series of thirty cartoons illustrating "the blot of Sinclairism"—generally a dismaying quotation, embedded in a big blob of black ink, and flung against some typical scene of American felicity.*
>
> *Thus, bride and groom, emerging from church, are assailed by a Sinclair comment that in capitalist society the institution of marriage has the qualities of "marriage plus prostitution." Or the picture of a madonna and child is defiled by Sinclair's observation that "of a score of religions in the world . . .* each is a mighty fortress of graft." . . .
>
> *Whitaker & Baxter had mats made of the cartoons, shipped them to papers around the state. At least three thousand appeared in print.*[22]

Many front groups were organized, mainly for the purpose of distributing anti-Sinclair campaign material. Thousands of leaflets and brochures were distributed by such organizations as the California League Against Sinclairism, the Young Liberal League, and the United for California League. These publications sometimes contained Sinclair quotes on an important subject—one, for example, was entitled "Free Love comes to CALIFORNIA?"—or might be aimed at a particular group or groups—such as "Upton Sinclair on The Legion, The A.E.F., The R.O.T.C. and THE BOY SCOUTS." [23]

Sinclair had always prided himself on being outspoken, and his works were a rich source of critical comments on American life. He had written several muckracking books in addition to *The Jungle:* they included *The Metropolis, The Industrial Republic, The Moneychangers,* and *The Machine,* all published before World War I. In the 1920's he wrote *The Profits of Religion*—probably the single book which was most used against him—*The Brass Check,* on the corruption of American journalism, *The Goose Step: A Study of American Education,* and *The Goslings: A Study of the American Schools.* The latter two publications contained his criticism of such institutions as the R.O.T.C. and the Boy Scouts.

[22] Irwin Ross, *The Image Merchants* (Garden City, N.Y.: Doubleday, 1959), pp. 69–70.
[23] Hatfield Papers.

These writings provided Sinclair's opponents with an enviable reservoir of material which could be reprinted and distributed to the groups most likely to be offended. Furthermore, Sinclair's opponents did not confine themselves to making use of the statements in his nonfiction works; the words of characters in his novels were also attributed directly to Sinclair, and taken out of context. Sinclair wrote of one such incident:

> In the novel Love's Pilgrimage, written in 1910, the idealistic young hero, twenty-two years of age, discovers that his wife is in love with another man, and he considers it his duty to step out of the way. He writes a letter to the other man, explaining his attitude, and in the course of it the solemn young jackass states as follows: "The crux of the whole difficulty I imagine must lie in what you say about your profound belief in the sanctity of the institution of marriage. That is, of course, a large question to attempt to discuss in a letter. I can only say that I once had such a belief, and that as a result of my studies I have it no longer."
>
> It wasn't enough for the Los Angeles Times to put that in a box in the year 1934. The cartoonists took it up, and portrayed me as a bespectacled creature with long pointed fingernails like the devil, enunciating the following words: "The sanctity of marriage . . . I have had such a belief . . . I have it no longer." One of my pointed fingernails is directed toward the picture of a happy family with a child climbing upon its father's back.[24]

Besides the thousands of brochures, leaflets, and reprints of cartoons which were distributed, the anti-Sinclair organizations also created such special campaign items as false paper currency—a reference to the scrip which he had proposed for use within the EPIC system. The paper money was printed—usually in red ink—with such inscriptions as:

ONE SINC*LI*AR

I O U   I O U

GOOD
ONLY IN
CALIFORNIA
OR
RUSSIA

Endure Poverty In California [25]

---

[24] Sinclair, *I, Candidate*, p. 135.
[25] Hatfield Papers.

Also—for perhaps the first time in history—motion pictures became a significant medium for the dissemination of campaign propaganda. Louis B. Mayer, president of Metro-Goldwyn-Mayer, was a vice-chairman of the Republican State Central Committee, and he and other leaders of the industry had threatened that if Sinclair were elected the studios would move out of California. During the campaign the studios raised a half-million-dollar fund for Merriam, part of which came from an assessment of one day's wages against their employees.

But an even more important contribution was made in the form of a series of films which were produced and shown as newsreels in theaters throughout the state. One of these showed mobs of vagrants —actually actors—supposedly on their way to California to get in on Sinclair's welfare schemes. Other films—also staged—showed an "inquiring reporter" interviewing voters: A little old lady told him she intended to vote for Merriam "because I want to save my little home. It's all I have left in this world." A bearded man with a Russian accent said he intended to vote for Sinclair: "His system vorked vell in Russia, vy can't it vork here?"

The *Hollywood Reporter* said of this campaign effort: "When the picture business gets aroused, it becomes AROUSED, and boy, how they go to it. This campaign against Upton Sinclair has been and is DYNAMITE. It is the most effective piece of political humdingery that has ever been effected. . . . All this activity . . . will undoubtedly give the big wigs in Washington and politicians all over the country an idea of the real POWER that is in the hands of the picture industry. Maybe our business will be pampered a bit, instead of being pushed around." [26]

Other business and industrial interests were equally strong in their support of Merriam, and some went so far as to urge their stockholders to vote for him. A letter sent by the president of the Standard Oil Company of California to stockholders on October 26, 1934, said:

> *Sinclairism must not only be beaten but the defeat should be overwhelming—a complete California repudiation of radicalism for the prosperity of the state and of the nation. His election, we believe, would be a calamity for the people of this State. We have never talked politics to our stockholders*

[26] Sinclair, *I, Candidate*, p. 154.

but this is not a political issue. It is a business issue that affects you and your company.[27]

The "Sinclairism" tag was heavily used throughout the campaign; there were also repeated efforts to convince the voters that Sinclairism and communism were more or less synonymous, or at least that Sinclair's victory would lead to communism. Earl Warren, then district attorney of Alameda County and chairman of the State Republican Central Committee, called EPIC "glorifying the Red flag of Russia with hopes to establish on American soil a despotism based on class hatred and tyranny." [28] One pamphlet distributed by a pro-Merriam group said Sinclair's election "Would be the entering wedge of the principles of Communist government in the United States, which might spread to other states, ultimately destroy our national democracy and transform the United States of America into the United Soviet States of America." [29] Another piece of campaign literature showed Governor Merriam standing under an American flag and Sinclair standing under the hammer and sickle, and was captioned: "Under Which Flag?" [30]

In the course of this campaign there was an enormous amount—hundreds and thousands of words spoken and broadcast and recorded, countless copies of leaflets and posters and pamphlets—of vituperative material directed against Sinclair. But very few harsh words came directly from Merriam. The governor himself campaigned as an incumbent, avoided name-calling, and made moderate speeches outlining his plans and hopes for the state's future progress.

As the campaign progressed so did the number of organizations created by Merriam's backers and—with the cooperation of the press—new releases were regularly issued giving the news of the endorsement of Merriam by new groups of voters. It gave the impression of a mass statewide swing away from Sinclair by every segment of the population imaginable, as papers around the state headlined:

FISHERMEN TO AID MERRIAM [31]
MINISTERS AND CHURCHMEN UNITE TO COMBAT SINCLAIR [32]
SONS OF WAR VETS OUT FOR MERRIAM HERE [33]

[27] Hatfield Papers.
[28] *San Francisco News,* Oct. 22, 1934, *ibid.*
[29] Hatfield Papers.
[30] *Ibid.*
[31] *Eureka Standard,* Oct. 26, 1934, *ibid.*
[32] *Atwater Signal,* Oct. 26, 1934, *ibid.*
[33] *Santa Ana Bulletin,* Oct. 26, 1934, *ibid.*

GREAT BODY OF WOMEN VOTERS, INDIFFERENT IN PAST, SUPPORT
MERRIAM [34]
YOUNG VOTERS IN BOTH PARTIES BACK MERRIAM [35]
FARMERS SWING TO MERRIAM [36]
PRACTICALLY UNANIMOUS SUPPORT OF EX-SERVICE MEN PLEDGED TO
MERRIAM [37]

These press releases were issued on behalf of an amazing
variety of organizations. In addition to those already mentioned, they
included the Civic League of Improvement Clubs and Associations,
the Loyal League of Democrats, Veterans for California, Merriam-
Hatfield Oil Workers' Club, and the American-Italian Voters' League.

There was particular emphasis upon conveying the impression
of labor support for Merriam. Headlines read:

LABOR SWINGS TO MERRIAM AS ELECTION NEARS [38]
LABOR UNANIMOUS FOR MERRIAM [39]
LABOR CHIEFS O. K. MERRIAM FOR GOVERNOR [40]
MERRIAM TO BE SUPPORTED BY WORKERS [41]

Sinclair's support among the ranks of workers was still strong.
A union president wrote in the *East Bay Labor Journal*:

> *We remember the riots instigated by the San Francisco police,
> so that Merriam would have an excuse to turn out the national
> guards, to enable his friends in the chamber of commerce and
> the industrial association to smash organized labor with
> machine guns and bayonets. . . . The unions were not
> crushed, and union men are not going to be such unmitigated
> idiots, that they will in November give their votes to a man
> who last July was quite ready to give them bullets and
> bayonets.*[42]

But the general impression conveyed in the press was of a coming
landslide for Merriam. Earl Warren on October 26 told a reporter
of "reliable reports that Gov. Merriam's strength is increasing daily
in Los Angeles and everywhere else." [43] One paper reported "LAND-

[34] *San Jose Mercury Herald,* Oct. 26, 1934, *ibid.*
[35] *San Francisco Chronicle,* Oct. 27, 1934, *ibid.*
[36] *Berkeley Gazette,* Oct. 24, 1934, *ibid.*
[37] *Yreka Journal,* Oct. 18, 1934, *ibid.*
[38] *Crescent City Triplicate,* Oct. 26, 1934, *ibid.*
[39] *Colusa Daily Times,* Oct. 27, 1934, *ibid.*
[40] *Gilroy Dispatch,* Oct. 27, 1934, *ibid.*
[41] *Redding Searchlight,* Oct. 27, 1934, *Ibid.*
[42] Letter from O. A. Rowan in *East Bay Labor Journal,* Oct. 26, 1934,
ibid.
[43] Herbert W. Slater, "Political Gossip," Santa Rosa *Press-Democrat,*
Oct. 26, 1934, *ibid.*

SLIDE FOR MERRIAM AND HATFIELD INDICATED," [44] and another told of the "increasing number of Democratic clubs dedicated to the saving of the state from the domination of the visionary fiction writer, Upton Sinclair." [45]

Amid these widespread predictions of impending defeat for Sinclair, there arose rumors that Sinclair might withdraw and throw his support to the Commonwealth party candidate, Raymond Haight. A poll conducted by Haight showed that if Sinclair were to withdraw, most of his votes would go to "middle-of-the-road" Haight, whereas a withdrawal by Haight would only insure victory for Merriam. Sinclair did hold a meeting with Haight—in the town of Marysville on October 25—and promised to consider withdrawing.

During this period there was behind-the-scenes pressure on Sinclair to pull out of the campaign in order to avoid bringing the whole Democratic ticket down to defeat with him. Among those who counseled him to withdraw were such close confidants of Roosevelt as A. P. Gianinni, president of the Bank of America, and J. F. T. O'Conner, comptroller of the currency; it appears that the President, in spite of his announced policy of neutrality in state election contests, supported the move to get Sinclair to withdraw.

Sinclair did not withdraw, but by the last days of his campaign most of the spirited optimism of his crusade had evaporated. On November 3, three days before the election, came another blow to his hopes: The *Literary Digest* published its election poll, which showed Sinclair to be badly trailing, a choice of 25.5 per cent of the sample compared to Merriam's 62.31 per cent.[46]

On November 6, the voters turned out to cast the highest vote of any election in California history to that time. No candidate won a majority, and Merriam's lead over Sinclair was far less than had been indicated by the *Literary Digest* poll, but it was sufficient to end the EPIC threat and maintain the control of the conservative business establishment over California politics. The returns gave 879,537 votes to Sinclair, 1,138,620 to Merriam, and 311,565 to third-party candidates.[47] The rather high percentage of votes for the minor parties would seem to indicate that (*a*) Haight had to some degree succeeded in campaigning as a moderate "middle of the

[44] Arroyo Grande *Herald-Recorder*, Oct. 19, 1934, *ibid.*
[45] Santa Cruz *Herald*, Oct. 26, 1934, *ibid.*
[46] *The Literary Digest*, Nov. 3, 1934, p. 5.
[47] Lee, *op. cit.*, p. A-120.

road" choice between conservative and liberal extremes, and/or that
(*b*) a considerable number of voters were not impressed by either
major party candidate.

Obviously, the Merriam forces had succeeded in branding Sinclair a dangerous radical and, equally obviously, his own works had
been of enormous help to them.

"All those wretched fabrications," Sinclair wrote later, "all those
garbled quotations from my books—millions of dollars were spent
to spread them; and how could I, having only a few dollars, attempt
to answer?" [48]

Merriam, on a nationally broadcast radio speech on election
day, said that while Sinclair "frequently charged—and to some extent
made his voters believe—that he was being misrepresented and lied
about, our most effective attack on him was the use we made of
his own writings and statements." [49]

Clem Whitaker said simply: "Upton was beaten because he had
written books." [50]

However, Sinclair would never have been beaten because he had
written books unless there existed some means for distributing to the
public—in the most damaging context—some of what he had written.
It is most unlikely that, even in an election year, any significant number of voters would take the time to read all of his books; and it is
also unlikely that reading any of them all the way through could have
been quite as frightening as merely reading the quotations which
appeared during the campaign.

The real significance of the Sinclair-Merriam campaign lies in
the fact that a candidate—perhaps for the first time in American
history, although certainly not for the last—was defeated, not by
his opponent, but by a planned and coordinated use of the mass
media of communication.

It took a certain set of conditions to give Sinclair this distinction. One most important contributing factor was the geography of
the state and the circumstances of its politics. California is a big
state, and carrying a campaign directly to the voters by the traditional
whistle-stop method is time-consuming and physically difficult; the
mass media—newspapers, radio, and movies—proved more effective.

[48] Sinclair, *I, Candidate,* p. 57.
[49] *Los Angeles Times,* Nov. 7, 1934.
[50] Ross, p. 69.

Another factor was the composition of the electorate: Many of the voters had recently moved to California, many of them remained mobile after they had arrived, and their mobility made Eastern-style political operations unworkable. As Carey McWilliams once noted, "There are neighborhoods in Los Angeles in which it would be quite safe to say that not more than two or three families in an entire block are known to each other. Try to boss such a neighborhood!" [51]

The possibilities of machine politics had also been diminished—deliberately—by the Progressive administration of Hiram Johnson, which early in the century had passed laws controlling the organization of political parties, making local elections nonpartisan and in many ways weakening party structure. This situation created a certain vacuum in political organization in the state and helped clear the way for the coming of the professional campaign-management organizations, of which Whitaker and Baxter was the first. Whitaker and Baxter had founded their company only a year earlier, and in their first campaign—on behalf of the Central Valley Project Act—they used radio more than any campaign in the state had done until that time. In 1934, they used all the mass media; they perceived that California offered the opportunity for a kind of politics in which persuasion could be far more important than "delivering the vote" of the party faithful, and in campaigning against Sinclair it was possible to put together a fully coordinated media attack.

It was possible partly because the business community's fear of Sinclair poured large amounts of money into the campaign against him, which Lord and Thomas and Whitaker and Baxter in turn poured into paid advertising. It was possible also because the newspapers were hostile to Sinclair and willing to use the press releases and artwork which Whitaker and Baxter delivered to them in great quantities. And it was possible, finally, because the motion picture industry, the third major medium of communication—and the one which, in the thirties, was at its peak of popularity—joined the crusade also. Sinclair's attempt to end poverty in California helped give birth to a new kind of campaigning, which, as the mass media became more pervasive and replaced older channels for the communication of political dialogue, would become an increasingly important part of the American democratic system.

[51] Carey McWilliams, *California: The Great Exception* (New York: Current Books, Inc., 1949), p. 195.

THE POLITICS
OF
LOYALTY

V

8

1950
California
Richard M. Nixon vs. *Helen Gahagan Douglas*

In the years after the end of World War II, as the Cold War with Soviet Russia became America's main preoccupation in the world of international affairs, a parallel obsession with domestic communism began to dominate internal politics. Actually, hostility toward anticapitalist ideology was nothing new in America; politicians had been calling their opponents Socialists with regularity—and sometimes with a good deal of accuracy—since the nineteenth century. But as Soviet Russia rose to world power this became an increasingly serious matter: The word "Socialist," in the imprecise vocabulary of political invective, gradually gave way to the word "Communist." And in the late 1940's, anticommunism became more than just political name-calling; it began to take on the appearance of a national inquisition. As it did, new political figures emerged: J. Parnell Thomas, chairman of the House Un-American Activities Committee; Joseph McCarthy, the Senator from Wisconsin; and Richard M. Nixon, the young Congressman from California.

Nixon raised the issue of communism in his very first political campaign when, as a young attorney recently discharged from the Navy, he defeated incumbent Jerry Voorhis for a Southern California congressional seat in 1946. In Congress, he became a member of the group most concerned with the threat of internal communism, the House Un-American Activities Committee. As chairman of HUAC's legislative subcommittee, he co-authored a major subversive activities control bill, the Mundt-Nixon bill. Its main provisions included registration of members of the Communist party, denial of passports and of federal employment to party members, deportation of aliens convicted of communist activity, and an increase in the penalty for peacetime espionage to a $10,000 fine and a maximum 10 years' imprisonment.

The bill ran into some strong opposition from Thomas Dewey, the Republican party's titular leader, who said of it: "Stripped to its naked essential, this is nothing but the method of Hitler and Stalin. It is thought-control . . . an attempt to beat down ideas with a club. It is surrender of everything we believe in." [1] The Mundt-Nixon bill did not become law, but many of its provisions did, in the form of the McCarran Act. The public discussion of the Mundt-Nixon bill made Nixon's name nationally known and strongly identified with anticommunism, but Nixon himself was still only a rather obscure young congressman; his own sudden national fame came not from his legislative activities but from his investigative performance in the case of Alger Hiss.

The Hiss case began—for Nixon—on August 3, 1948, when David Whittaker Chambers, a senior editor of *Time* magazine and confessed former Communist party member, testified before HUAC. Chambers gave the names of four men who he said had been members of his group, their purpose not espionage but "Communist infiltration of the American government." [2] One of the men named was Alger Hiss, then president of the Carnegie Foundation for International Peace, formerly a State Department official who had taken part in organizing the Yalta Conference and the San Francisco conference of the United Nations. Hiss was called in to testify two days later, and in an impressive performance convincingly denied that he had ever had any connection with Chambers or the Communist party.

Nixon, in his own account of Hiss's first appearance before the committee, says that he was intrigued by Hiss's choice of words: Hiss did not say, "I don't know Whittaker Chambers," but rather, "I have never known a man by the name of Whittaker Chambers." [3]

---

[1] From *The Facts about Nixon: An Unauthorized Biography* by William Costello, p. 189. Copyright © 1959 by Harrison-Blaine, Inc. Copyright © 1960 by William Costello. Reprinted by permission of The Viking Press, Inc. The occasion of Dewey's statement was a nationally broadcast radio debate between Dewey and his leading opponent for the 1948 presidential nomination, Harold Stassen.

[2] From *Six Crises*, by Richard M. Nixon. Copyright © 1962 by Richard M. Nixon. Reprinted by permission of Doubleday & Company, Inc.

[3] *Ibid.*, p. 8.

After the hearing most of the committee members were inclined to accept Hiss's testimony. The committee itself was under heavy criticism at the time—President Truman said the Republicans were using the spy hearings as a "red herring" to distract attention from their failure to deal with real problems. But Nixon persisted: The committee took more testimony from Chambers, going into details about his relationship with Hiss, and Nixon drove out three times to visit Chambers at his Maryland farm.

When Hiss appeared to testify again, in a closed session, he told of having once sublet an apartment to a man named George Crosley, who he said might have been Chambers. The committee then arranged a confrontation between the two. In the meeting, in a New York hotel room, Hiss identified Chambers as the man he had known, and Chambers repeated his accusation that they had been fellow Communists; Hiss challenged Chambers to make the same statement in public, where he would not have immunity from a libel suit, and a few days later Chambers did so, on a radio broadcast of "Meet the Press."

The next month Hiss sued for libel, and the case moved into its most bizarre and spectacular phase. Chambers had hinted that he had documentary evidence to support his charges, and Nixon ordered that a subpoena be served on Chambers ordering him to produce the documents. When the committee agent arrived in the night at Chambers' farm, Chambers led him out to a garden, cut open a pumpkin, and brought out five rolls of microfilmed copies of State Department documents. He also had produced some 65 pages of typewritten papers—all of which, he said, had been given him by Hiss.

On December 15, 1948, Hiss was indicted for perjury in denying that he had ever given government documents to Chambers. There were two trials: The first ended in a hung jury in July of 1949 and the second found Hiss guilty on January 21, 1950. The Hiss case had become world-wide news; Hiss's conviction was an embarrassment for the Truman administration, a political victory for the Republicans—and a personal victory for Richard Nixon. By the time Hiss was convicted, Nixon, then in his second term in Congress, had already decided to run for the United States Senate.

The incumbent senator whose term would expire in 1950 was Sheridan Downey, who had once run for lieutenant governor on the same ticket with Upton Sinclair. Downey had mellowed considerably since his fling at EPIC idealism; he was generally regarded as a political conservative, and his best work in the Senate had been on behalf of California oil interests.

Voter registration in California in 1950 was approximately 58 per cent Democratic to 37 per cent Republican,[4] but the Republican party generally won the elections. In 1950 the state's other senator was William F. Knowland, who had been appointed in 1945 to fill the vacancy created by the death of Hiram Johnson and then re-elected in 1946; the governor, preparing to run for his third term, was Earl Warren.

One of the curious features of California's elections—a legacy of the era of the Progressive reformers—was crossfiling, which allowed a candidate to file for the nomination of a party of which he was not a member. Crossfiling had made it possible for Nixon to run for reelection as the nominee of both parties after winning both primaries in 1948, and crossfiling would undoubtedly figure in the senatorial race; candidates usually filed for both nominations. But it appeared most likely that Downey would win the Democratic nomination, Nixon would get the Republican nomination, and the election would become the sort of partisan contest recognizable to people from the other side of the Sierras. It did become a partisan contest, but Sheridan Downey was not the Democratic nominee. That honor went to Congresswoman Helen Gahagan Douglas after a bloody primary battle between the liberal and conservative wings of California's Democratic party.

Mrs. Douglas, wife of actor Melvyn Douglas, was herself a successful former actress who had appeared in several Broadway stage productions, sung in European opera, and played the title role in a 1935 film version of H. Rider Haggard's *She.* Her husband was an active Democrat who had had the distinction of being the first movie actor to become a delegate to a Democratic national convention, and in the 1930's and 40's they were both prominent in California politics and strong Roosevelt supporters. In 1942, with the President's blessings and the backing of organized labor, she was elected to Congress from Los Angeles' 14th district. Since reelected three times, she was one of the best-known and best-dressed women in American politics; the newspapers often referred to her as the Democrats' answer to

[4] Eugene C. Lee, *California Voters 1928–1960* (Berkeley: Institute of Governmental Studies, 1963), p. A-27.

Clare Boothe Luce. Her announcement that she planned to try for the Senate meant that there would be a hard campaign for the Democratic nomination, and the aging Senator Downey decided he did not feel up to it. Two months before the primaries he announced that he was retiring from politics, and his place in the race was taken by Manchester Boddy, publisher of the *Los Angeles Daily News.*

Boddy, like Downey, was an ex-liberal whose views had shifted rightward over the years, and his campaign against Mrs. Douglas in the primaries was a small-scale rehearsal of the campaign Nixon would wage against her in the general election. He started out by referring to Mrs. Douglas and her backers as "red hots"—a term that in 1950 would be clearly interpreted as meaning procommunistic— and warned the voters of a "statewide conspiracy on the part of a small subversive clique of red-hots to capture, through stealth and cunning, the nerve centers of our Democratic party." [5] On a statewide radio broadcast he attacked her voting record in Congress, saying she had given "comfort to the Soviet tyranny by voting against aid to Greece and Turkey" and had "opposed an appropriation to enable Congress to uncover treasonable communistic activities." Boddy pointed out that in both these instances she had voted the same way as Vito Marcantonio. Marcantonio, who had once been Fiorello LaGuardia's protegé in East Harlem Republican politics, was now in Congress as a member of the American Labor party, and made no secret of his friendliness toward communism. Since Marcantonio was linked to communism, linking Mrs. Douglas to Marcantonio in a year when guilt by association had become a national pastime was tantamount to proving her to be a Communist.

Some insight into the state of the American mind in that spring of 1950 may be given by a story which ran in California newspapers during the time of the primary campaign: In the town of Mosinee, Wisconsin, in the home country of Senator Joseph McCarthy, the townspeople staged a mock "Communist coup" to alert the public to what might happen. On May Day local men dressed in improvised uniforms "shot" the police chief, took over the newspaper and published an issue of *Red Star,* issued orders that businesses were being nationalized, and posted private property with signs saying it had been taken over by the state. This was done with the full cooperation

[5] Costello, *op. cit.,* p. 62.

of city officials including the mayor, who was dragged out of his
house in the middle of the night to sign a proclamation and suffered a
fatal heart attack in the excitement.[6]

During that month of May, Boddy campaigned mainly on radio
and through his newspaper, and made some public appearances up
and down the state. Nixon and Mrs. Douglas campaigned in person,
traveling from town to town and making about ten speeches each per
day. Both of them had staked their political careers on the Senate
race, campaigning for it exclusively and declining to run for renomination to their respective seats in the House; in Mrs. Douglas'
14th district, a young state assemblyman named Sam Yorty was making a try to become her successor.

All three of the leading candidates—Boddy, Nixon, and Mrs.
Douglas—were filed for both nominations. Nixon made his appeal to
Democrats in a leaflet sent to registered Democratic voters which
began, "As One Democrat to Another. . ." The leaflet told of how
Nixon "broke the Hiss-Chambers espionage case" and showed photo-
graphs of him in his World War II Navy uniform and with his family.
It was identified as a publication of "Democrats for Nixon for United
States Senator." [7] Boddy and his campaign manager, Will Rogers, Jr.,
accused Nixon of misrepresentation, and the political editor of Boddy's
newspaper wrote:

> *Actually the impression is given that Nixon is a Democrat—*
> *and some of his critics are wondering if his antipathy to*
> *perjury would go far enough to prevent him from using this*
> *sort of advertising if he were under oath as Alger Hiss was*
> *when Nixon nicked him. It is surprising that a man who poses*
> *as the soul of truth and honor would permit such a deceitful*
> *device to be used to fool thousands of Democrats new to this*
> *county.*[8]

There was some speculation that Nixon might win the election
in the primaries. He was the only Republican of any stature in the
race and it appeared certain that he would win the Republican
nomination; a three-way split of the Democratic vote could give him
that nomination as well. Nixon, however, was not counting on this;
he expected to have a Democratic opponent in the general election—
that was the reason why, during the primary campaign, he did not

---

[6] *San Francisco Chronicle,* May 2, 1950.
[7] Costello, *op. cit.,* p. 61.
[8] Leslie Claypool, *Los Angeles Daily News,* quoted in *ibid.*

join with Boddy in trying to link Mrs. Douglas to communism. "Quite frankly," said Nixon's campaign manager, "we wanted her to be the Democratic nominee on the basis that it would be easier to defeat her than a conservative Democrat. So nothing was ever said pertaining to Helen Gahagan Douglas in the primary." [9] Instead, Nixon talked about the Hiss case, about the Taft-Hartley law, and about some of his ideas in the public welfare field—chiefly a pay-as-you-go pension plan to modify the existing Social Security setup, and government assistance to private health insurance programs as an alternative to Medicare.[10]

Nixon won the Republican nomination by over half a million votes, with Boddy in second place and Mrs. Douglas third. The Democratic nomination went to Mrs. Douglas, with Boddy again in second place and Nixon third. But Nixon, it should be noted, had made far greater inroads into the Democratic vote than either of his opponents had into the Republican vote.

A few weeks after the primary election, military forces from Communist-controlled North Korea moved southward across the 38th parallel. President Truman ordered United States intervention on June 27, and on the same day the United Nations Security Council, with the Russian delegation absent, voted sanctions against North Korea. By early August South Korean and American troops had been pushed back to a small enclave in the southeast portion of the country; the battle against communism was no longer merely ideological, and America was on the defensive.

The opening of the Korean conflict did not necessarily make things easier for the Republicans. President Truman had now become a wartime leader, against a Communist enemy, and at least for the time being it was impossible to equate Democrats with appeasement. The Democrats were now arguing that theirs was the superior brand of anticommunism. But, whatever the complications, it was necessary in 1950 for any politician who expected to get anywhere to display his anticommunism; and Richard Nixon was in the fortunate position of having established himself already as a crusading anticommunist.

Nixon had as his campaign manager Murray Chotiner, one of California's most skilled political professionals. Chotiner, whose busi-

[9] Earl Mazo, *Richard Nixon: A Political and Personal Portrait* (New York: Harper & Brothers, 1959), p. 76.
[10] *Los Angeles Times,* May 26, 1950.

ness activities included a law firm and a public-relations company, had run political campaigns for both Warren and Knowland; he was Knowland's southern California campaign manager in 1946 when he took on the side job of publicity director of Nixon's first campaign, for a fee of $500.[11] In 1950, he was Nixon's full-time adviser, and he remained Nixon's chief political confidant until he ran into trouble with a senatorial investigating committee in 1956. According to some accounts, Chotiner had personal reservations about the advisability of building the 1950 campaign on communism, but it was apparent from Nixon's opening speech that communism would be an issue.

The speech, broadcast from Washington on August 30, combined a call for unity behind Truman in the Korean War with an attack on past Democratic policies toward communism. He said that Truman's decision to fight "should have the wholehearted support of Congress and the American people." And, at the same time that the military battle is being fought in Korea, "we must enact legislation which will effectively deal with the Communist conspiracy at home. It is foolhardy to fight communism abroad and to allow it to go unchecked at home." [12] He called for the resignation of Secretary of State Dean Acheson and, getting to his opponent, charged that during Mrs. Douglas' six years in Congress she "consistently supported the State Department's policy of appeasing communism in Asia, which finally resulted in the Korean war." [13] He also proposed various measures for all-out mobilization to win in Korea. The speech was a most adroit piece of position-taking: It put Nixon in the commendable stance of wartime alliance with his commander-in-chief at the same time that it subtly placed the past blame for the conflict on the Truman administration and its supporters—including Mrs. Douglas.

On the same day, Nixon's southern California campaign manager issued a statement picking up—and elaborating on—Boddy's earlier charge that she voted the same way as Vito Marcantonio. The Douglas campaign leaders had expected this, and Mrs. Douglas had even made an amateurish attempt to blunt its effectiveness. In *her* opening speech, she had accused Nixon of voting with Marcantonio against aid to Korea and in favor of cutting Atlantic Pact funds in half. This strategy was supposedly designed to force Nixon to show his hand. According to Harold Tipton, Mrs. Douglas' campaign

11 Costello, *op. cit.*, p. 63.
12 *Los Angeles Times,* Aug. 31, 1950.
13 Costello, *op. cit.*, p. 63.

manager: "They fell for it. Nixon was right back with a defense. By September 1 he flooded the state with phony voting records. But our theory was that he couldn't keep up the red smear indefinitely." [14]

This proved to be a very inexpert appraisal of Nixon's ability to use an issue. The first statement issued from his southern California headquarters said that Mrs. Douglas' record revealed her "soft attitude" toward communism:

> *During five years in Congress Helen Douglas has voted 353 times exactly as has Vito Marcantonio, the notorious Communist party-line congressman from New York. . . . How can Helen Douglas, capable actress that she is, take up so strange a role as a foe of communism? And why does she when she has so deservedly earned the title of "the pink lady."* [15]

This was followed by a leaflet printed on pink paper, which became the central document of the campaign. The "pink sheet," as it became known, was headed "Douglas-Marcantonio Voting Record," and it began:

> *Many persons have requested a comparison of the voting records of Congresswoman Helen Douglas and the notorious Communist party-liner, Congressman Vito Marcantonio of New York.*
>
> *Mrs. Douglas and Marcantonio have been members of Congress together since January 1, 1945. During that period, Mrs. Douglas voted the same as Marcantonio 354 times. While it should not be expected that a member of the House of Representatives should always vote in opposition to Marcantonio, it is significant to note, not only the* great *number of times which Mrs. Douglas voted in agreement with him, but also the issues on which almost without exception they always saw eye to eye, to wit: Un-American Activities and Internal Security.*[16]

At a first glance, the pink sheet's argument that there existed a "Douglas-Marcantonio Axis" in Congress appeared to be borne out by the record. On closer examination it was considerably less impressive. According to an analysis of the record by *Editorial Research Reports,* there were 76 "outstanding" roll call votes in the House dur-

---

[14] Mazo, *op. cit.,* 80.

[15] Costello, *op. cit.,* p. 64.

[16] Morris H. Rubin, "The Trouble with Nixon, A Documented Report," *The Progressive,* Oct. 1956, pp. 6–7.

ing the period referred to in the pink sheet. Mrs. Douglas and
Marcantonio voted the same way on 66 of those—and so did a
majority of the House, both Republicans and Democrats. It would
have been more accurate, then, to say that Mrs. Douglas voted 85
per cent of the time with the majority.

The analysis continued: Of the 13 times when the Douglas-
Marcantonio votes coincided but were not part of the House or
Democratic majority, only two had to do with internal security: Mrs.
Douglas had voted against the Mundt-Nixon bill and against overrid-
ing Truman's veto of the subsequent McCarran bill. In both cases
there were numerous other Congressmen, both Republicans and
Democrats, who voted the same way. On foreign policy issues she
voted with the majority with one exception: She voted against the
Greek-Turkish aid bill. The remainder of the 354 votes which were
counted to make up the case were relatively minor and noncon-
troversial matters—on many of which her vote had been the same as
Nixon's. The pink sheet was statistically spurious, but it spoke with
the voice of irrefutable proof: "*Remember!* The United States Senate
votes on ratifying international treaties and confirming Presidential
appointments. Would California send Marcantonio to the United
States Senate?" [17]

While Mrs. Douglas' voting record was made, somewhat con-
fusingly, a central issue of the Nixon campaign, Nixon's own voting
record was not publicized. This was in accord with one of Chotiner's
basic principles of campaign techniques. As he said:

> *We never put out the complete voting record for our candi-
> date, vote by vote, in spite of the demands from people within
> our organization. The reason is—even if your candidate has
> voted 99 per cent right according to the person who reads the
> record, the one per cent will turn the prospect against you.*[18]

Mrs. Douglas' response to Nixon's campaign was inconsistent:
On one occasion she ridiculed "such pipsqueaks as Nixon and
McCarthy who are trying to get us so frightened of communism that
we'll be afraid to turn out the lights at night." [19] But at other times
she took the charges more seriously. She revived her earlier charge
that Nixon had voted with Marcantonio against aid to Korea and in

[17] *Ibid.*, p. 7.
[18] Costello, *op. cit.*, p. 46.
[19] *Ibid.*, p. 73.

favor of cutting Atlantic Pact funds, and added to it that they had voted the same way to reduce Marshall Plan aid, to reduce aid to China, and against extension of the Reciprocal Trade Agreement Act. "This does not," she said, "make Mr. Nixon a Communist. It only proves that he and Mr. Marcantonio and the majority in the Republican party see eye to eye in voting against measures of vital importance to our program to stem the tide of Communist aggression around the world." [20]

Murray Chotiner saw Mrs. Douglas' attempts to turn the Communist issue against Nixon as a serious error in campaign tactics. "Dick Nixon," he said, "was talking about communism . . . and what happened? Mrs. Douglas, in desperation . . . started to debate with Dick Nixon's issues. . . . She made the fatal mistake of attacking our strength instead of sticking to attacking our weaknesses." [21]

Also, Mrs. Douglas' occasional sallies at anticommunism were not part of an integrated campaign. In fact it is hard to see that she had an integrated campaign plan at all. Nixon's, on the other hand, was all of a piece: His billboards around the state showed his picture with the caption "On Guard for America," and in his speeches he reminded listeners of his work in the Hiss case and repeated the charge of the pink sheet: "My opponent did not vote as a Democrat. She did not vote as a Republican. . . . It just so happens that my opponent is a member of a small clique which joins the notorious party-liner, Vito Marcantonio of New York, in voting time after time against measures that are for the security of this country." [22]

Meanwhile, 550,000 copies of the pink sheet were distributed throughout the state, and their charges and Nixon's speeches were quoted in the largely Republican press. The state's major newspapers—the Hearst chain, the *Los Angeles Times,* the *Oakland Tribune,* owned by Senator Knowland's family—were pro-Nixon; a survey conducted by the Institute for Journalistic Studies at Stanford University showed that the total circulation of newspapers supporting Nixon outnumbered that of those supporting Mrs. Douglas and that, within those papers, there was a far higher percentage of articles favorable to Nixon.[23] The *Los Angeles Times,* for example,

[20] Harry W. Flannery, "Red Smear in California," *Commonweal,* Dec. 8, 1950, p. 223.
[21] Costello, *op. cit.,* p. 73.
[22] *Ibid.,* pp. 68–69.
[23] *Ibid.*

carried regular reports of Nixon speeches and either ignored the speeches of Mrs. Douglas entirely or mentioned them in the context of rebuttals from someone opposed to her. One pro-Douglas publication was the small *Independent Review,* which in an editoral condemned the conspiracy to defame her "by falsely accusing her through infamous insinuations and whispered innuendo of being a Communist," and in the process coined a nickname that was to stay with Nixon for the rest of his political life. "Representatives of her senatorial opponent, Tricky Dick Nixon," the editorial said, "are the chief mouthpieces for this partisan effort to crucify Mrs. Douglas. . . ." [24]

During the campaign Nixon failed to win an endorsement from Governor Warren, who was busy campaigning for a third term against the challenge of FDR's son, James Roosevelt; the coolness between the two leading California Republicans continued for many years thereafter. Nixon was supported strongly by most California Republicans, and also had the backing of Senator Joseph McCarthy, who visited Los Angeles on October 10 and made a radio speech in which he said that "the chips are down . . . between the American people and the administration Commiecrat party of betrayal." Mrs. Douglas was aided by outsiders also; Vice-President Alben Barkley, Mrs. Franklin D. Roosevelt, and Averell Harriman were some of the Democrats who came to help her California campaign.[25]

On election day and the day before, the Nixon campaign dropped communism and launched a statewide telephone drive. Advertising had announced that for anyone who answered the telephone with the words "Vote for Nixon" there would be:

> PRIZES GALORE! ! ! *Electric Clocks, Silex coffeemakers with heating units—General Electric automatic toasters—silver salt and pepper shakers, sugar and creamer sets, candy and butter dishes, etc., etc.* WIN WITH NIXON! [26]

The final voting returns showed that Nixon had won by a wide margin: 2,183,454 to Mrs. Douglas' 1,502,507.[27]

Nixon's victory in 1950 was an outstanding example of a campaign which had been successfully reduced to a single issue. As the strongly

---

[24] *Independent Review,* Sept. 29, 1950, quoted in *ibid.*
[25] Ralph de Toledano, *Nixon* (New York: Henry Holt and Company, 1956), p. 92.
[26] Costello, *op. cit.,* p. 73.
[27] Lee, *op. cit.,* p. A-212.

pro-Nixon *Los Angeles Times* editorialized on the day after the election: "The great issue between Senator Nixon and Mrs. Douglas was the Communist issue. . . . And the voters decided; the new Senator got the majority that most candidates can only dream of." [28]

At the time Nixon was elected to the Senate he was 37 years old, and he remained in the Senate only two years. His initial rise in politics was one of the most amazingly rapid in American history: In only six years from the time he returned from military service and made his first try for political office, he was Vice-President of the United States.

9

1950
Maryland
John Butler vs. *Millard Tydings*

At the same time that Helen Gahagan Douglas was being called the "pink lady" by her opponent in a California election, other candidates around the country were fighting similar battles: Senator Claude Pepper of Florida had been tagged "Red Pepper" in his campaign; Senator Elbert Thomas of Utah was being accused of communist activity by his Republican opponent—and even Senator Millard Tydings of Maryland, a conservative with 24 years in the Senate behind him, found himself on the defensive against charges that he was soft on communism.

There were great political differences between Millard Tydings and Helen Gahagan Douglas. Mrs. Douglas was, in 1950, a relatively inexperienced Congresswoman trying for a Senate seat, while Tydings

[28] *Los Angeles Times,* Nov. 9, 1950.

was an incumbent, and one of the most powerful members of the Senate. Then 60 years old, he was third in the Senate in seniority, chairman of the Armed Services Committee and a ranking member of the Foreign Relations Committee. Before coming to the Senate he had served in the House of Representatives; before that he had been a state senator and before that Speaker of the Maryland House of Delegates. Mrs. Douglas was a liberal and an avid New Dealer, whereas Tydings was a conservative who had had many battles with the Roosevelt administration. But for all their differences, in 1950 Mrs. Douglas and Tydings shared the experience of being caught up in the wave of anticommunism and of being opposed by candidates who employed public relations men as campaign managers. Richard Nixon's manager, lawyer and public-relations man Murray Chotiner, helped him make maximum use of anticommunism in California; and in Maryland a PR man named Jon M. Jonkel successfully manipulated the mass media to end the political career of Millard Tydings.

Tydings' political troubles began when he was appointed chairman of a Foreign Relations Committee subcommittee which had been formed in response to a Senate resolution to "conduct a full and complete study and investigation as to whether persons who are disloyal to the United States are or have been employed by the Department of State." The resolution was an attempt to create some order out of the pandemonium in which the country had foundered since the day—it was February 9, to be exact—when Senator Joseph McCarthy of Wisconsin officially opened the McCarthy Era by stating, in a speech to the Women's Republican Club of Wheeling, West Virginia, that he had in his hand a list of 205 Communists in the State Department. McCarthy had proceeded to make another speech at Salt Lake City, this time saying he had the names of 57 "card-carrying members of the Communist party" who were in the State Department. While State Department officials pressured him to release the names, he repeated his charges in a speech before the full Senate; by now the number had changed to 81. Two days later the Senate passed its resolution.

The Tydings Committee, as the special subcommittee came to be known, began its hearings in March, with McCarthy as the first witness; the proceedings dragged on into July, through four well-publicized and confusing months, as McCarthy introduced names without evidence, evidence without names. The best-known name he produced in substantiation of his promise to reveal throngs of card-carrying Communists in the State Department was Owen Lattimore. He charged that Lattimore, who had written books on Chinese history and Far East policy and was Director of the Walter Hines Page School of International Relations at Johns Hopkins University, had been "Alger Hiss' boss in the espionage ring in the State Department," the "top Russian espionage agent" in the United States. "I am willing to stand or fall on this one," he said. "If I am wrong on this I think the Subcommittee would be justified in not taking my other cases too seriously." [1]

The committee's conclusion was that (*a*) it found "no evidence to support the charge that Owen Lattimore is the 'top Russian spy' or, for that matter, any other sort of spy," and that (*b*) "Owen Lattimore is not now and never has been in any proper sense an employee of our State Department." His connection to the State Department, the committee said, had been "peripheral" and "sporadic." [2] Lattimore in his own statement before the committee said, "I think I can fairly claim—with great regret—that I am the least consulted man of all those who have a public reputation in this country as specialists on the Far East." He said that his own position toward the issue of communism in China was:

> . . . that the major American effort must be in one of . . . two directions: namely, to encourage a nationalism, even if it is a Communist nationalism, capable of standing up to the Soviet Union and maintaining independence in its dealings with us, or to encourage in every possible way the conditions that will make possible the survival of a so-called third force, a democratic group within China, that can change the character of the government. It seems to me that our long-term objective should be the latter. . . . [3]

Lattimore also accused McCarthy of being a spokesman for the strong pro-Nationalist China group in America, the "China lobby," which he called "McCarthy's Edgar Bergen." [4] Lattimore did not ever prove that McCarthy had been persuaded by members of the China Lobby to accuse him of being a spy in order to discredit the foreign-

[1] Richard Rovere, *Senator Joe McCarthy* (New York: Harcourt, Brace & World, Inc., 1959), pp. 151–52. Reprinted by permission.

[2] U.S. Congress, Senate, Committee on Foreign Relations, *State Department Loyalty Investigation,* 81st Cong., 2nd Sess., 1950, p. 72.

[3] "Lattimore Strikes Back," *New Republic,* April 17, 1950, p. 20.

[4] *Ibid.*

policy position he stood for; it left the McCarthy-Lattimore score at
one unproved charge apiece. The interim report issued by the Tydings
committee was strongly critical of McCarthy. It said:

> *At a time when American blood is again being shed to pre-*
> *serve our dream of freedom, we are constrained fearlessly and*
> *frankly to call the charges, and the methods employed to give*
> *them ostensible validity, what they truly are: a fraud and a*
> *hoax perpetrated on the Senate of the United States and the*
> *American people. They represent perhaps the most nefarious*
> *campaign of half-truths and untruth in the history of this*
> *Republic. For the first time in our history, we have seen the*
> *totalitarian technique of the "big lie" employed on a total*
> *basis. The result has been to confuse and divide the Amer-*
> *ican people, at a time when they should be strong in their*
> *unity. . . .*[5]

Support of the committee's position broke along strictly partisan
lines; Democrats agreed with it and Republicans called it a "white-
wash."

It had already become apparent, in that election year, that
communism would be an issue in many places, but it seemed unlikely
that it or any other issue would be a threat to Millard Tydings. He
was up for election that year, but he came from a state where the
registration was 70 per cent Democratic; and within the party he
was a powerful figure who had been able to overcome even the direct
opposition of the President: Roosevelt had campaigned for his opponent in the 1938 primary, but Tydings had won renomination by
65,000 votes and reelection by over 200,000.[6] He was not only powerful politically but prominent socially, with close connections to
Maryland aristocracy and Maryland financial interests; he would
have major newspaper backing and plenty of money for his campaign.
And at the urban precinct level he could depend on the support of
the Democratic machines. Machine organization was not what it had
once been in Maryland and the party was in the midst of a factional
split over the governorship, but the ward leaders could still be expected to deliver a significant number of votes.

The Republican party in Maryland was, at best, a rather loose
organization; it had delivered the state's electoral votes to Thomas

---

[5] "A Fraud and a Hoax," *New Republic*, July 31, 1950, p. 10.
[6] Stanley Kelley, Jr., *Public Relations and Political Power* (Baltimore:
Johns Hopkins, 1956), p. 110.

Dewey in the last presidential election, but within the state it depended for its existence on a state law requiring distribution of public jobs among political parties, the federal patronage, and the strength of individual candidates. In 1950 the most popular Republican was Theodore Roosevelt McKeldin, former mayor of Baltimore, who was preparing to run for governor.

Two candidates filed for the Republican senatorial nomination. One of them, General John D. Markey, was a well-known conservative who had run a good race against the junior U. S. Senator, Herbert O'Conor, in 1946. The other was John Marshall Butler, a 53-year-old Baltimore attorney who had never before run for public office— and who was about to bring off an amazing political upset.

Although Butler had little political experience and no statewide reputation, he did have two important people behind him: One was Ruth McCormick Miller, who was editor of the *Washington* (D.C.) *Times-Herald* and the niece of the famous Col. Robert McCormick, publisher of the *Chicago Tribune*. The other was Senator McCarthy. Mrs. Miller provided financial help, the support of her newspaper, a cut-rate printing job on a tabloid which was used in the last part of the campaign; and—most importantly—she helped bring about the importation from Chicago of Jon M. Jonkel, a public relations man who became Butler's campaign manager at a salary of $1,250 a month. McCarthy, in spite of the setback he had received from the Tydings committee, was becoming more powerful and influential every day; he provided a member of his staff to work for Jonkel as a "research assistant" and helped bring in some campaign contributions from wealthy out-of-state conservatives such as H. L. Hunt of Texas and Clint Murchison of Oklahoma. Murchison and his wife sent $10,000.[7]

Jonkel's first job in the primary campaign was simply to get his candidate known. One device used was a small, one-inch, one-column-wide advertisement reading simply "Be for Butler" in reverse-plate (white on black) type. These ads were inserted at least once —and sometimes twice—on every page of weekly newspapers throughout the state. Jonkel also used radio and direct-mail media while Butler traveled and delivered the speeches which Jonkel had written

[7] U.S. Congress, Senate, Subcommittee on Privileges and Elections of the Committee on Rules and Administration, *Hearings, Maryland Senatorial Election of 1950*, 82nd Cong., 2nd Sess., 1961, p. 1210. Hereafter cited as *Hearings.*

for him. The primary was a late one—September 17—and the Korean war was already well into its most disastrous phase as the campaigning got underway. Both Markey and Butler campaigned as anticommunists: Markey promised to "reveal hitherto unknown facts about the communistic influence in the State Department, with respect to Korea, where hundreds of American soldiers are dying daily to help correct the errors and mistaken policies of our Democratic Administration." [8] Butler announced as the first plank in his platform that he would "defend our country against Communism from Russia—across the seas—and from Communists and their friends within our Government." [9]

Ideologically there was not much difference between Markey and Butler, but the Butler campaign spent approximately four times as much money [10] and showed considerably more imagination. For example, in the last days before the election Jonkel sent to all members of county central committees in the state a special-delivery letter which implied that a Butler victory was certain and asked for their advice in matters pertaining to the campaign against Tydings. Jonkel said, "I tried to give the impression, and I guess I did give the impression, that we had inside information that Mr. Butler was going in in a walk, and we wanted to know where they wanted him to speak during the general-election campaign, what budgets they had set up, and how we would all work together."

Asked if he was actually confident of a victory, Jonkel said, "No. I was not confident, but it was sure fine to make it look that way. All the fellows in the county were sitting and waiting to see which side they should go with, and we convinced enough of them, I believe, that they had better stay with us." [11]

The Butler campaign also showed good judgment in concentrating on areas with the highest unit votes. Maryland had a primary election law similar to the electoral college system: Each county and each legislative district had a certain number of unit votes, all of which would go to the winner of a plurality of the popular vote within the district. The system made it possible for a candidate to win a nomination by campaigning successfully in the high unit-vote areas while losing in the state's over-all popular vote—which was exactly

[8] *Baltimore Sun,* August 1, 1950.
[9] Kelley, *op. cit.,* p. 116.
[10] Butler $15,643.24; Markey under $4,000. *Ibid.,* p. 117.
[11] *Hearings,* p. 289.

what happened in 1950: Markey got 34,791 popular votes and 70 unit votes, while Butler won the nomination with 32,899 popular votes and 82 unit votes.[12]

A similar spilt took place in the Democratic gubernatorial primary. George Mahoney, the challenger, won some 20,000 more votes than the incumbent, Preston Lane, but Governor Lane won the unit vote and was renominated. The questionable primary helped perpetuate the bitterness between the Lane and Mahoney factions in the Democratic party. Tydings won his renomination easily, getting a heavy majority of the popular vote and all the unit votes—but there were some subtle indications that the Senator's position was not so strong as it might appear. In the primary campaign, one of his Democratic opponents had charged that he had "covered up Communists and leftists" [13] in the recent subcommittee investigation, and Tydings had taken the charge seriously enough to answer it in a speech broadcast over statewide radio. He said that he had twice refused the appointment to the chairmanship of the special committee, and explained his reasons for ultimately taking the job:

> *I believe that the people of my State would not want me to run away from that assignment, just because it was difficult, disagreeable and might be unpopular. . . . [I] saw an opportunity to do a service, either by helping to expose subversives, or, if the McCarthy charges were unfounded, by seeing to it that nobody was convicted or injured by falsehood or suspicion or smear campaigns and by seeing to it that the liberties and freedoms, the rights and privileges of American citizens were not taken away or impaired by persons who talk freedom and democracy but who use totalitarian techniques and methods to satisfy their prejudices, their suspicions and their fears. . . . There will never be, if I can prevent it, government by unfounded character assassination.[14]*

Tydings, in the primary, won 172,572 votes, against 87,733 for his two opponents put together—but even that much of an opposition vote for a couple of young and little-known candidates was some cause for concern. The *Baltimore Sun* said: "The fact that two such candidates could between them get nearly 90,000 votes against an experienced and well-known candidate like Mr. Tydings shows that the attacks on the Senator growing out of the State De-

12 Kelley, *op. cit.*, p. 117.
13 *Baltimore Sun*, Aug. 29, 1950.
14 *Baltimore Sun*, Sept. 1, 1950.

partment investigation have carried some weight." [15] Jonkel and Butler noticed something even more portentous in the returns from the Democratic primary: Over 100,000 people who had voted for one or another of the gubernatorial candidates did not bother to cast any vote at all in the Senate race. As Jonkel saw it, "there were 100,000 people who did not want to choose a nominee for the Democratic Party for the United States Senate." [16]

Shortly after the primary McCarthy addressed a Republican rally at Hyattsville, and named Tydings as one of the men who "have done more than any others in this nation to shield the traitors, protect the disloyal, and confuse Americans in their desperate fight to clean out the Communists." [17] This was to become the basis of the whole Butler campaign—but not in McCarthy's direct-accusation style. Jonkel said:

> *Our slant on the Tydings' hearing was not this frontal approach at all. We worked with the fact that a very, very big doubt existed in the minds of the people of Maryland. . . . It would have taken, I don't know how many, but literally thousands of pages of words of testimony to try to prove . . . and I so informed Mr. Butler . . . I said, "Let's not get into the business of proving whether or not it was a whitewash, let's stay in the business that a doubt does exist."* [18]

The technique then became one of what Stanley Kelley in his study of the role of public relations in politics has called "merchandising doubt." [19] And if the attack was not frontal, it was also anything but subtle; there was a sledge-hammer bluntness in some of the materials used during the campaign to suggest that Tydings had for some reason—either to protect the Truman administration or because of a sinister concern for Communists—deliberately employed his committee's power to cover up disloyalty in government. One piece of literature distributed fairly early in the campaign was a reprint from an advertisement in Mrs. Miller's paper, the *Washington Times-Herald,* which asked Tydings:

> *WHY didn't you ask Secretary of State Dean Acheson to testify about loyalty?*

[15] *Baltimore Sun,* Sept. 19, 1950.
[16] *Hearings,* p. 273.
[17] *The New York Times,* Sept. 24, 1950. © 1950 by The New York Times Company. Reprinted by permission.
[18] *Hearings,* p. 272.
[19] Kelley, *op. cit.,* pp. 107 ff.

> *WHY didn't you allow the minority members of the Committee . . . the non-Administration members . . . to bring witnesses into the investigation?*
>
> *WHY is there all the talk about your keeping parts of the hearing out of the official record?*
>
> *WHY did you take the word of Earl Browder about whether or not any of these men were Communists? Didn't you think that as former top Communist in this country that he would cover up for anyone suspected of being a Red?* [20]

In addition to such generalized suggestions of disloyalty there were campaign pieces aimed at specific voter groups—such as the Catholics, who comprised more than one-third of the voting population of Maryland: An appeal to Catholic anticommunism gave Butler a good opportunity to chip away at Tydings' usually dependable Democratic support. Jonkel wrote a letter which went out with Butler's signature to Catholic clergymen. It read:

> *As the trusted guide of men and women, you are especially aware of the forces attempting to disrupt the spiritual and secular integrity of the American people. I believe you will agree with me that Communism is one of the most persistent and carefully-shielded pressures we must withstand if we are to survive as individuals and as a nation of many freedoms.*
>
> *I realize that the Church cannot take an active part in politics but I want you personally to know where I stand. I believe in my country and in my God. And I will not permit anything to corrupt the righteous influence of either.*
>
> *I pledge that if I am elected to the United States Senate, I will do everything within my power to defend us against the atheistic Russia overseas or from Communists and their friends within our Government.*[21]

Another important group of voters in Maryland were the Negroes; a leading figure in this part of the campaign was Col. Roscoe Conklin Simmons, a Negro who wrote an inspirational column for the *Chicago Tribune* and spent much of his time going around the country speaking to blacks on behalf of Republicanism. He had also had the distinction of seconding the nominations of many candidates—including Herbert Hoover and Robert Taft—at Republican conventions; Mrs. Miller referred to him as "a man of great distinction" and "in many respects a family retainer." [22] Col. Simmons came to Maryland

[20] *Ibid.,* p. 125.
[21] *Ibid.,* p. 128.
[22] *Hearings,* pp. 430–31.

and traveled about the state making speeches in churches, in saloons, on street corners, and even to groups of workers in the fields. Meanwhile the Butler campaign organization put out a brochure entitled "Back to Good Old Dixie," which criticized Tydings' voting record in matters of concern to black voters. The Democratic organization brought in young Congressman Adam Clayton Powell from New York; Powell made several speeches in Baltimore, but his involvement in the campaign was not as extensive as Col. Simmons', and on election day Negro precincts voted heavily for Butler.

The Butler campaign, which had had practically no organization whatever to begin with, filled out as the weeks passed but never did assume the dimensions of a traditional campaign organization. Jonkel continued to direct over-all campaign strategy, although there had been some thought that at a certain stage he would be replaced by someone from inside the state and would devote his own efforts more strictly to the public-relations aspects of the campaign. It became apparent, however, that giving someone else the title of campaign manager would only aggravate factional rivalries within the state's Republican party. Jonkel, as campaign manager, had some troubles maintaining control over campaign financing—his practice of "short-circuiting" contributions directly to persons to whom the campaign owed money caused him trouble later and made it impossible to calculate exactly how much the Butler campaign actually took in and spent. The amount reported, at any rate, was $82,913.61, as compared to $35,840.77 for the Tydings organization.[23]

While Jonkel dealt with the headquarters activities and the preparation and distribution of campaign literature, Butler concentrated on making public appearances. Much of the speechmaking was done as part of a unified Republican operation—Butler, McKeldin, and other candidates would travel together, thus helping Butler to draw larger crowds and benefit from McKeldin's popularity. Butler was continually on the road, and in fact visited his Baltimore headquarters only three or four times during the campaign. In his speeches, he played on the same basic theme of doubt and possible disloyalty that was being used in the other campaign material. According to Jonkel:

> *He talked about the situation in Korea, which was pretty*
> *hot at that time. What happened, I mean, we did not have*

23 Kelley, *op. cit.*, 135–36.

*to say anything, he never said that Senator Tydings had held
back arms from any place. You did not have to say that.
All you had to say was that Senator Tydings had been chairman of the Senate Armed Services Committee, and that so
much money had been spent on the Armed Forces. . . . $250
worth, or whatever it was, or a million dollars worth, or whatever it was, was not enough, as indicated by the news headlines and the news commenators of the day. Mr. Butler just
drew a parallel and wanted to know if that was a good Senate
Armed Services Committee. . . .*

*He campaigned also on the fact that Senator Tydings
had been the chairman of a subcommittee which investigated
the loyalty of the State Department employees. He com-
mented on that. There were some discrepancies in the report
of that thing. He would comment on that sometimes.*

*Most of the time he would say, "You are a father, you
are a mother, are you satisfied?"*

*Then he would say, for instance, that "Russia boasts that
all over the world it is going to take over the world by force,
by trickery, or by this or that. This is our country. We have
seen it happen in other countries. You are a father, you are a
mother, do you believe that we are well organized here? Do
you feel that you know for sure that there are no Communists
or Communist influence in the top levels of our Government?"*

*You just asked them those questions. Those are the ques-
tions he asked. That is the way he campaigned. We never had
anything personal against Senator Tydings.*[24]

An increasing amount of Tydings' energies in campaigning became tied up in trying to refute the oblique imputations of disloyalty.
He printed and distributed a pamphlet entitled "The Truth About the
Tydings' Investigation" and used a substantial amount of his campaign funds to finance television and radio speeches in which he explained in detail how the subcommittee had arrived at its conclusions.
Jonkel thought Tydings "probably was misinformed about the kind
of campaign he should conduct. He was campaigning on the defensive
. . . doing himself not very much good." [25]

Actually, Tydings had no one comparable to Jonkel in his
campaign organization to advise him about how to make best use
of the mass media. His campaign managers were his law partner,
F. Murray Benson, and Maryland Adjutant-General Milton A.
Reckord. An advertising agency, Joseph Katz and Company, was

[24] *Hearings*, p. 305.
[25] *Ibid.*, p. 233.

employed by the campaign, but all the major decisions about strategy were made by Tydings himself. In the Butler organization, Jonkel and a young advertising man named Marshall Hawk put together a much more effective mass-media campaign.

In the matter of radio time-buying, for example, while the Tydings campaign would purchase sizable blocs of time for Tydings to make traditional political speeches, Jonkel would buy time before and after each one for his own spot commercials. According to Jonkel, "every time Senator Tydings was on the air in the last four or five days of the campaign, he was preceded by a 20-, 30-, or 40-second spot about Butler, before and after everything Senator Tydings said."

> *I spent what money we had, I sent it into these little tiny things, these 20- and 30-second spot announcements, the same way they sell any other commodity on the air.*
>
> *We worked music into some of them and we worked drama into some of them. We had one that we used pretty consistently and I guess it might have been a little irritating, especially in Democratic headquarters, but we set up a positive slogan for Butler, "Be for Butler."*
>
> *It did not have anything to do with being against Tydings. But we used that in little jingles, something like they use for Bromo-Seltzer. "Be for Butler, be for Butler, be for Butler, be for Butler, be for Butler, be for Butler," and then end up with, "Be for John Marshall Butler . . . Republican candidate for United States Senator."* [26]

Other spot commercials evoked the war: Sound effects of machine-gun fire and exploding mortar shells would be heard, and then a voice would ask: "Do you, in your heart, believe that we were ready for what happened in Korea, or could have happened some place else? Vote for John Marshall Butler, Republican candidate for United States Senate." [27]

As the campaign progressed, according to Jonkel, Senator Tydings became "upset and . . . nervous. He was getting angrier and angrier all the time." [28] One of the many factors contributing to the Senator's unhappiness was radio commentator Fulton Lewis, Jr., who lived in southern Maryland. Lewis' broadcasts kept accusing Tydings of aspiring to become Ambassador to England, which position he was to be awarded by Truman in return for the favor he had

26 *Ibid.*, pp. 302–3.
27 *Ibid.*
28 *Ibid.*

done the administration in "whitewashing" its disloyal elements.
Tydings demanded equal time to answer the charge and protested
after the election that "perhaps one of the greatest indirect financial
contributions to Butler's campaign was made by the Mutual Broadcasting Corp. . . . 19 per cent of the stock of this broadcasting company is owned by Colonel McCormick's *Chicago Tribune,* which in
turn owns the *Washington Times-Herald.*" [29]

Four days before the election a newspaper-tabloid publication
appeared. It had been printed on the presses of the *Washington
Times-Herald* and was distributed under the nominal sponsorship of
a campaign organization called "Young Democrats for Butler."
Actually the copy and art had been prepared under the supervision
of McCarthy's loaned "research assistant," Jean Kerr.[30] The tabloid,
of which 500,000 copies were printed, was the strongest document of
the entire campaign; it seemed to prove that Tydings was a friend
of Communists and, because of his position as chairman of the
Senate Armed Services Committee, almost singlehandedly responsible
for America's troubles in Korea. One of its articles, headlined
"Tydings Group Held Up Arms," read:

> *One of the fundamental reasons for our early failures in the
> Korean War is being charged to the Senate Armed Services
> Committee, headed by Senator Tydings of Maryland. Last year
> Congress appropriated $87,300,000 to arm the South Koreans.
> The money was authorized in two bills. One set aside $75,-
> 000,000 to furnish planes, tanks, antitank guns, rifles and
> ammunitions, any part of which could be used in Korea. The
> second bill earmarked $100,300,000 for Korea alone.*
>
> *The check-up reveals that only $200 of this money was
> spent before the North Koreans attacked. It was spent for
> bailing wire. The Armed Services Committee did not use its
> power to see the money was used in time to prevent the debacle
> in Korea.*[31]

Another article, headed "Tydings Committee Blamed for High
Korean Casualties," said:

> *Veteran observers are holding Senator Tydings, chairman of
> the Senate Armed Services Committee, to blame for the
> horrible cost of the war in Korea. It has been pointed out
> that Tydings is head of this Senate Committee which controls*

[29] *Ibid.,* p. 20.
[30] *Ibid.,* p. 257.
[31] *Ibid.,* p. 8.

the Department of Defense, and which failed to provide this
country with the necessary equipment to protect the soldiers,
sailors, and marines who have been sacrificed in Korea.
      . . . Tydings led his committee away from the raging
controversy. He ducked any serious check-up of our defense
resources. His excuse was that he did not believe the Senate
should look into the matter as long as it was being thrashed
out by the House. Result? Korea and 343 casualties for Mary-
land.[32]

Tydings' retort—after the election—was to call the first article
a "deliberate, barefaced, scurrilous, damnable lie" and to remark
of the second that the statement that he had "led his committee away
from" the Korean controversy was "without a shred, a vestige, or an
iota of truth. The Senate Armed Services Committee, if you look
at its membership,[33] could not be led if I wanted to do so." [34] Unfortunately for Tydings—discounting the possible validity of Jonkel's
statement that being on the defensive was a mistake anyway—the
tabloid came out too late for him to mount any organized effort at
refuting it. He went on television the night before the election with
a copy of the tabloid and denounced it as a smear, but he had no
means in the time remaining to carry his argument to anyone except
those who watched his election-eve broadcast.

The most damaging part of the tabloid was not the articles but
the photographs—particularly the one which showed American Communist party official Earl Browder talking to Tydings. They both had
amiable facial expressions and it appeared that Tydings' arm might
be around Browder. The caption said:

Communist leader Earl Browder, shown at left, in this com-
posite picture, was a star witness at the Tydings committee
hearings, and was cajoled into saying Owen Lattimore and
others accused of disloyalty were not Communists. Tydings
(right) answered: "Oh, thank you, sir." Browder testified in
the best interests of the accused, naturally.[35]

Although the picture was identified as a composite, Tydings
complained that the word "composite" was not understood by many of

[32] *Ibid.,* p. 10.
[33] Membership of the committee at the time included Senators Lyndon
Johnson, Estes Kefauver, Styles Bridges, Leverett Saltonstall, William Knowland, and Wayne Morse.
[34] *Ibid.,* p. 11.
[35] *Ibid.,* p. 13.

the people who saw the tabloid. What the picture really did, he said, was "bring into clear focus the intent of the conspirators in their moral squalor to deceive the people of the State of Maryland in the selection of a candidate for one of the highest offices in the world." [36]

On November 7, 1950, the people of Maryland chose John Marshall Butler as their new United States Senator. It was an unusually heavy voter turnout: According to a Baltimore election official, nearly 75 per cent of those registered voted. Tydings got 283,258 votes, Butler 326,286.[37] McKeldin, by an even wider margin, defeated his Democratic opponent for governor.

Tydings had complained bitterly about the Butler campaign tactics and continued to do so, to the point of filing a formal complaint with the Senate Subcommittee on Privileges and Elections—and yet he told reporters after the election that the main cause of his defeat had been the factional split in his own party which had opened up during the primary. Although this seems contradictory, it may not be: The kind of campaign which Jonkel ran appears to work best in areas where party organization is feeble. The business of campaign management by public-relations companies first prospered in California, where Progressive legislation had combated machine rule by restricting party organization. And when Jonkel came on the Maryland scene in 1950, the leadership of the Republican party was nonexistent and the leadership of the Democratic party had been disintegrating for years as rivalries and reform movements broke up the once-strong machine organizations. As Stanley Kelley wrote:

> Such a situation calls for a strategy of propaganda capable of supplying voting cues to the unorganized voter, supplementing the efforts of the boss. But it was Butler and not the Tydings forces which were best equipped for this kind of politics. Lacking any important source of "sure" votes, their campaign became essentially a propaganda campaign with the professional public relations man as its strategist.[38]

The voting returns showed that the old system still had some vitality. In the first, second, and third wards in Baltimore, Tydings won by small majorities. These were areas with a high percentage

[36] *Ibid.*
[37] Kelley, *op. cit.,* p. 135.
[38] *Ibid.,* p. 138.

of Catholics, who might be expected to be influenced by Butler's "soft on Communism" allegations—but they were also areas where the Democratic machine was best organized.[39]

But the machines function best when the voting is done by a small percentage of the population—preferably those who for one reason or another can be depended on to be faithful to their party. When the voter turnout increases, so does the likelihood that the outcome of the election will be determined by "swing" voters who have no special party ties and are subject to persuasion through the mass media. If fewer people had voted in 1950, and if the Democrats had been less divided, Tydings might have remained in office. But the national excitement about the war and McCarthyism and communism, the high-pressure Butler campaign and Tydings' furious reactions to it, and McKeldin's challenge to the dispirited state Democratic administration all intermingled to generate much publicity and popular interest, a high voter turnout, and the greatest Republican victory in Maryland history.

As a result of Tydings' complaint, the Senate Subcommittee on Privileges and Elections held hearings at which Jonkel was questioned in detail about his financing and propagandizing operations, and Tydings aired his charge that he had been the victim of "false statements, faked pictures, direct assertion, and transparent innuendo." [40] The Senate took no action as a result of the hearings, but Jonkel was subsequently indicted in Maryland on misdemeanor charges of conducting a campaign while not a resident of the state and failing to report campaign donations and expenditures on time; he was fined $5,000.[41]

[39] *Ibid.,* p. 140.
[40] *Hearings,* p. 27.
[41] Kelley, *op. cit.,* p. 135n.

A
CATHOLIC
PRESIDENT

VI

10

1960

West Virginia

John F. Kennedy vs. *Hubert Humphrey*

The 1960 presidential primary in West Virginia, in which John F. Kennedy defeated Hubert Humphrey, has found a secure place in the Kennedy folklore. "If our political disputes are ever remembered as our battlefields are now," Associated Press correspondent Arthur Edson wrote, "West Virginia will become a national shrine. For it was in West Virginia's beautiful mountains, in its thriving cities, in its impoverished coal fields that the decisive battle was fought that gave Senator John F. Kennedy the Democratic presidential nomination." [1]

The historical importance of the West Virginia primary has to do with the religious issue—specifically, with the doubts among Democrats of a Catholic's ability to get Protestant votes, and with the blow Kennedy dealt to those doubts by winning strongly in a Protestant state. It is undoubtedly true that important blocs of delegates did fall behind Kennedy as a result of the West Virginia victory, and yet the simple cause-and-effect explanation does not entirely fit. The sequence of events was rather more elusive, because presidential primaries are elusive kinds of elections—their value never lies squarely in the victory itself, but rather in the peripheral matter of how the victory is interpreted. And although there is usually no

---

[1] Harry W. Ernst, *The Primary That Made a President: West Virginia 1960* (Cases in Practical Politics Series, Eagleton Institute of Politics, 1962), p. 1. Reprinted by permission.

question about who has won an election, there can be many questions about how the victory should be interpreted.

In 1912, when Theodore Roosevelt campaigned in the primaries, he did so knowing that the presidential primaries alone could not yet provide the delegates to control a nomination. He expected that such a time would soon come, but he understood that in 1912 the primaries were useful mainly for their publicity value: they were a stage on which he could perform for the nation, preaching his ideas, electrifying his followers, and defeating his foe in open democratic conflict. And although TR's campaign in the primaries did not win him the Republican nomination, it did generate enough momentum to tear apart the Republican party.

The nationwide conversion to presidential primaries which had been expected by TR and his Progressives never quite came off; in the decades that followed, as some states passed new presidential primary laws, other states repealed theirs; when John F. Kennedy began his campaign for the Democratic presidential nomination in 1960 the number of states with primaries was about the same as it had been in 1912. And the main value of primaries was still publicity, not delegate votes—the increased importance of mass communications in American society had made the primaries more than ever highly newsworthy, exciting previews of the coming attractions of conventions and the national campaign.

In the 1960 Democratic convention, West Virginia's delegates would have 25 votes out of the total of 1,520. And the West Virginia presidential primary preference vote was not even binding on the delegates. But for a while, in the spring of 1960, the entire country was watching West Virginia. The primary itself, the tangible rewards of it, were insignificant, and yet in a circular way the attention that was paid to it made it worthy of attention. Such a primary possesses many of the characteristics of what historian Daniel Boorstin, talking of how news reporting shapes reality, calls a "pseudo-event." A pseudo-event, according to Boorstin, possesses the following characteristics:

> (1) It is not spontaneous, but comes about because someone has planned, or planted, or incited it. . . .
> (2) It is planted primarily (but not always exclusively) for the immediate purpose of being reported or reproduced. Therefore, its occurrence is arranged for the convenience of the reporting or reproducing media. Its success is measured by how widely it is

reported. . . . The question, "Is it real?" is less important than, "Is it newsworthy?"
(3) Its relation to the underlying reality of the situation is ambiguous. Its interest arises largely from this very ambiguity. Concerning a pseudo-event the question, "What does it mean?" has a new dimension. . . . Without some of this ambiguity a pseudo-event cannot be very interesting.[2]

The West Virginia presidential primary, it should be said in fairness, was not created for the purpose of being reported. Yet there is no possibility that John F. Kennedy and his supporters would ever have bothered to channel their vast resources of wealth and talent into the humble political machinery of West Virginia but for one reason: the impression that a victory would make on people in other parts of the country.

Five men, in 1960, were regarded as potential Democratic presidential nominees: Adlai Stevenson, the former governor of Illinois who had won the nomination in 1952 and 1956 and been twice defeated by Dwight Eisenhower; Senator John F. Kennedy of Massachusetts; Senator Hubert Humphrey of Minnesota; Senator Lyndon Johnson of Texas; and Senator Stuart Symington of Missouri. Stevenson was uncertain as to whether he should seek or accept the nomination a third time; Johnson and Symington were pursuing it, in their various ways, through the dark corridors of power politics. Only Humphrey and Kennedy were staking their hopes on the presidential primaries, each man attempting to collect some delegates thereby and—what was much more important—each man attempting to demonstrate to the power brokers who would control decision-making at the coming national convention that he was a superior vote-getter who could lead the party to victory over the Republican nominee— probably Richard Nixon—in November.

Kennedy was a more glamorous and attractive campaigner, with more money behind him, a surer feel for politics, and a brilliant corps of campaign assistants—but he was a Catholic, and in 1960 no one was quite sure how much of a disadvantage that might be. In 1928 the Democrats had nominated Al Smith, a Catholic, and Smith had been defeated by Herbert Hoover; many professional politicians computed this to mean simply that a Catholic could not be elected

[2] From *The Image* by Daniel Boorstin, published by Atheneum. Copyright © 1961 by Daniel J. Boorstin. Reprinted by permission of Atheneum Publishers.

President. Their conclusion may not have been correct, and their willingness to accept it may not have been morally commendable, but the average politician would rather be a successful pragmatist than a successful crusader. Kennedy, who came from a family background of professional politics, understood this and accepted it. According to Theodore Sorensen:

> He was not enlisting crusaders in a drive to remove the ban on Catholics from the White House. He had no deep desire to avenge the discrimination his grandparents had encountered in Boston. And he was not, contrary to some reports, interested in whatever glory attached to being the first Catholic President. He simply wanted to be President and happened to be Catholic.[3]

Kennedy's run for the nomination began with the New Hampshire primary in March; he won it handsomely, but his only opponent was an obscure ballpoint-pen manufacturer from Chicago, and the victory was not considered significant. His first real test was when he came up against Hubert Humphrey in the Wisconsin primary.

The Wisconsin primary helped create the context in which the West Virginia election would be interpreted. Wisconsin was next door to Humphrey's home state of Minnesota and consequently regarded by some as Humphrey country—a consideration which would give value to a Kennedy victory. But there was also the fact of the state's high proportion of Roman Catholics, 32 per cent against the national average of 23 per cent—if people voted according to their religion, this might outweigh Humphrey's local popularity. The tempo of modern news dissemination requires instant interpretation as well as instant reporting, and the news media had the votes already analyzed before they were cast. *Time*'s election-eve report said: "At week's end, Kennedy was holding strong in populous urban areas. . . . Wisconsin's Roman Catholics (30 per cent of the electorate) were enthusiastically behind him, and neutral politicos guessed that many Catholic Republicans would cross over in the primary to vote for him. . . ."[4]

Kennedy won the primary with a total popular vote of 476,024 to Humphrey's 366,753;[5] most reports of the election were built

---

[3] Theodore C. Sorensen, *Kennedy* (New York: Harper & Row, Publishers, 1965), p. 14. Reprinted by permission.

[4] *Time,* April 4, 1960, p. 14.

[5] James W. Davis, *Springboard to the White House* (New York: Thomas Y. Crowell Company, 1967), p. 303. Reprinted by permission.

around the assumption that religion had been an important—perhaps
the important—factor. *Time* said:

> Last week Jack Kennedy proved beyond doubt in the Wiscon-
> sin primary that an attractive, hard-campaigning Catholic
> candidate can count on a powerful Catholic vote that cuts
> across labor-union loyalities, the farm problem, and even—to
> a lesser extent—party lines . . . with his 106,000 plurality,
> Kennedy showed some remarkable strengths and some re-
> vealing weaknesses. His support from Wisconsin's large Roman
> Catholic population (32 per cent) almost amounted to a bloc
> vote—from the German and Polish Catholics in Milwaukee's
> Fourth District to the thousands of rural Republicans who
> crossed over to vote for him. (One interesting exception to the
> rule: in economically hard-pressed Ashland and Iron counties,
> both over 40 per cent Catholic, Hubert Humphrey won.)
> Though Humphrey was endorsed by U.A.W.–C.I.O. leaders,
> Kennedy swept the labor vote, which is heavily Catholic.[6]

The New York Times likewise editorialized that "Wisconsin's primary
. . . showed that many Catholic voters—Republicans included—
cast their ballots for Senator Kennedy as a Catholic," [7] and political
analyst Arthur Krock warned:

> The concentration of votes for Kennedy in strongly Catholic
> areas of Wisconsin presage, if he is nominated at Los Angeles,
> a Catholic versus Protestant division in this country that will
> tend to solidify the Protestant voting majority in this country
> against him. . . . The Democratic party will not assume re-
> sponsibility for the risk.[8]

This kind of analysis, tying Kennedy to the Catholic vote, was turning his victory into a defeat. And the analysis itself was debatable.
According to Sorensen:

> Humphrey ran best, it was correctly reported, in the least
> Catholic areas. But few pointed out that all these areas were
> near the Minnesota border—that Humphrey also ran well in
> the Catholic areas near Minnesota—and that Kennedy ran
> well in the cities and in the eastern part of the state among
> non-Catholics as well as Catholics. Humphrey did well in the
> cities near Minnesota; Kennedy did well on the farms further
> away. Geography was more decisive than religion.[9]

[6] *Time*, April 18, 1960, pp. 16–17.
[7] *The New York Times*, April 7, 1960. © 1960 by The New York Times
Company. Reprinted by permission.
[8] *Ibid.*
[9] Sorensen, *op. cit.*, pp. 155–56.

But, whether the public verdict was correct or not, Kennedy was stuck with it; he had yet to prove conclusively that he could win Protestant votes. West Virginia, the only other primary which both Kennedy and Humphrey planned to enter, might be more decisive. *Time* said of this one: "The supporters of Humphrey see West Virginia as their big chance, because a large portion of the state lies within the Southern Bible Belt, with an electorate composed mainly of mountaineer Protestants likely to be wary of a Roman Catholic candidate." [10]

Actually, the picture of West Virginia as a stronghold of old-fashioned Protestantism was equally doubtful. According to a survey conducted by the National Council of the Churches of Christ in the United States of America, church membership in the state was about half the national average; the population was 4.9 per cent Catholic and 27.5 per cent Protestant—and some 67 per cent of the people were not affiliated with any church at all.[11] Furthermore, when Al Smith had entered the West Virginia primary in 1928, he had defeated his opponent, Senator James A. Reed, a Missouri Baptist, by nearly 6,000 votes.[12] But the press continued to discuss the importance of religion. "It will be a miracle," Walter Lippman wrote, "if the outcome in West Virginia shows that there is no religious issue which divides seriously the people of this country." [13]

According to a poll which had been taken for Kennedy in West Virginia several months earlier, he had a wide lead over Humphrey. But after the Wisconsin primary and all the attendant publicity about the religious issue, Kennedy's popularity in West Virginia dropped sharply; it appeared that the voters were learning that Kennedy was a Catholic and being reminded that they were not expected to vote for one. Even though Kennedy's chances of winning in West Virginia seemed to be diminishing, most of his advisers were glad to hear that Humphrey still planned to come into the state and campaign. An opponent makes a primary victory much more meaningful; as one Kennedy aide is reported to have said: "If Hubert Humphrey didn't exist, we'd have had to invent him." [14]

10 *Time,* March 28, 1960, p. 23.
11 *Ibid.,* May 2, 1960, p. 13*n.*
12 Ernst, *op. cit.,* p. 2.
13 Quoted in *ibid.,* p. 5.
14 Stewart Alsop, "Kennedy's Magic Formula," *Saturday Evening Post,* August 13, 1960, p. 60, quoted in Davis, *op. cit.,* p. 68. Reprinted by permission.

With Humphrey's decision to campaign in West Virginia, the primary became a do-or-die situation for both candidates. Actually, Humphrey was probably dead already, after the Wisconsin defeat, but he could still knock Kennedy out of the running—and Kennedy charged more than once that Humphrey was in the race mainly as the front man for a "stop Kennedy" drive backed by Symington and Johnson.

Kennedy's strategy in regard to the religious issue was to meet it head-on. He flatly told a Washington meeting of the American Society of Newspaper Editors that he was "not the Catholic candidate for President" and went on to characterize the campaign as one in which the real issue was not religion, but religious bigotry: "If there is bigotry in this country," he said, "then so be it—there is bigotry. If that bigotry is too great to permit the fair consideration of a Catholic who has made clear his complete independence and his complete dedication to separation of church and state, then we ought to know it. But I do not believe that this is the case." And when he went campaigning in West Virginia he repeatedly talked of religious tolerance. He asked an audience in the town of Fairmont: "Is anyone going to tell me that I lost this primary 42 years ago on the day I was baptized?"

It had been expected that Humphrey might subtly try to raise the religious issue in West Virginia—*Time* thought there was something suspicious about his campaign song, "I'm Gonna Vote for Hubert Humphrey," which was set to the tune of "Give Me That Old-Time Religion" [15]—but Kennedy's tactic reversed everything, and soon Humphrey was accusing Kennedy of talking too much about religion. His campaign managers, William Jacobs and Marshall West, charged the other side with "deliberately stirring up doubts as to the fairness and tolerance of our voters," and the *Charleston Sunday Gazette-Mail* complained of "the popular psychology which suggests that a West Virginia vote against Senator Kennedy is a vote for bigotry." [16]

But the religious issue occupied only the surface level of the campaign, the level of speechmaking and publicity; below that there was another level of campaigning, the obscure realm of machine-style party politics. Kennedy's looks and wit and personal charm worked

[15] *Time,* March 28, 1960, p. 23.
[16] Quoted in Ernst, *op. cit.,* p. 9.

for him on the first level; on the second he used his good political judgment, his money, and his large and competent team of advisers. West Virginia is a state in which a lot could be done on the second level. On any fair scale of political corruption and election mismanagement in contemporary America it would deserve an extremely high rating, somewhere up there among the most machine-dominated urban areas in the northern states and the comfortable, wheeling-and-dealing rural oligarchies of the South.

West Virginia was primarily a coal-mining state, but the decline in importance of coal as a source of power had been accompanied by a decline in employment, and there was great poverty; many people were on relief, and in some counties over one-fourth of the population lived on skimpy government food packages. Poverty creates a favorable climate for political corruption, and money could always buy votes—legally—by hiring precinct workers and miscellaneous other campaign employees, and by hiring a man's car at the standard rate of $40 a day to get voters to the polls. There were other votes for sale, less openly. According to Harry W. Ernst:

> In the handful of organizational counties where the worst abuses of machine politics have not been softened by public outcry, vote-buying and crooked election officials still play a small part in the democratic process. Voter registration lists in those counties are bloated with the dead and departed. While West Virginia's population declined 7.2 percent from 1950 to 1960, the number of registered voters increased 2.4 percent. The 1960 Census counted 6,629 noses in Williamson, including more than 3,700 residents under voting age. But the coal field town reported 7,298 registered voters.[17]

After the election there were several attempts—by reporters, FBI agents, a Republican state attorney general, and private investigators hired by Richard Nixon—to uncover firm evidence of improper spending, but nothing was ever proved. However, there was no doubt that the Kennedy campaign poured a lot of money into West Virginia—some $100,000 for advertising, $50,000 to $100,000 in contributions to county organizations, probably over $250,000 in all, as compared to Humphrey's total of about $30,000.[18]

The Kennedy advertising campaign, handled through a West

17 Ernst, *op. cit.*, p. 16.
18 *Ibid.*, p. 30.

Virginia ad agency, went into every newspaper, radio, and TV station in the state. There were statements of Kennedy's position on separation of church and state, reminders of his war record and his literary accomplishments, pictures of his family, and, occasionally, repetitions of the charge that Humphrey was campaigning on behalf of a Johnson-Symington "stop Kennedy" combine. Humphrey had almost no newspaper advertising campaign, and little radio or TV; one of his major efforts was a dismal election-eve telethon which turned out to be a sad substitute for a complete mass-media campaign.

One of the important, if less conspicuous, uses of campaign money was for slate mailers. Slate mailers—cards or leaflets with a list of "recommended" candidates—are standard campaign pieces everywhere in the country, but in West Virginia, with its long ballots and bewildering variety of elective offices, they become particularly important. They can tie an uncertain presidential candidate to a popular local candidate, or vice versa; local candidates are of course more likely to allow their names to be put on slate mailers with a doubtful presidential candidate if the presidential candidate pays the bill. Getting on a slate required (*a*) winning the support of the local Democratic machine and (*b*) contributing to its campaign—and not always necessarily in that order.

In 1960 the Republicans controlled the state government, and there were five different candidates in the running for the Democratic nomination for governor. The state's Democratic party was split up into a number of factions, cliques, and local organizations—out of which came a variety of slates. Kennedy's forces had been at work on the local level well in advance of the campaign: Lawrence O'Brien, the architect of Kennedy's nationwide campaign master-plan, and Robert McDonough, his West Virginia campaign manager, had in some cases made arrangements with the leading local faction, in some cases backed a dissenting faction, and in some cases put together new organizations. It was a job that took money, time, patience, and organization, and the Humphrey campaign could make no comparable effort. Humphrey did have the support—which he did not want—of Senator Robert C. Byrd, a vociferous Johnson admirer and former Ku Klux Klan member, and he did have enough money and local connections to get slated in five or six counties, but his effectiveness in this part of the campaign was extremely limited.

The Kennedy organization can be accounted for only partly in terms of money. It was large and well financed, but many of the key men in the organization were Harvard classmates or Kennedy relatives, young men of independent wealth whose talents and enthusiasm could never have been purchased. They manned numerous campaign offices, did the advance work to produce large turnouts wherever Kennedy spoke, and overwhelmed local politicians by sheer force of numbers. "Everywhere the politicians went," said one, "they saw someone working for Kennedy. They sensed he was going to win and wanted to be on the winning side. On the other hand, they seldom saw any Humphrey people. But everywhere there was enthusiasm and excitement for Kennedy." [19]

Under the conditions, Humphrey hardly had any choice but to present himself as the candidate of the common man. "There are three kinds of politics," he said. "The politics of big business, the politics of the big bosses, and the politics of big money, and I'm against all of them. I stand for the politics of the people." At first he merely talked of his own humble origins, but then he began to make more pointed statements about his inability to "run through this state with a little black bag and a bankbook. I can't buy an election," he said, and: "Kennedy is the spoiled candidate and he and that young, emotional, juvenile Bobby are spending with wild abandon. . . . Anyone who gets in the way of . . . papa's pet is going to be destroyed . . . I don't seem to recall anybody's giving the Kennedy family—father, mother, sons or daughters—the privilege of deciding . . . our party's nominee." [20]

But Humphrey and Kennedy both knew that the poor people of West Virginia had, not too many years earlier, enthusiastically backed another wealthy, Harvard-educated Democrat with a strange accent, Franklin Delano Roosevelt—and Roosevelt's administration had poured hundreds of millions of dollars of federal money into the state and had made it possible for the workers to help themselves by organizing effective labor unions. The memory of FDR was still a powerful emotional force in West Virginia, and both candidates tried to tap it. Humphrey frequently cited the New Deal record in what reporters called his "Roosevelt speech"; Kennedy in his speeches

19 Ernst, *op. cit.*, pp. 19–20.
20 Sorensen, *op. cit.*, pp. 159–60.

promised major new relief and recovery plans for West Virginia—
and to help evoke the Roosevelt image he brought in Franklin D.
Roosevelt, Jr., who stumped the state for him, sent out letters to
voters postmarked from Hyde Park, and signed a newspaper ad stating: "I am positive that John F. Kennedy is the only candidate for
President who can do for West Virginia in the '60's what my father
did for West Virginia in the '30's." [21]

Labor had been Humphrey's great hope at the beginning of the
primary campaign. West Virginia has one of the highest proportions
of union membership of any state in the country, and the unions had
not only members but money and political influence. The strongest
single union in the state was the United Mine Workers, organized
in the New Deal era by John L. Lewis; a smaller, but also potent,
labor group was the state branch of James R. Hoffa's Teamsters
Union. The state AFL-CIO leadership stayed firmly neutral, the
UMW leaders were officially neutral but more or less openly leaning
toward Humphrey—Humphrey had the personal support of the aging
John L. Lewis—and the Teamsters gave Humphrey a public endorsement. Kennedy's tactic was to appeal to the union men directly—the
help of Roosevelt was especially valuable here—and to recruit young
union members around the state to work for him as volunteers; so,
although Humphrey had come into the campaign as the labor candidate, Kennedy undoubtedly won more votes among union members.

Humphrey's endorsement by the Teamsters was of course a
mixed blessing. Kennedy told a labor audience: "I'm sure the people
of West Virginia are not going to let Jimmy Hoffa determine who
should be the Democratic nominee for President," and one of his
top campaign executives said: "The intervention of Mr. Hoffa in
West Virginia is just added evidence of the character of the gang-up
against Senator Kennedy in West Virginia, which has brought together
the strangest array of political bedfellows in the history of American
politics." [22]

Humphrey never quite managed to get free of the "gang-up"
charge. It had not helped him any when Senator Byrd told the voters:
"If you are for Adlai Stevenson, Senator Stuart Symington, Senator
Johnson or John Doe, this primary may be your last chance to stop
Kennedy." [23] And the issue came up when Kennedy and Humphrey

[21] Ernst, *op. cit.*, p. 11.
[22] *Ibid.*, p. 27.
[23] Sorensen, *op. cit.*, p. 159.

appeared on television together in the last week before the primary, for a debate broadcast to a national audience from Charleston station WCHS-TV. The debate—for Kennedy, valuable practice for the debates he would be having with Richard Nixon a few months later—was for the most part a mild affair; the exchange about the "gang-up" provided its most heated moments, and both of the candidates directed their strongest remarks at the Republicans.

There was one important difference in the way the two chose to use their time in the debate: Kennedy talked mostly about his proposed solutions to West Virginia problems, while Humphrey aimed most of his remarks toward the national audience. Since the national audience was small (six TV stations outside of West Virginia carried the broadcast) and the state audience was larger than any Humphrey had been able to reach with his limited TV budget, it is hard to understand why he did not concentrate on West Virginia issues—especially since he knew that a loss in that primary would be the end of his campaign for the nomination. The next day, he offered the unconvincing explanation that he did not feel West Virginia should be given any special sales job; it seems quite possible that Humphrey did not use the debate to give the state a special sales job mainly because it did not occur to him or to anyone on his staff that it might be good campaign strategy to do so.

A few days before the election, Lyndon Johnson came into West Virginia and addressed a fund-raising banquet in Clarksburg. He predicted at the time that he would get 12 to 15 of the state's 25 delegates, regardless of who won the nonbinding preference vote—but Johnson, too, was in for a setback in West Virginia.

On election day the voters gave Kennedy a 61 per cent majority —236,510 to Humphrey's 152,187.[24] Also, Kennedy's work with the local groups paid off: 15 of the 25 delegates elected were Kennedy men, who proceeded to elect as chairman of the delegation one of their own number instead of Senator Byrd.

As soon as the returns were in, Humphrey announced that he was no longer a candidate for the Democratic presidential nomination and would withdraw from the remaining primaries which he had planned to enter. Kennedy held a press conference and told reporters: "I think we have now buried the religious issue once and for all."

24 Davis, op. cit., p. 303.

The press—and the politicians—tended to agree. *The New York Times* report said:

> The Massachusetts Senator, a Roman Catholic, scored his triumph in a heavily Protestant state where it had been forecast that he would lose. In so doing, Senator Kennedy blunted the religious issue nationally, and eased the fears of some top Democrats that the nomination of a Catholic would lead to defeat as it did in 1928 when Alfred E. Smith lost to Herbert Hoover.[25]

Immediately after the election, Democratic boss Charles Buckley of the Bronx announced for Kennedy. At a Democratic dinner national committeeman Carmine DeSapio said that Kennedy now had more than a majority of the New York State 114-vote delegation. At the same time, he picked up heavy second-ballot support in New Jersey. The Associated Press running poll of delegate strength gave Kennedy 241½ votes before the West Virginia primary, 329½ votes later in the month.[26]

The New York Times, which did not question the generally accepted interpretation of Kennedy's victory, did raise questions in a postelection editorial about the whole primary process:

> The wise politicians were saying before the West Virginia primary that a Kennedy victory there would be essential to him, not because it would necessarily insure his nomination but because his defeat might destroy his chances at Los Angeles for the top place. If this observation was accurate, as we believe it was, it is simply one more commentary on the absurdity of the American primary system. Why should the fate of any candidate, least of all so able and attractive a candidate as Mr. Kennedy, depend in the last analysis on a few score thousand voters in a state that is typical of nothing but itself? West Virginia has special economic problems all its own, a population make-up uncharacteristic of the country, an interesting if unique political tradition. It is unreasonable that a Kennedy defeat in West Virginia should have defeated Kennedy, or that a Kennedy victory in West Virginia should nominate him.
>
> No candidate should be made or broken by such an expensive, exhausting, distracting, haphazard, unsystematic primary "system" as the one we have. The Presidential nomination is too important a prize to be determined in such a way.[27]

[25] *The New York Times,* May 12, 1960. © 1960 by The New York Times Company. Reprinted by permission.

[26] Davis, *op. cit.,* p. 85.

[27] *The New York Times,* May 12, 1960. © 1960 by The New York Times Company. Reprinted by permission.

There is good reason to be even more skeptical than the *Times* was, because the appraisal of importance of the West Virginia primary depended on an extremely doubtful set of premises: the predominant importance of religion in Al Smith's defeat in 1928, the importance of religion in the Wisconsin primary, the importance of religion in the West Virginia primary, and the "surprise" of Kennedy's victory. In regard to the last, it should be remembered that one poll had showed Kennedy to have a strong lead before the campaign began, and that Kennedy's win was much more surprising to the newspapers than it was to local political observers in West Virginia.

Many accounts of the election attributed Kennedy's victory to his clever tactical move of taking the aggressive on the religious issue, making his campaign a crusade against bigotry. But that, too, may be overemphasizing a single factor. Actually, Kennedy outcampaigned Humphrey on all fronts. Kennedy's campaign manager had a simple explanation for the victory. "We just set up a classical political operation," he said, "and pushed it to the hilt." [28]

Yet, whether the explanations for it were sound or not, the West Virginia primary was important. As a result of it the objections to Kennedy based on his religion lost their force, and Kennedy gained a winner image which stayed with him through the convention. One thing that emerges clearly from the uncertainties of the West Virginia primary is the picture of John F. Kennedy, moving with increasing momentum toward his historic and personal destiny.

[28] Ernst, *op. cit.,* p. 31.

MOVEMENTS
AND
COUNTERMOVEMENTS

11

1966
Georgia
Lester Maddox vs. *Howard Callaway*

Lester Maddox' definitive day in history was July 6, 1964. The Civil Rights law forbidding discrimination in public accommodations was scarcely 24 hours old when at about 6 P.M. three Negroes tried to enter Maddox' Atlanta restaurant, the Pickrick. While a host of reporters recorded the scene for the mass media, Maddox not only refused to serve the three but, waving a pistol, ordered them from the premises with the help of his son, Lester, Jr., who was wielding an ax handle. Overnight, Maddox emerged as a symbol of white southern resistance equal to Selma Sheriff Jim Clark, Birmingham Public Safety Commissioner Bull Connors, Mississippi Governor Ross Barnett, and Alabama Governor George Wallace.

Although few Americans outside of Georgia had ever heard of Maddox until that day he and the ax handle found their place in the sad chronicle of racial conflict, he was already well known within his own state. He had achieved a peculiar kind of notoriety with his antics as restaurateur and propagandist, and he had made three un-successful attempts to run for public office—twice for mayor of Atlanta, once for lieutenant governor of Georgia. Each time he had lost, but somehow he came back to triumph over all the people who regarded him as a harmless political curiosity—and his eventual victory was one of the most significant political achievements of modern segregationist sentiment.

Georgia was regarded by many northerners as the one Deep

South state that had somehow managed to solve its racial problems—but Georgia had no magic formula; in the 1960's any issue related to integration was politically explosive, and nobody knew how strong die-hard segregationist sentiment was or might become. The state managed to delay action on the Supreme Court's school desegregation order until 1960; in that year the Atlanta Board of Education was ordered to integrate its school system. In January of 1961, after federal court intervention, two Negroes were admitted to the University of Georgia; the following fall, the first Negro children began attending white high schools in Atlanta. Civic leaders organized and sponsored public-relations campaigns to urge cooperation with the law, and an article in *The New York Times Magazine* reported that "most white Atlantans have shown calmness, common sense and respect for the law." Atlanta, the writer said, "is today setting an example for its Deep South neighbors in making the racial adjustments dictated by necessity." [1]

But Atlanta is not all of Georgia; in rural areas there continued to be deep resentments—of the speed with which traditional color barriers were being forced down by federal legislation, and of the constant pressure being exerted by the various Negro groups and their leaders, such as Martin Luther King, Jr., and Stokely Carmichael. Even in Atlanta, the official policy of peaceful change faced strong opposition.

One Atlanta businessman who did not go along with the changes was the owner of the Pickrick restaurant; Maddox, a high-school dropout and former factory worker, had started out in business for himself with a small investment and built up his restaurant into a thriving operation, serving southern-fried chicken and other simple meals to a faithful clientele of working people, families, and students from nearby Georgia Tech.

His clients knew him as an energetic, talkative, table-hopping host who loved the role of restaurateur, and the people who read his weekly "Pickrick Says" ads in the newspapers knew him as a purveyor of folksy salesmanship along the lines of:

> *PLEASE forgive us. It's not always our fault when the waiters are delayed in serving your table. Quite often it is the customer. If you look around and listen, you will find that some*

[1] Claude Sitton, "Atlanta's Example: Good Sense and Dignity," *New York Times Magazine,* May 6, 1962, pp. 22, 123. © 1962 by The New York Times Company. Reprinted by permission.

> *good lady or gentleman has your waiter all tied up with—*
> *Where do you get this wonderful chicken?—What do you use*
> *for the batter?—What makes it so tender?—How do you fry*
> *it?—And who makes these fine biscuits?—And bring me*
> *another bowl of that delicious chicken gravy. . . .*[2]

In 1957, after the Pickrick had been in operation for ten years and its success had made Maddox a moderately wealthy man, he began to consider running for mayor of Atlanta. He discussed the idea in one of his "Pickrick Says" ads:

> *I've done about all the building there is room for out here,*
> *and being one who likes to build and grow, I've been thinking*
> *maybe I could build some highways, some park areas, finance*
> *an airport or two, and do a lot of other progressive things—*
> *if I could find a job that affords such an opportunity. There is*
> *only one job that affords such an opportunity. There is only*
> *one job in Atlanta that offers me what I'm interested in and I*
> *would very much like to have your comments on what you*
> *think about the idea. . . .*[3]

The comment from Maddox's admiring clients was overwhelmingly encouraging, and so he entered his first political campaign. He was defeated, but the campaign brought him a good deal of publicity, and increasingly the Pickrick became known as a center of political activity as well as southern-fried chicken. And Maddox's opinions began to show a sharp drift toward the right. His "Pickrick Says" ads talked more and more about the evils of intermixing the races, the Communist conspiracy, and the wrongdoings of the federal government. Soon he ran into trouble with the Internal Revenue Service, which claimed that his ads were political messages and hence not deductible as ordinary business expenses. He fought their rulings in the court, and ended up with a portion of the ads allowed as a deduction. He became an active member of the local White Citizens Council and helped found a group called GUTS—Georgians Unwilling To Surrender. In 1961, he tried again to become mayor of Atlanta.

His 1961 campaign was reasonably well financed, and he had strong support from the city's segregationists. He came in second in the primary election but was beaten by Ivan Allen in the runoff, 64,313 to 36,091. A year later, he ran for office again. This time the post he sought was that of lieutenant governor of Georgia, and during

---

[2] Bruce Galphin, *The Riddle of Lester Maddox* (Atlanta: Camelot Publishing Co., 1968), p. 19. Reprinted by permission.

[3] *Ibid.*, p. 21.

the campaign his talents for getting free publicity developed rapidly: He made the headlines when he sent President Kennedy a telegram urging him to appoint Martin Luther King, Jr., "ambassador to Africa, Russia or elsewhere," and again when he wired the President to ask for an emancipation proclamation for whites. Again he made it into the runoff election, but in the final count he came in second, trailing the winner by over 40,000 votes.

Even the third defeat did not seem to diminish Maddox' appetite for political activity. In 1963, as civil rights demonstrations were being stepped up in Atlanta, he helped organize a group to picket businesses which integrated. The integrationists, he charged, were in league with "the Kennedys, Khrushchev, Martin Luther King and Castro." He also became an enthusiastic early follower of Alabama Governor George Wallace, who was already being talked about in the South as a potential presidential candidate. Maddox had become a leading figure among die-hard southern anti-integrationists, and on July 6, 1964—one day after the Civil Rights Act had been signed into law—he became nationally famous.

Negroes were walking into restaurants and hotels all over the South that day, putting the new law to the test, and in the great majority of places they were being served; any proprietor who refused, as Maddox did, was knowingly leaving himself open to prosecution. In Maddox' case, the three Negroes who had been escorted from the Pickrick premises swore out warrants against him for pointing a pistol and the Justice Department charged him with refusing to comply with the Civil Rights Act. The pistol-pointing charge was long delayed and finally ended in acquittal, but the federal action proceeded quickly and in a matter of weeks Maddox was enjoined from refusing to serve Negroes. During the intervening period business had been booming at the Pickrick, with lines often stretching out into the parking lot. The kitchen was working at top speed, and Maddox was jovially greeting his supporters and passing out leaflets. There were ax handles on sale for $2 apiece, and on a bench in front of the restaurant was a dummy with a knife in its back and a sign announcing: "This manikin represents what has happened to the American free enterprise system."

On August 11 another group of Negroes tried unsuccessfully to enter the Pickrick, and proceedings were begun to hold Maddox in contempt of court for failing to obey the injunction. Again on the 13th, two Negroes tried to enter the restaurant, and this time Maddox decided to close up. With tears streaming down his face, he announced to the crowd gathered in the parking lot that "My President, my Congress and the Communists have closed my business and ended a childhood dream." By closing the restaurant, he was at least avoiding further conflict with the law—he could not be accused of discriminating against Negroes if he was not doing business at all.

He was becoming involved in the Goldwater campaign now—he had helped found a Georgia Democrats for Goldwater organization—and the Pickrick became a propaganda center and souvenir shop. For a while it did a healthy business in ax handles, Goldwater campaign materials, American flags, and right-wing literature. Later that year Maddox constructed in front of the building a strange white tower which he called a monument to the death of free enterprise. It was draped in red, white, and blue bunting and had on its side a sign reading: "In Memory of—PRIVATE PROPERTY RIGHTS." Inside it were copies of the U.S. Constitution, the Declaration of Independence, and framed quotations of the words of various prominent Americans, including Maddox.

He got a new license and reopened the Pickrick under the name of the Lester Maddox Cafeteria, with a posted sign announcing that service would be refused to interstate travelers—an attempt to remove the restaurant from the jurisdiction of the Civil Rights Act, which was based on the federal government's power to regulate interstate commerce. But the Lester Maddox Cafeteria ran into the same problems as the Pickrick—Negroes tried to integrate, they were refused service, and a new court order was issued for Maddox to appear at a hearing on contempt charges. Again there was a booming segregated business during the legal proceedings, and again the decision went against Maddox: This time the court ordered him to pay a fine of $200 for every day the cafeteria continued to operate as a segregated establishment. Maddox said he would comply with the law, but the next day, when a Negro entered the cafeteria, he announced that it was no longer in business. He hung up a sign reading:

CLOSED

OUT OF BUSINESS
RESULTING FROM ACT PASSED
BY THE US CONGRESS
SIGNED BY PRES. *JOHNSON*
AND INSPIRED AND SUPPORTED
BY DEADLY AND BLOODY—COMMUNISM

That was Maddox' last day as a restaurateur. For a while he leased the Pickrick to a pair of former employees—who ran it as an integrated cafeteria—and then he sold the property to Georgia Tech, who turned the main building into a job placement center. He put the profits from the sale into a new business, the Pickrick Furniture Store, which opened in the fall of 1965, and announced at about the same time that he intended to run for governor of Georgia. His platform, he said, would be "constitutional government, free enterprise, God, liberty and Americanism."

The incumbent governor was Carl Sanders, who was prevented by Georgia's one-term law from running for reelection. The law did not, however, prevent an ex-governor from running for the office again after another term had elapsed, and in 1966 the state seemed to be full of ex-governors who wanted the job back again. The most unusual feature of the impending election was that it would be the first time since Reconstruction that a strong Republican candidate was in the running for governor—in fact, as election day drew nearer, he looked more and more like a probable winner. Howard "Bo" Callaway had not been a Republican for long, and he was the kind of Republican—conservative—who made sense in the Deep South of the mid-1960's. He was 39—a trim, black-haired West Point graduate, and heir to the vast Callaway textile empire at La Grange. He had joined the Republican party in 1964 as a Goldwater follower, and when Goldwater carried Georgia in the presidential election Callaway became the first Republican congressman from Georgia since Reconstruction. He was popular and articulate, he was young, he was as much opposed to integration as anybody, and he had the backing of important business and financial leaders. He would be a hard man for any Democratic candidate to beat, and the Democrats did not seem to be doing their best to come up with a strong candidate.

When Maddox first entered the race, it appeared that the most likely winner of the Democratic primary would be ex-Governor Ernest Vandiver, who had served from 1959 to 1963. But then Vandiver's doctors told him that another political campaign might be fatal, he reluctantly withdrew, and the faction which he represented—the one led by Senator Herman Talmadge—was left without a major candidate. For a while Talmadge himself—also an ex-governor—toyed with the idea of returning from Washington to seek his old job back. When he dropped the idea it meant the nomination would probably go to still another former governor, Ellis Arnall, who was an old enemy of the Talmadge clan—he had defeated Senator Talmadge's father, Eugene Talmadge, for the governorship in 1942.

Arnall was an old New Dealer, strongly identified with the Roosevelt years, and although his political style seemed a little out of date to many people in 1966, he was still one of the most progressive politicians in Georgia. He had privately told friends he hoped to "make it popular again to be a liberal in Georgia," and his stand in favor of cooperation with integration laws made it safe to assume that he would have strong support from Negroes—but he did not campaign in Negro communities or call himself a liberal.[4] His Democratic opponents were:

Maddox.

State Senator Jimmy Carter—young, attractive, lacking finances, a liberal who would be likely to draw some voters away from Arnall.

James Gray, a wealthy and elegant Massachusetts-born publisher and TV station owner, a conservative whose "law and order" campaign and hard-line opposition to school integration made him a strong competitor for the segregationist vote. Gray's extensive financial resources had been visible in a precampaign publicity build-up and continued to show up in heavy radio, TV, and press advertising.

Garland Byrd, former lieutenant governor, with support from some factions of the party establishment, also a strong competitor for the segregationist vote.

Hoke O'Kelley, 71, making his fifth race for the governorship.

Maddox was not the only candidate lacking in governmental experience—neither Gray nor O'Kelley had ever held any public office—but he obviously felt some need to defend his qualifications. In one newspaper ad, headed "From Lester (Pickrick) Maddox to All Georgians," he stated:

> *I will use my thirty years' study of Government, my background in education, and my experience in industrial planning, production and maintenance, steel manufacturing, aircraft production, ship building and agriculture, along with my positions of leadership and training and real estate, and the restaurant, furniture and grocery businesses, to try and make you the best Governor ever to serve our great state.*[5]

[4] Pat Watters and Reese Cleghorn, *Climbing Jacob's Ladder: The Arrival of Negroes in Southern Politics* (New York: Harcourt, Brace & World, Inc., 1967), p. 347.

[5] *Atlanta Constitution*, Sept. 1, 1966. Reprinted by permission.

According to Georgia's election laws, there would be a runoff primary unless one of the candidates should win a majority the first time around. The early polls showed that Arnall had the support of a plurality of the voters, but it indicated that the combined opposition to him was big enough that whoever made it into the runoff might well take the nomination. This situation intensified the competition among Maddox, Gray, and Byrd, since it appeared that the segregationist vote could well be the deciding factor; it also lent a certain amount of credibility to Maddox' charge that a week before the election he was offered a bribe of $100,000 to get out of the race.

The incident took place in the Dempsey Hotel in Macon. According to Maddox, the first overtures had been made to a relative of his by representatives of the Gray campaign. He said two men came to his room in the hotel with a zipper bag containing $100,000 in cash and presented him with a letter to the secretary of the state Democratic party, which said, "Due to my physical condition it would be both impossible and unwise for me to complete my campaign for governor of Georgia." [6] Maddox was to sign the letter, go downstairs and announce his withdrawal to the newsmen, and then come back to the room and collect his money. Instead, he went downstairs and announced that an attempt had been made to buy him out.

Gray denied that he had any knowledge of the bribe attempt, and no prosecution resulted from the incident. Gray, Maddox, and Byrd continued to compete for the "resistance" vote, and there was ample evidence to Georgians that their way of life was being threatened from many sides. There were riots in the Negro districts of Atlanta, and meanwhile in Washington Georgia's two senators—Talmadge and Richard Russell—led in organizing the filibuster against the new Civil Rights bill.

But there was still no evidence that most Georgians were swinging toward a stronger segregationist position. On the contrary, one of the big surprises of the election was the strong last-minute showing made by young Senator Carter. He came very close to making the runoff a contest between two liberals. At the end of election day, September 14, the returns showed Arnall in first place and Carter second—but as the late results trickled in from the rural precincts, Maddox moved ahead. The final returns were: Arnall 231,480, Maddox 185,672, Carter 164,562, Gray 152,973, Byrd 39,994, and

[6] *Ibid.*, Sept. 9, 1966.

O'Kelley 13,271.[7] On a percentage basis, the vote was 30 per cent for Arnall, 23 per cent for Maddox, and 21 per cent for Carter. The fact that Arnall's and Carter's votes added up to a majority was interpreted as an encouraging sign by the moderate *Atlanta Constitution.* The paper editorialized that Georgians had "destroyed a misconception: They showed that anger and negativism are not dominant characteristics of Georgia politics, 1966. In the governor's race, two middle-of-the-road men who pointedly refused to make a whipping boy of the national government have jointly won a majority of the votes cast." [8]

The same arithmetic was used by some disappointed Arnall backers as a basis for the accusation—which became much more meaningful after the final election—that Carter's entry into the race had prevented Arnall from winning the majority which would have made a runoff primary unnecessary.

The runoff primary was scheduled for September 28, two weeks later. In all the confusion, legal and political, of the contest for the governorship, it was the only episode which provided a fairly clear choice. The way Arnall put it, the fundamental issue was "whether Georgia will have responsible government or ax-handle government." Maddox in turn called Arnall "a wild Socialist who is the granddaddy of forced racial integration in the Georgia sellout, a candidate who would never raise his voice or a finger—much less an ax handle— to protect the liberty of Georgia children and all Georgians."

In the second week of the short campaign, Maddox began to pick up on the "law and order" theme which Gray had used in the first primary. "If we continue to compromise and surrender," he said, "we will get into problems. I will demand strict law and order, and people will be punished."

The bribery charge against Gray had been forgotten, and Maddox made peace with the wealthy publisher. He flew to visit Gray in Miami, and Gray agreed to provide financial support for the battle against Arnall.[9]

It had been expected that Carter would give his backing to Arnall, but Carter refused to make an endorsement. He did go so far as to express his concern, just before the election, about reports that Republicans in large numbers were planning to "cross over," as was permissible under Georgia primary laws, in order to vote for

[7] Galphin, *op. cit.*, p. 114.
[8] *Atlanta Constitution*, Sept. 16, 1966.
[9] Galphin, *op. cit.*, p. 115.

Maddox. Since Callaway's nomination was already assured, there was nothing to prevent interested Republicans from influencing the Democratic runoff. Carter said, "To vote deliberately for the weakest in hopes that he may later be more easily defeated is an irresponsible act contrary to the best interests of Georgians." [10]

There is no precise measurement available of the crossover vote, but some indication of its size is given by the fact that in 55 counties Maddox got more votes in the runoff than he did in the general election—although the total vote was larger in the latter. The runoff, at any rate, was a Maddox victory—the only time in his political career he had come in first in an election. The returns gave him a margin of more than 70,000 votes over Arnall. God, said Maddox, had been his campaign manager. His first act as the nominee was to announce the appointment of James Gray as the new state chairman of the Democratic party.

The Callaway-Maddox alternative that was now presented to the voters was not the choice most of them had expected, and to many it was hardly a choice at all. There were—especially in Atlanta—many liberals, who favored either integration or at least some kind of peaceful accommodation to the new law of the land; and there were also, throughout the state, some 290,000 Negroes registered to vote —17.4 per cent of the total voter registration.[11] This was a body of votes which, although a minority, could be important in a close race. For most of these voters, neither candidate had much appeal, and neither candidate tried to develop much appeal. When the campaign was just beginning Richard Nixon, touring the South for the GOP, said approvingly that Callaway "will run the same kind of campaign against Mr. Maddox that he would have if Mr. Maddox had lost." Nixon was right. Callaway had planned to run against Arnall, and had expected to lose the liberal vote; when presented with an opponent who was even less acceptable to the liberals than he was, he still campaigned as if he expected to lose the liberal vote.

The Callaway campaign started out full of optimism and high spirits; it was well financed and well organized. The national Republican party, eager to encourage the renewal of the party in the South, provided some support. George Murphy of California flew to Atlanta to speak at a hundred-dollar-a-plate fund-raiser, and among

---

[10] *Atlanta Constitution,* Sept. 26, 1966.
[11] Watters and Cleghorn, *op. cit.,* Appendix 11.

those who gathered at the Dinkler Motor Hotel to hear him were some of the state's wealthiest and most influential men; the business and financial establishment—including most of the newspapers—was for Callaway. His campaign had all the advantages of ample financial backing—many paid staff members, a big and busy headquarters, computer and surveying services, and professional and well-coordinated radio, TV, and press advertising.

In some ways this 1966 contest between a Goldwater Republican and a Wallace Democrat seemed to be a modern version of the ancient southern rivalry that Pitchfork Ben Tillman had exploited in the previous century—with Maddox as the leader of the rural and lower-middle-class voters and Callaway the spokesman of the urban financial and business interests. This theme was apparent in Callaway's pointed references to his own country background and was strongest in Maddox's speeches, as in the time he waved a copy of a national magazine which contained an expensive full-page ad for Callaway, and called Callaway a "puppet" of the "national liberal czars of politics and finance." As for his own supporters, Maddox said: "We've got a few with dirt under their fingernails—thank God—but none with dirt in their hearts."

As the official nominee of the Democratic party Maddox now had more resources at his disposal than he had enjoyed in any of his previous campaigns, but he still had much less money then Callaway. His main chance of victory lay in being able to consolidate the support of the party, and after the runoff it appeared that most of the party's leaders would close ranks behind him. The "Big Four" of the state capital—the agriculture commissioner, the comptroller, the state treasurer, and the public service commissioner—agreed to give him their support, and one former Arnall man told the press: "It's amazing how many people I never thought would ever support Lester are back of him now." [12]

The support was most evident at the state Democratic convention, where the assembled candidates hailed Maddox as the new leader of their party; and Arnall's former campaign manager delivered a keynote speech, a classic piece of partisan oratory, in which he said, "Mr. Maddox possesses the common touch of William Jennings Bryan, the humanity of Franklin D. Roosevelt, the sincerity of Adlai Stevenson and the tenacity of Harry Truman."

[12] *Atlanta Constitution,* Sept. 30, 1966.

Many other Democrats, however, could not bring themselves to support Maddox. The more conservative among these found their places in the "Democrats for Callaway" organization, which in this case was rather more potent than is usually true of that tired cliche of American political campaigns, the party-dissenter group. The reaction of Negroes was expressed by Martin Luther King, Jr., who called Georgia "a sick state produced by the diseases of a sick nation." Maddox's victory, he said, made him "ashamed to be a Georgian." One spokesman for white liberals was Atlanta Mayor Ivan Allen, who, in an obvious reference to Maddox, warned that the principles of the founding fathers should not be "surrendered to the rabble of prejudice, extremism, buffoonery and incompetency."

The most dramatic protest against Maddox' nomination came from a young Congressman named Charles Weltner. Weltner, a moderate representing an Atlanta district, was, like all Democrats, bound by an oath to support Maddox as the nominee of his party. Weltner decided that he could not support Maddox; what made his decision national news was his announcement that, rather than break his oath, he would resign his own Democratic nomination—give up his seat in Congress. Weltner's announcement said:

> *Today, the one man in our state who exists as the very symbol of violence and oppression is the Democratic nominee for the highest office in Georgia. His entire public career is directly contrary to my deepest convictions and beliefs.*
>
> *And while I cannot violate my oath, neither can I violate my principles. I cannot vote for Lester Maddox.*[13]

Weltner also made it clear that he was not going to support Callaway, who, he said, was "the same as Maddox on race except in a slicker way." He said that on election day he would write in the name of some Democrat.

The idea of a unified write-in campaign was being discussed among liberals and Negro voters. Many of these voters felt that a write-in was all they had left as an alternative; the question was who the candidate should be. Many names were mentioned—among them Weltner, Allen, Carter, and Arnall. At a meeting of a citizens' group in Atlanta, Martin Luther King, Sr., stunned the audience by proposing that the candidate should be Herman Talmadge. Finally, the candidate selected by the newly organized Write In, Georgia move-

13 *Atlanta Constitution,* Oct. 4, 1966.

ment—WIG for short—was Arnall. He did not formally accept the
WIG group's backing, but he did not refuse it—which was good
enough for the write-in organizers. For the rest of the month of
October, while Maddox and Callaway campaigned by traveling
through the state and making speeches, Arnall campaigned by staying
out of the state as much as possible and by refusing to make any
statement repudiating the WIG drive.

The write-in move received some help from the Fulton County
(Atlanta) Democratic party organization—many of whose leaders
were also WIG organizers—which announced that it would not support Maddox and urged a write-in vote. The justification for the
Fulton County organization's move was, curiously, party loyalty—
specifically, Maddox' failure to support the national party platform.
Cited as evidence was a June 30 letter from Maddox, in which he
had written: "I do not support the racial planks of the platform, other
socialistic and communistic planks . . . and planks that promote the
centralization of government and a resulting loss of freedom, through
watering down states rights and constitutional government." [14]

A few days after the Fulton County group made its announcement, a crowded WIG rally was held at the Biltmore Hotel in Atlanta.
There were, of course, many speakers—and there were also folk
singers, who entertained the audience with such songs as the following,
which was offered as Callaway's musical message to his opponent:

> Oh, Mr. Maddox!
> Oh, Mr. Maddox!
> Can I please have back the votes I lent to you?
> Now the runoff's in your sack,
> I would like my Republicans back,
> Or I really don't know what I'm going to do.[15]

The WIG movement continued active, especially in the Atlanta
area, but it was never able to compete with either the Maddox or
Callaway campaigns. Some of its leaders believed it could win the
election; few of its opponents did, but they did fear that it might
prevent any candidate from getting a majority—which would then
throw the election into the General Assembly.

Still, neither of the major candidates made any real effort to
woo the liberals. Maddox had said the day after he won the nomination that, "If anyone asks me about the Negro problem . . . those

[14] *Ibid.,* Oct. 7, 1966.
[15] *Ibid.,* Oct., 10, 1966.

views are the same as those of Gov. George Wallace of Alabama." He repeatedly stated his opposition to the federal guidelines for school integration, and so did Callaway. Callaway said he was "very much opposed" to the guidelines, and was "the only one who has fought them effectively"—referring to his consistent anti-civil-rights record in Congress.

Callaway's campaign did begin to show some sign of having adjusted to Maddox as the opponent rather than Arnall, but this did not take the form of any modification of Callaway's positions. What did emerge was a personalized attack on Maddox; "irresponsibility" became a favorite word in Callaway's speeches. Again and again, he referred ambiguously to the chaos that might result if Maddox became governor. Callaway's chief fear seemed to be that Maddox' election might be poor public relations for Georgia and might possibly discourage the growth of business and industry in the state. In mid-October, for example, he said that some engineers and technicians scheduled to be transferred to the huge Lockheed-Georgia plant at Marietta had said they would refuse to come if Maddox was elected. The whole issue of industrial growth and immigration from the North was, of course, relevant to the issue of school integration, but Callaway's treatment of it was undoubtedly of more interest to the businessmen already supporting him than to the Negroes and liberals who were working for Arnall.

Maddox, who was naturally interested in some free campaign exposure and far less cautious than Callaway about his public statements, had repeatedly challenged Callaway to a TV debate. Finally, a pair of joint TV appearances were arranged.

Neither of them was much more than a disorganized exchange of accusations. The accusation that got the most publicity was Callaway's charge that Maddox had flown to Miami to confer with Gray after the first primary, in a plane chartered by Gray. The "mystery flight" became the subject of much newspaper attention after the debate: Callaway said the flight had been arranged by Gray, and wanted to know how much Gray had contributed to the Maddox campaign fund to get the job of state Democratic chairman. Gray said he hadn't arranged the flight, Maddox said he didn't know who had arranged it, and the newspapers said it had been arranged by one Ed Bridges, Gray's publicity man—who later went to work as publicity man for Democrats for Callaway. Finally an associate of Gray's, Ray Harris of Augusta, said he had arranged the flight as a go-between.

For whatever it was worth, Callaway had proved his point—but Maddox had also made charges against Callaway, particularly in reference to his alleged hiring of off-duty policemen to keep Negroes out of a Columbus recreation area called Callaway Gardens, and on balance neither candidate came off really well. One indication of the reaction of moderates to the debate was the *Constitution's* decision to run a letter from a reader as a guest editorial. The letter, printed under the headline "Guest TV Critic Looks at Debate," said:

> Dear Sir,
>
> I watched the show of maddox and bo. I thought it was the most childish thing I saw.
>
> Stephen Malone
>
> grade 3   age 7½
> Roswell Elem School [16]

The second debate, a few days later, brought out the same charges and countercharges, and when it was over Maddox and Callaway continued shouting at each other before a small audience of studio technicians and reporters. The postbroadcast fray also made the papers—again, there was no victor in the debate. It is quite possible that the write-in campaign benefited from them more than either of the participants.

The write-in movement proved to be the decisive, if not the victorious, element in the campaign. On November 8 the people of Georgia went to the polls—and failed to elect a governor. The returns came in slowly, as usual, and nearly a week had passed before it was fairly certain what had happened. Callaway was first, but he did not have the majority necessary to elect. The vote as it was finally certified was Callaway 453,665, Maddox 450,626, and Arnall write-ins 52,831.

Georgia's election laws provided that, if no candidate received a clear majority in a general election, the decision would then be made by the state legislature, choosing between the two leading contenders. And the state legislature was overwhelmingly Democratic.

The law providing for throwing the election to the General Assembly was something of a peculiarity—only two other states, Massachusetts and Vermont, had similar laws, and no election had been decided by a state legislature anywhere since 1913. Since then,

[16] *Ibid.,* Oct. 30, 1966.

there had been a number of Supreme Court decisions affecting the apportionment of state legislatures and advancing the "one man, one vote" doctrine. It had been expected that there would be challenges to the law if the election ended in a no-majority vote, and the challenges came soon after the election: First the American Civil Liberties Union filed a suit on behalf of WIG, and then another group of lawyers filed a suit on behalf of Callaway. Both groups wanted a new election instead of the legislative vote. While the suits moved through the courts, Maddox and Callaway both insisted on being treated as governor-elect, and both began cautiously to campaign all over again, making speeches and public appearances in preparation for still another election.

The U.S. Circuit Court ruled that the section in the Georgia constitution calling for the election to be decided by the legislature was invalid, but no runoff was called yet; instead, the case moved quickly to the Supreme Court. On December 12, the Supreme Court reversed the lower court's decision; by a 5–4 vote, it held that the existing law was constitutional. Justice Hugo Black, speaking for the majority, said: "There is no provision of the United States Constitution or any of its amendments which either expressly or impliedly dictates the method a state must use to select its governor." Justice William O. Douglas believed that the legislative-election provision was contrary to the one-man, one-vote principle, but his was the dissenting opinion. The two governors-elect, who were attending a legislative gathering at the University of Georgia, were informed of the decision at the same time, and both knew that it meant Maddox was the winner.

There was no doubt about what would be the outcome of the January 10 joint session of the Georgia General Assembly, and in general everything went off as expected. The votes were counted, it was found that there was no majority, and the legislators proceeded to cast their own votes. A few—ten Negroes and one white—abstained, and some Democrats—explaining that their vote reflected the vote of their constituents—went for Callaway; but Democratic party loyalty prevailed, and Maddox was elected by a vote of 182 to 66.

Maddox' victory, as has been said, has to be regarded as an important political expression of anti-integrationist sentiment—especially in view of the fact that it occurred in the state which had probably the strongest cadre of Democratic liberals in the Deep

South, and especially in view of the fact that Maddox represented the clearest and simplest possible statement of resistance. He changed his positions as often as any politician, but he never deviated far from the position he had taken on the day he and his son chased the Negroes away from the Pickrick. That Lester Maddox was very much the same man who two years later became the governor of Georgia.

Without detracting from the significance of the social and psychological processes which aided his quick rise to power, it must be remembered that every election is also shaped by its election laws—and Maddox' victory was in part the result of a series of fortunate events in which the legal technicalities all worked to his advantage:

First, the one-term law prevented Sanders from running for reelection in 1966.

Second, the Georgia election laws required a majority for nomination. This is not uncommon in the one-party South where it is assumed that the Democratic nominee will be elected, but in many states of the North a plurality is sufficient for a nomination and runoff primaries are not required.

Third, the "open primary" provision made it possible for Republicans to vote in the runoff—which they were most likely to do, since their own candidate had already been nominated.

Fourth, the legislature was empowered to decide an election where no candidate had a clear majority.

In each case, Maddox happened to be the man who benefited from the existing laws. Good arguments can and have been advanced on behalf of each of the laws cited above—and yet their cumulative effect, in 1966, was to make a man who had never won a general election the governor of Georgia.

12

1966
California
Ronald Reagan vs. *Edmund G. Brown*

The forces of history sometimes seem to be moving in several directions at once, all with equal enthusiasm, and political campaigns—which are remarkable condensations of history—sometimes reveal a combination of reaction and revolution in a single candidate. There is no better example of this, no clearer incarnation of history marching forward and backward together, than Ronald Reagan, who came to political power as a representative of a powerful popular urge toward old and understandable American values—in a word, reaction—but who did so by campaigning with the most modern techniques, so skillfully used as to make the operation of his opponent look like a creaking political Model T by comparison.

Reagan found his way to politics by a curious route. Born in a small Illinois town, he received his higher education at Eureka College, a Disciples of Christ institution in Illinois where his main interests were student-body activities and sports. After college he became a radio announcer for station WHO in Des Moines, where he was regarded as one of the best practitioners of a craft that flourished for a while in the early days of radio—simulating a play-by-play description of a baseball game while in reality broadcasting from a studio and recreating the action from information supplied by wire. It required an ability to take the rather sparse information that came in over Western Union and transform it into exciting, action-filled narration, and it also required an ability to keep up the narration without pause on the frequent occasions when the wire broke down and there was no information from the game at all.[1] In 1937 he visited Hollywood and was given a screen test by Warner Brothers which led to an acting contract and a leading role in a movie called *Love Is on the Air,* in which he was cast as a radio announcer. Through the thirties and forties and fifties he labored competently in picture after picture, nearly all of them undistinguished. He married actress Jane Wyman and became a leading member of the Screen Actors Guild. He was also a strong New Deal Democrat and took an interest in politics. He backed Harry Truman in 1948, and in 1950 he campaigned actively for Helen Gahagan Douglas when she ran for the Senate against Richard Nixon. As president of the guild he traveled to Washington to testify before the House Un-American Activities Committee, during its investigation of possible Communist influence in the motion picture industry: With past SAG presidents Robert Montgomery and George Murphy, he defended his industry and reported on its continuing efforts to resist communism.

In 1948 Reagan's first wife divorced him, and in 1952 he married Nancy Davis. Miss Davis was also an actress, and the two co-starred in Reagan's last movie, *Hellcats of the Navy.* The new marriage was one of the factors that influenced Reagan's political conversion from liberal to conservative: Nancy Reagan held conservative views, and so did her father, Loyal Davis, a wealthy Chicago doctor. Another factor was Reagan's move into television. In the mid-fifties, with his movie career at a standstill, he went to work for General Electric in a high-level corporate image job which involved acting as host on the *G. E. Theater* weekly show, visiting factories to boost employee morale, and representing the corporation in various public appearances around the country.

During these years of traveling for G.E. and addressing countless meetings and banquets, Reagan developed a standard oratorical performance he called simply "The Speech." The Speech, which he continued to use after leaving the General Electric job—because it was equally useful at political gatherings—was a stirring if somewhat unclear collection of economic statistics and anecdotes about Welfare State waste and inefficiency; quotations from various philosophers, poets, and politicians; Bob Hope-style jokes; and an ending call to arms which usually brought audiences to their feet applauding. The following version of The Speech, as delivered at a testimonial

[1] Bill Boyarsky, *The Rise of Ronald Reagan* (New York: Random House, Inc., 1968), p. 58. Used with permission of Random House, Inc.

dinner for a Republican candidate in Ohio, quoted Thomas Wolfe
on "the promise of America" and led from there into the climax:

> *An earlier generation of Americans pledged their lives, their*
> *fortunes and their sacred honor to give us that promise and*
> *Americans since have paid with their lives and their fortunes—*
> *all of them have preserved their honor. We pray devoutly, as I*
> *am sure they did, that we'll never be asked to make such a*
> *sacrifice. But one thing is certain: unless we are willing to*
> *make the same pledge they made and make it within the hear-*
> *ing of the enemy that freedom will disappear from this earth*
> *in our lifetime and our failure will be recorded in a book yet*
> *to be written called the Rise and Fall of the United States of*
> *America.*
>
> *The pathway of history is littered with the bones of dead*
> *empires. If we're to follow we'll have no decades or centuries*
> *for leisurely decay. The enemy at our gates is combat lean and*
> *hard and hungry for everything that we produce here. Every*
> *time, history tells us, that a cultured, advanced society has met*
> *the less cultured, the barbarians triumph. The words of the*
> *poet Bellocq:*
>
> *"We sit and watch the barbarians. In the long stretches*
> *of peace we laugh. But as we laugh we are watched by large*
> *and awful faces from beyond and on those faces there is no*
> *smile."*
>
> *You and I have reached our moment of truth, our*
> *rendezvous with destiny. We and we alone must make the*
> *decision as to whether freedom will perish from the earth.*[2]

Reagan used the speech for nearly ten years, with occasional
variations to suit the event. He had acquired, to use sociological
terminology, a new reference group. Moving in the world of corporation executives, he absorbed and formed—and expressed in The
Speech—a conservative business philosophy. He was still registered
as a Democrat, but in 1962 he emerged as an active Republican; he
served as state campaign chairman for Lloyd Wright, a conservative
who unsuccessfully opposed Senator Thomas Kuchel in the Republican
primary, and he also campaigned for Congressman John Rousselot,
who later became public relations director of the John Birch Society.
In 1964 he was named co-chairman of the California Committee for
Goldwater-Miller.

It had often been suggested, while Reagan was touring the
country for General Electric, that he ought to run for office sometime,
and the talk of him as a possible political candidate was heard with

[2] *Vital Speeches*, Sept. 1, 1965, pp. 685–86.

increasing frequency as he made his move to the Republican party. When he took a new job in 1964, as host of the *Death Valley Days* series sponsored by the United States Borax Company, it was after careful consideration of how his public image might be enhanced by association with the show's Western-history format.

The state in which Reagan was preparing to launch his political career was now the most populous in America—in itself a modern industrial society with greater land area, more people, more wealth, and more complex social problems than most nations in the world. It had a fantastically productive agriculture, vast natural resources including oil and lumber, important major aircraft and space-technology industries, and the world's most ambitious and fastest-growing system of public higher education: The University of California, with its nine campuses, had an enrollment of nearly 80,000 students, and the system's mother campus at Berkeley had become recognized as one of the country's best universities.

Berkeley was the scene, in 1964, of a dispute which turned into a major upheaval in higher education. The Berkeley Free Speech Movement, as it came to be called, began with a conflict between students and administration over rules restricting the rights of various groups, political and other, to debate, recruit, and raise funds on campus. The dispute climaxed in a mass sit-in at the administration building which led to the arrest of some 800 students. The Free Speech Movement was the prototype for similar revolts in other universities in America and abroad; it opened a discussion on basic educational values within the university system and at the same time touched deep feelings of fear and resentment in many older Californians, who saw the public-supported university as a haven for ungrateful young anarchists. The public image of Berkeley became increasingly identified with hippies and beatniks, anarchy and protest —all thriving at the expense of the respectable taxpayers of California.

The next year there was another upheaval, in another part of the state. As Berkeley had become a world-wide symbol of students in rebellion, now the obscure community of Watts, in south-central Los Angeles, became a symbol of blacks in rebellion. California's Negro population had risen sharply during World War II with the rise in defense-industry employment, and it was still on the increase. As the black population rose, the question of integration in housing became an explosive political issue. There were laws passed in 1959 and 1963 which outlawed discrimination in the sale or rental of residences, but in 1964 the California Real Estate Association sponsored an initiative to repeal those laws. The initiative, as Proposition 14, was approved by the voters by a 2 to 1 majority but subsequently declared unconstitutional; in the 1964 senatorial election his stand against Proposition 14 undoubtedly contributed to the defeat of Pierre Salinger, former Kennedy press secretary, by George Murphy, businessman and former movie star; and the strong endorsement of the anti-integration measure by white voters undoubtedly contributed to the sense of frustration felt by blacks who lived in the vast ghetto areas of California's cities.

In August of 1965 a dispute between a policeman and some Negro residents of Watts turned into six days of rioting and burning, a widespread outburst of violence that ended with 34 deaths, about $40,000,000 in property damage, and 3,952 arrests.[3]

Governor Brown was out of the country at the time of the Watts riots, and the lieutenant governor, Glenn Anderson, assumed the responsibilities of governor—which included the decision as to whether to order out National Guard forces for duty in the riot area. After the riots there was controversy over whether Anderson acted rapidly enough in calling out the guard, and the issue was raised both by his opponents in the Democratic primary and by his Republican opponent, Robert Finch, in the general election.

As there were conflicts in the state between young and old, between black and white, so there were also the more traditional conflicts between the north and south—the north the older center of finance and politics, the south growing more powerful with its rapid industrial and population growth—and of course between Democrats and Republicans. The conflict between the two parties deserves to be listed last; in California, party ties have usually been weak, and often the state's bitterest political battles have been not between parties, but within them.

The Democratic party—after a couple of decades of being the state's majority party while losing elections regularly to the Republicans—seemed, in the mid-1950's, to have finally found the key to political success. Unity and organization were part of it: in 1953 the California Democratic Council was formed, a statewide organiza-

[3] *Report by the Governor's Commission on the Los Angeles Riots* (Los Angeles: State of California, 1965), p. 1.

tion of volunteer clubs whose members, many of them enthusiastic
political newcomers recruited by the Stevenson campaign, were dedicated to helping Democratic candidates get elected. By the time of the
1954 election the old Progressive law prohibiting party affiliations of
candidates from appearing on the ballot in primaries had been repealed; that, too, helped the Democrats. Some inept politicking by the
Republican candidates in 1958 contributed also, and suddenly there
was a Democratic governor of California: Edmund G. "Pat" Brown
of San Francisco, the former state attorney general. The round-
faced, deep-voiced Brown, who came in with the support of labor
leaders and political professionals and Democratic-club liberals, saw
himself as a unifying force in his party.

For a while, in the wake of victory, there was unity among
California's Democrats, but by the mid-1960's the party was really
no longer one organization so much as a loose confederation of power
factions and ideological groupings. One major faction within the
party centered around Governor Brown, and Brown himself was
closely identified with the Johnson administration. The strongest
opposing faction was that led by Speaker of the Assembly Jesse
Unruh, a Kennedy man. And then there were the liberals, who were
becoming increasingly dissatisfied with Johnson and the war in
Vietnam.

The CDC, which had functioned well a few years before by
bringing the liberal club members into the mainstream of political
activity as precinct workers, was now becoming something of an
embarrassment to the politicians because of its noisy preoccupation
with issues—such as Vietnam. The organization, while still supporting Brown, had taken a strong anti-Vietnam stand at its 1965 convention. In the 1966 CDC convention there was a nominal victory for
Brown when activist president Simon Casady—who had interpreted
the responsibilities of his office to constitute representing the CDC in
civil-rights marches and traveling about the state speaking against the
Vietnam war—resigned after a no-confidence vote; Brown was endorsed for reelection by the CDC, but some 200 of its delegates walked
out of the convention; for many liberals, in and out of the CDC, the
honeymoon with Brown was over. In the coming election they would
either not work in the campaign, or not vote, or both.

In the primary Brown had to contend with another wing of the
party, this one led by Los Angeles mayor Sam Yorty. Yorty, who
was customarily described in the press as a "maverick Democrat,"

occupied a place on the political spectrum somewhere to the right of both Brown and Unruh, and far to the right of the CDC, which he regarded as a gathering of subversives, demagogues, and naive do-gooders. Yorty was also sometimes described as a "Nixon Democrat" because he had supported Richard Nixon in the 1960 presidential campaign. When he challenged Brown in the primary he pulled 981,088 votes to the governor's 1,355,262.[4]

Reagan's candidacy was in part an outgrowth of his work in the 1964 Goldwater campaign. He was noticed by Republican leaders, as he had been by corporation executives, for his attractive personal manner and effective low-key speaking style. However, the interest in Reagan could hardly have built as quickly as it did without some encouragement—and that was provided by Reagan's two closest financial backers, auto dealer Holmes Tuttle and oilman Henry Salvatori, and by the fast-rising political public relations firm of Spencer-Roberts. Spencer-Roberts, too, had played a part in Goldwater's campaign—for the opposition. They had handled the California primary campaign of Nelson Rockefeller, but their performance had so impressed Goldwater that he personally commended them to Reagan.[5]

Stu Spencer and Bill Roberts had a series of meetings early in 1965 with Reagan, his brother Neil "Moon" Reagan—a vice-president in the Hollywood office of the McCann-Erickson advertising agency —and others who were taking an interest in Reagan's political future. At about the same time Spencer and Roberts were in touch with former San Francisco mayor George Christopher, another candidate for the Republican gubernatorial nomination, but they chose to go to work for Reagan. They were influenced by Reagan's assurance that he would not take "extremist" positions, and by an agreed-upon fee of approximately $50,000 a year. Soon letters were going out from the Spencer-Roberts office with the letterhead of the Friends of Ronald Reagan and the signature of former Union Oil president A. C. Ruble, informing selected Republicans that "Ronald Reagan, out of a deep sense of duty and dedication, is willing to serve as Republican candidate for governor, providing a substantial cross section of our

[4] Totton Anderson and Eugene C. Lee, "The 1966 Election in California," *Western Political Quarterly,* XX (June 1967), 538.

[5] James M. Perry, "Ronald Reagan, in a Dazzling Performance," *National Observer,* Jan. 10, 1966.

party will unite behind his candidacy." [6] Throughout 1965 the Reagan organization, building on its central core of wealthy pro-Goldwater businessmen, attracted money and supporters, and in January of 1966 Reagan formally announced his candidacy in a televised speech.

The Republican primary was conducted in keeping with the "eleventh commandment" which had been set down by state chairman Dr. Gaylord Parkinson: "Thou shalt not speak ill of any Republican."[7]

The commandment, an expression of Parkinson's determination to unite his party's contentious liberal and conservative wings, helped Reagan by effectively restraining Christopher from attacking his inexperience, but did not help Christopher, who was open to a much more damaging attack.

Christopher was in the dairy business, and he had been convicted of violating milk price stabilization laws in 1940; the police "mug shot" taken at the time of his arrest had followed him throughout his political career. It was predictable that whenever George Christopher ran for office one of his opponents would produce the story and the photographs in an attempt to characterize him as an arch-criminal. It was something of a standing joke among San Francisco politicians, but the joke was not shared by other Californians. During the primary campaign the Brown organization leaked the story to newsmen, including columnist Drew Pearson, and Pearson ran two columns about Christopher's past troubles with the law. Soon the Christopher mug shots were in circulation again, this time with "WANTED" underneath in block letters.

The Brown strategists had revived the arrest story in the belief that Reagan was the more beatable candidate, and therefore the best way to insure the governor's reelection was to knock Christopher out of the primary. But, Parkinson's Law notwithstanding, the Brown forces were not alone in circulating the mug shots: Some of them were sent out from Sacramento together with pro-Reagan and other conservative material, and Christopher claimed after the campaign that some of them were found in the Reagan headquarters in Los Angeles.[8] It cannot be said that the arrest business was enough to cost Christopher the primary, but the polls did show that, although he

[6] Boyarsky, *op. cit.,* p. 106.
[7] Anderson and Lee, *op. cit.,* p. 539.
[8] *Ibid.,* p. 540.

had been gaining steadily on Reagan, his popularity slipped badly after the Pearson columns were published.

Reagan used the primary mainly to campaign against Brown, and to perfect the techniques and delineate the issues which he would use in the general election. His way of anticipating criticism of his lack of experience lay in the use of the brilliantly chosen term "citizen politician," which, although virtually meaningless, helped convey an image of dedicated, incorruptible amateurism that made Reagan even more attractive than he would have been if he had spent a life in public service.

The citizen-politician image justified a lack of experience in office, but it could not, of course, accommodate a lack of knowledge of the issues; the Ronald Reagan who first came before the public as a candidate in January of 1966 talked with easy familiarity of the problems facing California and presented his own view of the issues. After the election, Bill Roberts of Spencer-Roberts said the campaign boiled down to three main issues: "morality; then taxes, spending, that whole ball of wax; and then the eight years of incumbency." [9]

Those themes were evident in the speeches Reagan made early in the primary campaign. In April he told a Southern California women's club about an anti-Vietnam-war protest dance in Berkeley which he called an "orgy" and which, he said, showed that the university had "finally reached a point where the morality gap is so great that we can no longer ignore it." [10] He asked the audience in his first TV speech whether the people should meet the students' "neurotic vulgarities with vacillation and weakness," and he called the streets of California's cities "jungle paths after dark, with more crimes of violence than New York, Pennsylvania and Massachusetts combined." [11] There were also early references to the taxes, particularly property taxes, which were "squeezing" Californians, to the high costs and abuses of welfare programs, to the "messes" created by the Brown administration.

In the June 8 primary, Reagan defeated Christopher easily, with 1,419,623 votes to the former mayor's 675,683; Christopher led in the San Francisco area but Reagan had huge majorities in the more populous southern counties and—surprisingly to those who looked

[9] Walt Anderson, "Dynamic Duo of California Politics," *Los Angeles Times West Magazine,* Dec. 11, 1966, p. 22.
[10] Boyarsky, *op. cit.,* pp. 22–23.
[11] *Ibid.,* pp. 139–40.

for a simple north-south split—also won in the rural central valley and far northern counties.[12]

Reagan, whom Brown and his advisers had refused to take seriously in the primary, emerged from it not only as the Republican nominee but also as the man most likely to win in the general election. According to the polls, Spencer and Roberts had chosen well in the matter of key issues. A survey conducted by the California Poll in mid-June asked voters what issues concerned them most: The results showed crime, drugs, and juvenile delinquency first (selected by 57 per cent); next, racial problems (49 per cent); state taxes and financing (44 per cent); and welfare programs (40 per cent). In the same poll, 55 per cent chose Reagan as the man most capable of handling the problems, compared to 38 per cent who picked Brown.[13]

As Reagan's campaign progressed, the morality issue became increasingly identified with Berkeley. His campaign organization, unlike Brown's, was unified, sensitive to shifts in public opinion, and flexible. At the strategic center of it were Stu Spencer and Bill Roberts, who controlled the itinerary, the schedule, the selection and timing of issues, and the statewide organizing. Spencer and Roberts had considerable authority in making decisions about the use of campaign funds, but did not involve themselves deeply in the work of raising money; that was left to Salvatori, Tuttle, Ruble, and others. Spencer and Roberts would normally have purchased advertising time and space through their other company, the S-R-H Advertising Agency,[14] but in this particular campaign the advertising billing went through McCann-Erickson, under the supervision of Reagan's brother.

Spencer and Roberts obtained the services of a pair of psychologists, operating under the firm name of Behavior Science Corporation, who accompanied Reagan on campaign trips and provided advice and expert appraisals of the state of voter psychology.

Early in the campaign, particularly in the primary campaign, speeches to small groups included a question-and-answer session, which, according to Spencer, was designed "so people could see he was thinking for himself and not reading from a script." [15] The feedback from the question-and-answer sessions, which was being closely studied by the psychologists, provided a clue which led to the in-

---

[12] Anderson and Lee, *op. cit.*, p. 540.
[13] *California Poll*, quoted in *ibid.*, p. 550.
[14] The "H" represents a third partner, Fred J. Haffner.
[15] Walt Anderson, *op. cit.*, p. 21.

creased emphasis on the Berkeley issue. "Every place Ron went," said Spencer, "somebody asked him about Berkeley." [16] Out of this came stronger statements in which Reagan attacked "the appeasement of campus malcontents and filthy speech advocates under the pretense of preserving academic freedom," and called for a special investigation of the University to be headed by former CIA chief John McCone.[17] This choice provides interesting evidence—if any is needed—of the close link in the campaign between Negro unrest and student unrest; it was McCone who had been named by Brown to investigate the causes of the Watts riots. McCone, who was now a member of Reagan's campaign executive committee, announced his willingness to help, but the idea was dropped after the election.

Reagan also took a stand on the controversial fair housing law —one of the few issues in the campaign on which there was a clear-cut difference of opinion between the two candidates and one in which, according to the polls, Reagan was in agreement with the great majority of the voters. He told delegates to a California Real Estate Association Convention in San Francisco that in his opinion the law "invaded one of our most basic and cherished rights—a right held by all our citizens—the right to dispose of property to whom we see fit and as we see fit." The realtors, according to a newspaper account, "roared their agreement" and chanted "we want Ronnie." [18]

Reagan was still making speeches regularly at this point in the campaign, but much of the burden had been shifted to television. TV was a medium in which Reagan was enormously effective: His quiet, conversational manner makes him one of the best examples of what might be described as the new oratory—the political style which has made control of the small screen more important than control of the large audience, and of which John F. Kennedy (whose style, if not ideology, Reagan admired and deliberately copied) was one of the early masters. The TV part of the Reagan campaign was undoubtedly Spencer-Roberts' single most valuable contribution: Its effectiveness lay in its very simplicity, which made maximum use of Reagan's relaxed on-camera presence and at the same time made it impossible for the opposition to accuse him of running a "show business" campaign. As Spencer said, if they had presented Reagan in any fancy TV productions, "everybody would have yelled *Hollywood*

16 *Ibid.*
17 *Los Angeles Times,* Sept. 23, 1966.
18 *Ibid.,* Oct. 7, 1966.

at us." Instead, "all our TV stuff was very simple: We just put Ron in front of the camera and let him talk." [19] The use of television was a major reason for the extremely high cost of the Reagan campaign budget, but it paid off: It allowed the candidate to campaign in a relatively leisurely fashion—early experience had shown that he sometimes became irritable under pressure—and it presented him in his best medium. The sincere, soft-spoken man who appeared on the screen before millions of Californians could obviously not be the dangerous villain the Brown campaign was talking about.

There were vast differences between the Reagan campaign and the Brown campaign; one of the most important was the degree of *personal* attack involved. Reagan attacked everything around and about the Brown administration, but had little to say against the governor himself. But Brown never seemed to recover from a deep sense of the incredibility of his situation: that he, who in his two previous campaigns for governor had defeated the Senate minority leader, William F. Knowland, and a recent presidential candidate, Richard Nixon, should be running—as an underdog—against a movie actor who had never held office. He attacked Reagan personally, and the attack backfired.

The personal attack against Reagan took two lines: The attack on Reagan the actor, inexperienced in politics; and the attack on Reagan the right-wing extremist.

Sometimes the attacks were tied together, as when Brown, in a San Joaquin Valley speech, reminded voters that while his administration was building California, Reagan was making second-rate movies. "While we've been building a dynamic working society in California, he was off making such film epics as 'Bedtime for Bonzo' and 'Tugboat Annie Sails Again.' " And when Reagan was not acting, the governor said, he was working as a "voice for hire" against such programs as Medicare, the Tennessee Valley Authority, the graduated income tax and Social Security, and supporting "some of the most rightwing candidates this country has ever seen, including those proud to declare themselves members of the John Birch Society." [20]

Most of Brown's references to Reagan's acting background in speeches were fairly light blows of the "I can't act and he can't govern" variety, but some of the printed and filmed material which

19 Walt Anderson, *op. cit.,* p. 21.
20 *Los Angeles Times,* Oct. 7, 1966.

came out of the Brown campaign was much stronger. There were full-page newspaper ads which asked the voters whether they wanted a "real governor" or an "acting governor" and showed pictures of Reagan in costumes—such as a Confederate officer's uniform—from his past movie roles. Campaign material attacking Reagan as a right-winger was stronger yet. The California Democratic State Central Committee put out a *Time*-magazine-sized booklet entitled "Ronald Reagan, Extremist Collaborator: An Expose," which contained names of leading right-wingers around the country who were allegedly backing Reagan. The booklet's cover showed a right-wing bookshop's offering of bumper stickers, which conspicuously featured "REAGAN for GOVERNOR" among such items as "EARL WARREN SHOULD BE IMPEACHED," "THIS IS A REPUBLIC NOT A DEMOCRACY! LET'S KEEP IT THAT WAY," "REGISTER COMMUNISTS NOT FIREARMS," "I'D RATHER FIGHT THAN SWITCH . . . TO SOCIALISM," and "WILL IT BE CHRIST OR ANTI-CHRIST?" [21]

Reagan was not the only candidate who made use of professional campaign-management firms. Although Brown's top campaign executives were members of the Democratic hierarchy and his personal staff, two political public-relations firms, Baus and Ross and Harry Lerner Associates, were employed in the preparation of special "attack" material. Ironically, Baus and Ross, the firm which had worked for Goldwater in the California primary of 1964—against Rockefeller and Spencer-Roberts—was now working against Spencer-Roberts again. But political public relations, like any other profession, becomes more sophisticated with time, and the Spencer-Roberts soft sell proved far more effective than the heavy-handed productions, reminiscent of the early days of Whitaker and Baxter (see Chapter 7), which were used against Reagan. For example, on the eve of the election, full-page ads warned:

> IF REAGAN TAKES OVER. . .
> TOTAL DISASTER THREATENS OUR PUBLIC SCHOOLS!
> If Reagan and his extremist supporters are allowed
> to carry out their policies. . .
> *You can expect these horrible set-backs*
> A SHORTER SCHOOL YEAR!
> REDUCED TEACHER SALARIES!
> MORE HALF-DAY SESSIONS!

[21] *Ronald Reagan, Extremist Collaborator: An Expose,* published by the California Democratic State Central Committee, San Francisco and Los Angeles, 1966.

END OF *FREE* COLLEGE TUITIONS! . . .
Doesn't Reagan's *Threat* to Our Schools Terrify You?
SAVE OUR SCHOOLS FROM DISASTER!
STOP REAGAN AT THE POLLS! [22]

Unfortunately for Brown's public-relations experts, these strident warnings could never overcome the contrary image presented by Reagan himself over millions of TV screens—the quiet, sincere, well-informed "citizen politician." Bill Roberts of Spencer-Roberts said after the campaign that the extremist issue was an "over-the-hill issue" by 1966 anyway, and that if he had been working *against* Reagan instead of *for* him, he would have used an entirely different approach: "In the first place I would never have attacked Reagan. I would have killed him with kindness. I would have said he's a decent, fine person and no doubt has a future in politics, but maybe he should start at a lower level." [23]

Much attention has been given to the fact that Reagan employed a political public-relations firm, tending to obscure the fact that Brown employed two of them. The real difference lies in the fact that Spencer and Roberts actually ran the campaign—planned its strategy from the beginning and made the key decisions which unified issues and candidate image—while the firms employed by Brown were merely peripheral parts of a large, cumbersome organization, hired to fire a few blunderbuss shots at the opposition.

There are some obvious reasons why it was easier for Reagan to allow Spencer-Roberts to run his campaign: A candidate emerging from private life into politics has no existing organization, and therefore a firm such as Spencer-Roberts, which can expertly assemble a statewide campaign, from television commercials to precinct chairmen, fills a great vacuum. For a candidate such as Brown, carrying all the habits and obligations of a lifetime in politics and eight years in the governor's office, surrounded by jealous advisers who considered themselves to be the equals of Spencer and Roberts and all the other free-lance campaign experts, it would have been almost impossible to bring in a PR company and put it in full control of a campaign; previous (Republican) governors had done so, but Brown, who tended to be influenced by those close to him, never seriously considered doing so in 1966.

Theoretically, there is no reason why the Brown organization

---

[22] *Los Angeles Times,* Nov. 6, 1966.
[23] Walt Anderson, *op. cit.,* p. 22.

could not have produced a planned and unified campaign anyway— but it did not. It was disunited in its structure and vacillating in its strategy. Among Brown's closest political advisers were Don Bradley, who had been a major figure in many California Democratic campaigns including President Johnson's in 1964, State Finance Director Hale Champion, and attorney Frederick Dutton, University of California regent and former member of the Kennedy administration. The three disagreed over many things, including the question of who should become the new state chairman of the Democratic party in August. Brown wavered between the two leading candidates—Charles Warren and Mrs. Carmen Warschaw—and when the post went to Warren, Mrs. Warschaw defected from the Brown campaign and turned up on election night at Reagan's victory celebration. Mayor Yorty, who might have been expected according to political tradition to close ranks behind Brown after the primary, also personally congratulated Reagan that night. The CDC wing of the party was represented in the inner circles of Brown's campaign organization by Controller Alan Cranston, but although Cranston remained faithful to Brown, the group of which he was one of the founders was itself divided.

On September 27, another Negro riot broke out. This time it was in the Hunters Point area of San Francisco, and again it was touched off by a police incident, the shooting of a 16-year-old boy who was fleeing from police in a stolen car. Brown quickly ordered out California Highway Patrol reinforcements and then the National Guard, and at the same time expressed his sympathetic concern for the residents of the San Francisco ghetto. Neither whites nor blacks were satisfied; the new outbreak of violence only speeded the polarization process, leaving Brown stranded in an ideological middle ground that seemed to grow lonelier by the day.

On election day the pollsters were proven wrong: Reagan won by a greater margin than anyone had predicted—3,742,913 to Brown's 2,749,174 [24]—and so did Republican candidates for nearly every other state executive office. Lieutenant Governor Anderson was replaced by Robert Finch, and Controller Cranston by Houston Flournoy. The only remaining Democrat in the administration was Attorney General Tom Lynch.

[24] Anderson and Lee, *op. cit.*, p. 536.

Undoubtedly the length of time Brown had been in office—
eight years—was a factor in his defeat, although not long before
Earl Warren had managed to be elected to a third term. There seem
to be two separate but interconnected factors which account for the
Reagan-Republican triumph in 1966. First, Reagan's campaign was
better run, in terms of strategy and organization. Second, Reagan was
campaigning with what was just becoming one of the overwhelming
issues of the decade: law and order. The two factors, it should be
emphasized again, were closely interrelated: A less astute campaign
might never have detected the potency of the issue so soon or exploited it so effectively—or managed to overcome its own side's
shortcomings so well while doing so.

After the election there were amazed reactions, particularly in
the East and in Europe, to the news that an actor had been elected
governor of America's most populous state. And much of what was
written to explain the phenomenon stressed Spencer-Roberts and characterized the whole campaign as a sort of extravaganza in which
Reagan the actor played the leading role, merely mouthing the
lines which had been prepared for him by the public-relations man.
The truth was that Reagan himself had been for years much more of
a public-relations man than an actor, and his relationship with
Spencer-Roberts was much more of a collaboration with fellow
workers in a profession which he knew and respected and understood. And of his personal advisers, the closest was his brother Neil
Reagan, an advertising man.

The kind of campaign they put on was of course costly—the
total was in the neighborhood of 2.6 million dollars for Reagan, 2
million for Brown.[25] It was the most expensive campaign in California history, and quite possibly the most expensive state campaign
ever.

It was built on the recognition that many voters were increasingly fearful of the threat—to morality, to institutions, to property,
to themselves—that was posed by the angry demands for social change
which were coming from within the state. Protests and dissent and
riots were making some Americans look deeply at the problems
underlying them, but they were making millions of others recoil in
fear and disapproval. Ronald Reagan was elected governor of Cali-

[25] *Ibid.*

fornia mainly because he promised to restore and keep the peace; his campaign anticipated by a full two years the "law and order" issue which would dominate the 1968 national elections, and it showed any politician capable of reading its message that the issue, properly used, could be a key to victory and power.

13

1967
Cleveland
Carl M. Stokes vs. *Seth Taft*

In the mid-1960's the struggle of American Negroes to attain full equality gave birth to a multitude of slogans. One of them was Black Power, and of all the phrases in that phrasemaking decade it seemed to have the greatest ability to evoke emotional reactions and also the greatest range of meanings—anything from peaceful voter registration to armed rebellion. But for all its ambiguity the term was generally understood to be primarily relevant to one kind of power: political power. Malcolm X said:

> *The cornerstones of this country's operation are economic and political strength and power. The black man doesn't have the economic strength—and it will take time for him to build it. But right now the American black man has the political strength and power to change his destiny overnight.*[1]

[1] Malcolm X, *The Autobiography of Malcolm X* (New York: Grove Press, Inc., 1964), p. 315. Copyright © 1964 by Alex Haley and Malcolm X; copyright © 1965 by Alex Haley and Betty Shabazz. Reprinted by permission of Grove Press, Inc.

Political strength and power was, of course, most attainable in the places where blacks made up the largest segments of the population. The South was one such area, and the industrial cities of the urban North were another. Blacks had been moving northward into the factory cities since the early 1900's—and in greatest numbers during and since World War II—attracted by the job opportunities and the hopes of greater equality.

What they found as they poured into the cities was room at the bottom. There were some openings for unskilled workers in industry, but as many black men worked, if they worked at all, as janitors and garbage men, dishwashers and shoeshine boys. Their wives created a new servant class in the cities as housemaids in the homes of wealthy whites. And the neighborhoods they occupied were usually the dismal leftovers of transition and change. Perhaps nowhere else in history have whole segments of cities moved so rapidly from open land to hopeless slum in such short periods of time—progressive America has, among other accomplishments, broken all speed records for urban decay.

One such blighted city was Cleveland, Ohio. Chartered in 1836, the city on the shores of Lake Erie became an important iron, steel, manufacturing, and shipping center—and, in the McKinley era, a city of broad streets and elegant homes in residential areas not far from the central business district. But by the middle of the twentieth century the lake was dead, polluted with industrial wastes, and the once-genteel residential areas had become overcrowded Negro slums—the big houses were now rickety tenements, and dope pushers and prostitutes roamed the streets.

Two things are spectacularly apparent in Cleveland's population statistics in mid-twentieth century: the influx of blacks and the exodus of whites. Between 1950 and 1965, the number of Negro residents rose from 147,847 to 279,352—and during the same period, the white population declined by nearly a quarter of a million.[2] The total population of Cleveland fell, but the total population of the greater Cleveland area rose as the middle-class whites moved out into the growing suburbs. Cleveland was left with the lowest percentage of middle-class whites of any major city in the United States.

The city's population by 1965 was approximately 35 per cent Negro. The whites who made up the 65 per cent majority were for

[2] Jeffrey K. Hadden, Louis H. Masotti, Victor Thiessen, "The Making of the Negro Mayors 1967," *Trans-Action*, January/February 1968, p. 22.

the most part "cosmos," the Cleveland slang term for various ethnic groups—Poles, Czechs, Germans, Romanians, Hungarians, Italians. To be a cosmo meant to have been born in the old country or to have at least one foreign-born parent. Most cosmos lived in identifiable neighborhoods, and many of them read foreign-language newspapers and attended foreign-language religious ceremonies. Although the cohesion of the various white ethnic groups was disintegrating, the several strains of working-class whites together made up the majority of Cleveland's voting population and set the tone for its politics: Senator Frank Lausche was one prominent ex-mayor, and Kennedy cabinet member Anthony Celebrezze was another. The incumbent mayor when Carl M. Stokes entered the picture was Romanian-born Ralph S. Locher.

Cleveland city government was anything but brilliant at its best, and Locher was rather less brilliant than the average. He has been called a "nonmayor," an "amiable and ineffective time-server," [3] and had been accused, it was said, "of almost every municipal offense except being dishonest or colored." [4] Locher was first elected in 1961 and elected to a second term in 1963.

During his incumbency the contrast between the urgency of the city's problems and the apathy of its government became more and more pronounced. Public facilities, especially schools and hospitals, were old and inadequate. Unemployment and housing shortages were acute. Cleveland had the honor of recording the worst performance mark of any major city in the United States participating in the federal urban renewal programs. The federal government eventually cut off all funds allocated to Cleveland for renewal projects. Blocks of homes had been bulldozed, and the building sites stood empty.

On several occasions, Mayor Locher bluntly rejected requests from black community leaders and white civil-rights groups for face-to-face discussions on the needs of the ghetto. There were sit-ins and demonstrations at the city hall—which produced arrests, but no changes. Then in 1965 the civil-rights groups turned to conventional politics as a possible way of changing the city government: A petition was circulated to place the name of Carl Stokes, a young Negro legislator, on the general election ballot as a candidate for mayor.

---

[3] John Skow, "The Question in the Ghetto: Can Cleveland Escape Burning?" *Saturday Evening Post,* July 28, 1967, p. 38. Reprinted by permission.
[4] Calvin Trillin, "U.S. Letter: Cleveland," *The New Yorker,* Oct. 14, 1967, p. 210. Reprinted by permission.

Stokes was then 38. He was a native of Cleveland, born and raised in the slums, and had become a high school dropout before enlisting in the army at the age of 18. After his discharge from the service he returned to finish his education. He received a B.A. from the University of Minnesota in 1954, and after attending Cleveland-Marshall Law School at night while working in the daytime, he passed the Ohio state bar examination. He entered private law practice with his brother in 1957, and the following year he was appointed assistant city prosecutor of Cleveland. He would say later that his family background, his experience as a city prosecutor, and his earlier work as a state liquor control agent and municipal court probation officer made him "a by-product" of all the kinds of problems of a city.[5] In 1963 he was elected to the Ohio state legislature, becoming the first Negro Democrat to sit in that body.

By 1965 the seriousness of Cleveland's situation was apparent to everyone—the city was so underfinanced that it could afford to collect rubbish only once a month [6]—but the complacent Democratic organization supported Locher for another term. Locher was re-elected, but only by a slim margin of 2,143 votes, less than one per cent of the total. He received 38 per cent of the votes, Stokes, running as an independent, was a close second, and the remainder of the votes were divided between another independent and Ralph Perk, the Republican nominee. Although Stokes had come amazingly close to beating Locher, he had lacked backing in significant areas: The two major newspapers and most business and community leaders had supported Locher. Stokes, running as an independent, had no official backing from his party; even six of the nine Negro city councilmen had refused to endorse him.

Locher survived the challenge, but during his third term Cleveland became the scene of one of the country's worst riots. In the Hough ghetto the following summer there was a four-day outburst during which buildings were burned and looted, four Negroes were killed, 46 people were injured, and 187 arrested.[7]

In the days and months that followed the July riot, the Locher administration and Cleveland politics in general were publicly denounced all over the country. TV broadcasts reporting on conditions

[5] James Naughton, "In Cleveland and Boston, the Issue Is Race," *New York Times Magazine,* Nov. 5, 1967, p. 100. © 1967 by The New York Times Company. Reprinted by permission.

[6] Skow, *op. cit.,* p. 41.

[7] *Time,* July 29, 1966.

in Hough told of the apathetic city government and searched for combinations of adjectives with the right note of kindly ridicule to describe Locher. National magazines ran articles on Cleveland. John Skow in the *Saturday Evening Post* described the Hough ghetto as a "fifty block by ten block infection of crumbling three story buildings and huge rotted frame houses still owned by rats that can't be frightened and landlords that can't be found." [8] He also mentioned, as one example of the Locher administration's style of dealing with urban problems, the recent application that had been made for federal funds under the Model Cities project. The application had been submitted on the last possible day, without details and without the required approval of the city council. The mayor had attached a note saying he would try to fill in details by the end of the month.[9]

The official response of local government to the Hough riot was a Cuyahoga County Grand Jury investigation which concluded that it had all been caused by professional agitators and Communists. The report said:

> *This jury finds that the outbreak of lawlessness and disorder was both organized, precipitated and exploited by a relatively small group of trained and disciplined professionals at this business. They were aided and abetted, wittingly and otherwise, by misguided people of all ages and colors, many of whom are avowed believers in violence and extremism, and some of whom also are either members of or officers in the Communist Party.*[10]

Mayor Locher wholeheartedly accepted the grand jury report, and efforts were made to prevent further riots by increasing police strength. Every night a special police helicopter, equipped with a strong searchlight, patrolled the Hough area. The helicopter was armed with a Thompson submachine gun. Too costly a piece of equipment for Cleveland's unsteady city treasury, it had been paid for by private groups, including the local Rotary Club and a young businessmen's association called Group 66.[11]

Meanwhile, the federal Civil Rights Commission was holding hearings on Cleveland police practices. It was brought out that the

8 Skow, *op. cit.*, p. 38.

9 *Ibid.*, p. 48.

10 Ruth Fischer, "Why Hough Got Tough—the Real Agitators," *New Republic*, Sept. 10, 1966, p. 9. Reprinted by permission of the *New Republic* © 1966, Harrison-Blaine of New Jersey, Inc.

11 Roldo Bartimole and Murray Gruber, "Cleveland: Recipe for Violence," *The Nation*, June 26, 1967, p. 814.

Police Department made frequent use of a "waiver card" to avoid the possible legal repercussions of arresting and holding people without charges. When such arrestees were released, they were to sign a card which declared, "I am guilty of the charge of (blank) and the conduct of all members of the Police Department in any way connected with my arrest was in all respects reasonable and proper." [12] Although the waiver was legally ludicrous, it was effective with people who did not understand their rights. At that time the Cleveland Police Department had about 100 patrolmen, four sergeants, and no officers who were Negro out of a uniformed force of about 2,200.[13]

The "get tough" policy which the city adopted toward the ghetto widened the gulf between the black community and the administration, and the outside criticism of Locher gradually weakened his support from many segments of city leadership which had previously backed him. It was obvious that Locher would have a hard time getting reelected again in 1967.

The general election would be held in November of 1967, the party primaries in October. But the campaign began early in the spring. Stokes was in the running again, but not as an independent; this time he planned to challenge Locher for the Democratic nomination. A third Democrat, Frank Celeste, representing a rather feeble "dump Locher" movement among some party regulars, also announced his candidacy.

It was no secret that national Democratic officeholders and the national Democratic party organization favored Stokes's entrance in Cleveland's Democratic primary campaign. The 1968 presidential elections were approaching, and national party leaders eagerly sought the large black vote which Stokes could help deliver to the Democratic nominee. Stokes was in constant touch with Washington Democrats—particularly Vice-President Hubert Humphrey—long before the primary.

In entering the Democratic primary, Stokes hoped to take maximum advantage of the anti-Locher sentiment which had grown to monumental proportions as a result of the Hough riot. In the primary the anti-Locher vote would not be siphoned off by white Republican or independent candidates.

[12] Skow, *op. cit.*, p. 46.
[13] *Ibid.*, p. 42.

A second major tactical move by Stokes was to concentrate his personal appearances in the white sections of the city. In 1965 he had campaigned almost exclusively in the ten predominantly Negro wards, and only three per cent of Cleveland's white voters had supported him on election day.[14]

This time, instead of public appearances in the black community Stokes relied on an extensive registration campaign and a tight-knit organization of the black population. During the late spring and summer months a massive voter registration drive led by Martin Luther King qualified thousands of Negro voters. Stokes was aided in this drive by a Ford Foundation grant to the Cleveland chapter of CORE. The Stokes organization then threw a well-coordinated network of campaign workers across the black community to provide election information and to insure the highest possible black voter turnout. The black section of town was organized down to the block level; each volunteer was assigned the responsibility of turning out a specific number of voters from his district. In all, an estimated 3,000 campaign workers were actively assisting in the Stokes campaign, which the candidate coordinated through ten branch offices.[15]

The decision to campaign personally in the white communities in Cleveland would have been disastrous had Stokes not been able to count on the political solidarity of Cleveland blacks. Given the conditions in the ghettos and the alienation of most blacks from socially sanctioned political channels, their unification behind the Stokes campaign was truly remarkable. Many militants who looked upon the electoral process as a hoax worked diligently throughout the summer of 1967 to prevent another racial explosion, urging discontented ghettoites to "Cool it for Carl." Slum dwellers, many of whom had never before voted, responded *en masse* to the registration and electoral drives. Middle-class Negroes who *had* voted before became active in new ways, wherever the campaign could use their efforts. What had begun in 1965 as a negative expression of racial discontent developed following the 1966 riot into a positive sense of racial solidarity. Without it, all of Stokes' organizational skills would have failed to produce the black vote he had to have to win.

The riot and its aftermath made an impact on Cleveland's business and community leaders also. Many business leaders abandoned

[14] *Los Angeles Times,* Nov. 9, 1967.
[15] *Time,* Oct. 3, 1967.

Locher and reluctantly endorsed the only candidate whom they felt could reduce the threat of more violence and destruction.

A major boost was given Stokes's campaign by the *Cleveland Plain Dealer,* one of the city's two daily newspapers. Endorsing Stokes one month before the primary election, the editor noted that "he was the right age, was born and brought up in the community and understood its problems, had made politics his profession and would understand the Negro community better than anyone else." [16] The other daily, the *Cleveland Press,* did not directly endorse Stokes but asked its readers to vote for anybody *but* Locher.

In carrying his campaign to the white sections of the city, Stokes had two objectives in mind. First he wanted to enlarge his white vote from the miniscule three per cent he had received in 1965. But more importantly, he hoped to counteract a possible backlash vote motivated by fear and prejudice. To this end, he stressed three themes: his moderateness on the race issue; the need for wholesale political change; and governmental efficiency.

On the race issue, he was primarily concerned with convincing whites that he was not attempting a "black power takeover." He denounced militant black leaders, stating that "H. Rap Brown would not be welcome in Cleveland" if he were mayor.[17] He reminded voters that in the state legislature he had sponsored both a fair housing bill and one increasing the governor's power to dispatch National Guard troops to riot areas, and he stood on the record of his speech to a Los Angeles NAACP meeting on Black Power, when he had said:

> *To the extent that this new philosophy is intended to shake the Negro into political action and to excite pride in his being black, I support it. To the extent that it connotes separation and "control by blacks," I reject it. I find no difference in a bigot whether that bigot be black or white.*[18]

One of his newspaper ads began with the startling headline: "Don't vote for a Negro," adding in smaller type: "Vote for a Man. Vote for Ability." [19]

On the question of change, Stokes attempted to capitalize on the general discontent and dissatisfaction with Locher's administration. "It is absolutely essential," Stokes stressed, "that the voters know that

16 Quoted in *The New York Times,* Oct. 14, 1967.
17 Naughton, *op. cit.,* p. 97.
18 *Ibid.,* p. 100.
19 Trillin, *op. cit.,* p. 211.

they are voting for change, total change in the old political system in order to serve the needs of the people." [20] To emphasize his intention to change the city's politics, Stokes promised to fire every member of the incumbent's cabinet. Indicating his dissatisfaction with the city's traditional leadership, he charged that:

> There are just too many people around here, mostly the men in government, who think that everything is normal or soon will be normal. They really cannot see the problems of this community because they do not believe that the people are suffering. This is the most dangerous dream a leader can have.[21]

In personal and public meetings with Cleveland businessmen, Stokes indicated that he hoped to work closely with the business community in order to insure governmental efficiency: "Maybe cities don't make profits, but they still need money-wise managers for such things as port authorities, urban renewal, and financial management. I intend to recruit experts from industry to come into City Hall and help us out." [22]

Recognizing that Cleveland's traditional Democratic party dominance would be ended by a Stokes victory in the primary, local party regulars mobilized all their resources in support of Ralph Locher. The candidate himself carefully avoided any overt racial appeals, choosing rather to stress the indirect question of law and order. For all who listened, however, it was clear what Locher meant when he pleaded with the electorate to "keep the hoodlums out of City Hall."

The county Democratic organization was less subtle. Endorsing the candidacy of Locher, the Democratic executive committee of Cuyahoga County labeled Stokes's campaign a black power conspiracy aimed at overthrowing the system and establishing a "Negro dictatorship." In a party newsletter the executive committe urged the electorate to "save the city," calling Stokes a mere pawn of Martin Luther King: "Will Dr. Martin Luther King actually be the mayor of Cleveland if Carl B. Stokes is elected? This would give the noted racist control of his first city in the United States." [23]

Locher, following the advice of his campaign manager, City Law Director Bronis Klementowicz, relied on the same strategy that

[20] *Los Angeles Times,* Oct. 5, 1967.
[21] *Ibid.,* Nov. 9, 1967.
[22] *Business Week,* Oct. 7, 1967, p. 37.
[23] Quoted in Trillin, *op. cit.,* p. 214.

he had used before: mobilize the regular party personnel and cultivate the various cosmo communities. He attended countless numbers of ethnic picnics, and made the usual rounds to address such groups as the Polish Falcons, the Croatian Club, and the Slovenian National Home.[24]

Many liberal middle-class suburbanites who would be unable to vote in the primary nevertheless took active part in the Stokes campaign, working in the office or aiding the registration and voter drives. Among these were many members of the one ethnic group that was conspicuously absent in Cleveland: Jews. The total Jewish population within the Cleveland city limits was scarcely 500, although there were some 85,000 Jews in the various suburbs.

Stokes gained rapidly in the last month of the campaign. On the weekend before the primary election, a newspaper poll predicted a narrow Locher victory. Most observers expected a large turnout to favor Stokes; and the night before the election Martin Luther King led a huge get-out-the-vote rally in the Negro community. On election day, thousands of Stokes volunteers filled the streets to turn out the vote for their candidate.

Early evening returns on the night of the election favored the incumbent Locher; a local television station prematurely proclaimed the renomination of the mayor, even while the Locher lead was melting away. By ten-thirty that evening, Stokes had been unofficially acclaimed the winner of the Democratic party nomination. The final vote count showed 110,769 votes for Stokes, 92,033 for Locher, and 8,565 for Frank Celeste.

The black vote for Carl Stokes was approximately 94,000—good enough by itself to defeat Ralph Locher by 2,000 votes. Of the whites who went to the polls, 16,000 cast their ballots for the black candidate; Stokes' margin of victory was 18,000 votes. Blacks in Cleveland represented only 40 per cent of the registered Democratic voters, but their vote alone was sufficient to defeat the incumbent mayor in the Democratic primary.[25]

The black voter turnout was a record 74 per cent; only 58 per cent of the qualified whites voted. Ninety-six per cent of the black participants voted for Stokes; less than 80 per cent of the whites voted for Locher.[26]

---

24 *Ibid.*, p. 210.
25 Hadden *et al.*, *op. cit.*, p. 24.
26 *Ibid.*, p. 24.

Seth Taft, the 44-year-old grandson of President William H. Taft, won the Republican party primary election unopposed—and unnoticed. Republicans have never inspired Clevelanders, and throughout the summer and early fall of 1967 Taft's presence as a candidate for mayor did nothing to change that tradition. The Republican party can count only 11 per cent of the electorate as party registrants; even when contested the party primary causes little excitement. Taft's candidacy was further obscured by the dramatic unfolding of a black-white contest for the other party's nomination. Consequently, Taft began his general election campaign against Stokes with almost no exposure before the Cleveland electorate.

But there were even greater drawbacks to Taft's candidacy. He had only *lived* in Cleveland for a few months; he moved into the city from a Cleveland suburb for the specific purpose of running for mayor. Nor had he ever held public office; the only political connection the Cleveland population could make was through politician relatives of his with the same name, and even this was more a negative than a positive factor—especially with union men who found it hard to develop any love for the nephew of the author of the Taft-Hartley Law.

Stokes, on the other hand, had a number of factors working for him in the general election campaign. He now had the open support and financial assistance of the national Democratic party organization. Both his primary rivals endorsed him, and he was even successful in gaining a shaky reconciliation with the county Democratic executive committee. The *Cleveland Press* joined the *Plain Dealer* in support of his candidacy, and labor leaders joined the large business sector standing behind him against Seth Taft.

The first polls taken after the primary election showed Stokes leading Taft by over 30 percentage points. According to traditional political patterns there was no conceivable way for Taft to overcome such a lead—but there was no precedent for a two-way mayoral race between a black man and a white man.

During the month-long general election campaign Stokes continued to concentrate his efforts in Cleveland's white districts, paying special attention to the cosmo population which had been Locher's main support in the primary. Most ethnic groups were reluctant to commit themselves either way in the Stokes-Taft contest, but Stokes' efforts among the cosmos did pay off occasionally. The Hungarian daily *Szabadsag* endorsed him, saying that under his leadership all races could "live up to the ideals that inspired the ethnic groups to settle in Cleveland in their search for freedom and in pursuit of happiness." [27]

Among the cosmos, Stokes argued that Taft's aristocratic background made him incapable of understanding the problems of the poor. "No one," said Stokes, "can explain a hunger pain to Seth." [28]

Taft was trying to establish himself as a new-style Republican liberal on the order of his former Yale classmate, New York mayor John Lindsay. He talked about the need for new jobs, better housing, and improved law enforcement. He proposed to bring government closer to the people by establishing 15 neighborhood branches of City Hall. As a civil-rights advocate he circulated a "bill of rights" pledging to use the mayor's power to open up building and trade unions to Negroes. He promised he would personally investigate all charges of police brutality.

To overcome his lack of previous public exposure, Taft conducted a strenuous personal-appearance campaign, climaxed by a door-to-door drive in the closing weeks. He appeared on television in a series of debates with Stokes which allowed thousands of Clevelanders to see that he was young, presentable, articulate, well-informed, and white. In the second of the four debates Stokes angered Taft and many members of the studio audience by stating: "The personal analysis of Seth Taft—and the analysis of many competent political analysts—is that Seth Taft may win the November 7 election, but for one reason. That reason is that his skin happens to be white." [29]

It was later revealed by Stokes' campaign manager that the remark was not an intemperate slip—it was a deliberate attempt to keep the race issue sufficiently alive to combat any possible slip back toward apathy of the black voters.[30]

Taft claimed that he was more handicapped by race than Stokes. "If I say something on the subject," he complained once, "it is racism. If Carl Stokes says something, it is fair play." On another occasion he said that "just because I'm running against a Negro is no reason to call me a bigot." [31]

The fact was that race was the overriding issue in the election and both candidates knew it. Taft, running against a white Democrat,

[27] Quoted in Naughton, *op. cit.*, p. 32.
[28] *Ibid.*, p. 114.
[29] Hadden *et al.*, *op. cit.*, p. 25.
[30] *Ibid.*
[31] Naughton, p. 110.

would have been just another token Republican candidate. His color was undoubtedly his greatest asset, but he refused to campaign as if it were his only one. He also insisted on taking a strong civil-rights stand where a more cynical politician might have run a "you know where I stand" anti-integration campaign. Although he did not make any inroads into Stokes's support in the black community, he very nearly came from behind to win the election.

On November 7 more than 78 per cent of Cleveland's 326,000 registered voters went to the polls, one of the highest turnouts in the city's history. As the count of the ballots began, extra police patrols toured the ghetto areas, and units of the Ohio National Guard readied for possible disturbances in the city.

By late evening, Taft had built up a sizable lead, which he retained into the first hours of the next morning. With only 21 of the city's 901 electoral districts left to count, Taft held a 5,000 vote lead —but most of the late-reporting districts were in black neighborhoods. At 2:30 A.M. Stokes finally caught up, and for a while, until the last seven precincts were tallied, the two candidates were even. At about 3:00 A.M., Stokes was unofficially the mayor-elect.

Stokes defeated Taft by 1,644 votes; 129,318 to 127,674. Despite his strong early lead, his official backing from key elements of the city's leadership—the newspapers, the unions, the Democratic party—he won by a margin of 0.6 per cent. The racial alignment of votes was striking: Nineteen out of twenty blacks voted for Stokes, sixteen out of twenty whites for Taft. Some 221,000 Clevelanders voted for the candidate of their own color.

The real accomplishment of Stokes's campaign was mobilizing an unprecedentedly large segment of the black electorate to political activity. His victory was due to some 30,000 white voters and more than 90,000 black voters—whites who saw his election as desirable or acceptable, and blacks who saw it as possible. The former was a modestly encouraging token of tolerance, but politicians of all colors were more impressed by the latter. Thousands of Negroes in Cleveland had been roused to political awareness by the Stokes campaign, and it is incalculable how many millions more saw his victory and that of Negro lawyer Richard Hatcher in Gary, Indiana, as evidence that black power could be not merely a slogan but an election-deciding reality in American politics.

14

1968

New Hampshire

Eugene McCarthy vs. *Lyndon B. Johnson*

There is a sort of upsetting of the order of values in American presidential primary elections. The factor which should be of first importance—the number of delegates involved—becomes a secondary consideration, and factors which should be relatively inconsequential —such as the date of the election—become paramount. For this reason, New Hampshire—which happens to have the earliest presidential primary election in the country—occupies a special place in American politics, and for a few weeks in most presidential election years it becomes the center of national and world-wide attention. It was thrift, not a lust for publicity, that brought this about originally: When New Hampshire adopted the presidential primary in 1916, the state government scheduled it to be held on Town Meeting day, the first Tuesday in March, thereby saving the cost of an extra election. Thus New Hampshire's primary became the opening act in the five months or so of elections, conventions, caucuses, and deals that all together make up the prenomination stage of the long presidential campaign.

At first the New Hampshire primary was merely an election for convention delegates. In 1952 a preference, or "popularity," vote was added, and that was credited with being the main reason for one President's decision to retire from politics. Senator Estes Kefauver of Tennessee, coming into the primaries fresh from his highly publicized hearings on organized crime, defeated President Truman, and Truman subsequently decided not to seek reelection.

In 1968 Senator Eugene McCarthy's performance in New Hampshire contributed in a somewhat similar way to President Lyndon Johnson's decision to retire. But where Kefauver's campaign had been merely a challenge, McCarthy's was somewhat more in the nature of a crusade: Its ideals were an end to the war in Vietnam and the intermingled cause of reversing the growing disaffection of young Americans with the styles and structures of American politics.

Opposition to the country's policy in Vietnam had been increasing steadily for years, to the point of becoming a movement in itself within national politics. Actually, it was more a multitude of movements, varying expressions of dissatisfaction or of hope for change. Some voters, remembering that Republican President Eisenhower's election had led to the end of the Korean conflict, looked to George Romney or Nelson Rockefeller or Richard Nixon; others were abandoning the two-party system entirely in favor of such groups as the new Peace and Freedom Party; and many liberal Democrats were banding together in dissenting organizations designed to either force the President into a new policy or throw support to an alternative candidate.

The man most often mentioned as a possible Democratic opponent to Johnson was New York Senator Robert F. Kennedy—but Kennedy planned to restrain his presidential aspirations until 1972 instead of entering into an intraparty battle that would be bitter and divisive and, by all the odds of history, probably unsuccessful. He repeatedly said he would not run in 1968, and the peace movement in the Democratic party remained a cause without a rebel until, in the fall of 1967, Senator Eugene McCarthy entered the picture.

McCarthy was a tall, soft-spoken man who had spent a year in a Benedictine monastery in his youth and had considered becoming a monk. He was teaching sociology and economics at St. Thomas College in St. Paul when he first became active in politics, as a supporter of Minneapolis Mayor Hubert Humphrey, who was then organizing the Minnesota Democratic-Farmer-Labor party. In 1948, the same year that Humphrey (and Lyndon Johnson) were elected to the Senate, McCarthy was elected to Congress as a DFL candidate from a predominantly Irish Catholic district in St. Paul. Through the era of Joseph McCarthy he was known to liberals as the "other" or "good" McCarthy; in 1960, then Minnesota's junior Senator, he made a stirring nomination speech for Adlai Stevenson at the Democratic National Convention in Los Angeles. That convention chose

John F. Kennedy as its nominee, and afterward, although McCarthy campaigned for Kennedy, it was rumored that there was a certain coolness between the two prominent Catholic Democrats. In 1964 McCarthy was considered by Lyndon Johnson—who had been his second choice at that 1960 convention, and with whom he had worked closely in the Senate—as a possible vice-presidential nominee. But that prize ultimately went to Hubert Humphrey.

McCarthy was a prominent Senate liberal, but he was not, like Fulbright of Arkansas and Morse of Oregon and Gruening of Alaska, an early critic of the Vietnam war. He was a member of Fulbright's Foreign Relations Committee, and in August of 1967 he was present when Undersecretary of State Nicholas Katzenbach testified on U.S. commitments—specifically, Vietnam. Katzenbach spoke strongly— one reporter described his testimony as "aggressive, arrogant, almost contemptuous"—about the President's authority to direct action as he saw fit, with or without consulting Congress. McCarthy angrily left the hearing room and said outside, "This is the wildest testimony I ever heard. There is no limit to what he says the President could do. There is only one thing to do—take it to the country." [1]

In September the country's largest unofficial organization of party volunteers, the California Democratic Council, held a special convention and decided to enter in the California primary an independent delegation pledged to peace—an indication of potential political strength in the nation's most populous state. In October, a statement by Secretary of State Dean Rusk which resorted to imagery of "millions of Chinese brandishing atomic weapons" led McCarthy a step closer to deciding to challenge the basic assumptions about the purpose of the war in Vietnam.[2]

In early November—still not a declared candidate—he traveled through the East and Mideast, meeting with potential supporters and making speeches. Speaking to faculty and students at Macalester College in St. Paul, he stated what would be the main theme of his campaign:

> *In the year 1968, we must raise the basic question as to whether or not what is called our commitment in South Vietnam is morally defensible; to ask not only whether is it legally, militarily and politically defensible, but also is it*

[1] E. W. Kenworthy, "Eugene McCarthy Hits the Road," © *New Republic*, Nov. 25, 1967, p. 12. Reprinted by permission.
[2] *Ibid.*

*morally defensible and in the national interest. We must
raise the essential moral question as to whether or not there is
a proper balance in what we may gain in what is projected
as victory, in contrast with the loss of life, the loss of material
goods, the loss of moral integrity and moral energy which goes
with the effort.*[3]

On November 30 he formally announced that he would be a
candidate for the Democratic nomination for President and would
enter primaries in six states. Although he said he did not intend
to "demagogue the issue," he made it clear that he would be challenging administration Vietnam policy; he also made it clear that
he was seeking the support of young people, who, he said, were "on
the edge of almost complete alienation from politics." It was expected that the first primary he would enter would be Wisconsin's,
on April 2. Then he suddenly stepped up the pace of his campaign—
and national interest in it—by announcing on January 3 that he would
enter the New Hampshire primary. He had previously dismissed New
Hampshire as "not particularly significant," but now he said he hoped
to use that primary to bring about a "more direct confrontation" with
Johnson.

For several reasons, McCarthy's decision to enter the New
Hampshire primary did not seem wise. For one thing, New Hampshire
voters were generally regarded as being on the "hawkish" side and
less likely than voters in more liberal areas of the country to respond
favorably to McCarthy's peace-oriented campaign. For another, there
were strong forces already organized in the state and ready to make
the going difficult for any anti-administration challenger. The President had not yet announced his candidacy for renomination, but a
New Hampshire "Citizens for Johnson" organization had been set up
in November and was preparing to secure for Johnson the state's 26
delegate votes without his declaration—which, if he should subsequently announce his intention to seek another term, would give
the announcement a flavor of response to public demand.

The organization was run by the state's top Democrats: The
chairman was Governor John W. King; co-chairman was Senator
Thomas J. McIntyre, and campaign director was Bernard Boutin.
Boutin, a former head of the federal Small Business Administration,
was now an executive in Sanders Associates, an electronics firm doing
a $140-million annual business, mostly from federal defense and space

[3] *Ibid.*

contracts.[4] The organization was large and well financed, and its leaders did not appear to be disturbed by the news that McCarthy was entering the campaign. One told the press that his entry would only help by providing competition.

The New Hampshire presidential primary is one of those which has a presidential preference vote and a separate selection of delegates. Since Johnson had not declared his candidacy his name would not appear on the ballot for the preference vote, but the Citizens for Johnson organization were preparing a formidable write-in campaign: Each Democratic voter was to receive from the state committee a packet containing Johnson buttons, bumper stickers, and literature— and also a perforated, three-part numbered card. The first part of the card was to be retained by the voter for instructions on how to write in Johnson's name on election day, the second part was to be sent to the President as a demonstration of support, and the third part was to go into the state committee's permanent files.

Since Johnson had not given his official consent to the campaign on his behalf, his delegates would have to appear on the ballot as "favorable" to him rather than as "pledged," but there was no likelihood that the loyal party men who were running as Johnson delegates would abandon him at the national convention. The powerful but discreet Johnson campaign seemed foolproof. A *New York Times* editorial said, "This cautious approach will enable Mr. Johnson to claim all the credit for a victory and to blur the significance of a defeat." [5] Most observers did not even consider the possibility of a defeat. When a New Hampshire paper, the *Newport Argus-Champion,* decided to conduct a voter poll, it concerned itself with Romney, Rockefeller, and Nixon and did not bother to sample the Democratic vote. "The rhubarb's all Republican," the editor said. "Who has any doubts about the Democratic candidate?" [6]

The biggest doubts that did exist had to do with Robert Kennedy. Many political observers interpreted McCarthy's function in New Hampshire as that of a stalking-horse for Kennedy, to test the strength of anti-Johnson sentiment. But both McCarthy and Kennedy denied there was any such arrangement. McCarthy did seek Kennedy's endorsement, but Kennedy was trying uncomfortably to

[4] *The New York Times,* Jan. 4, 1968.
[5] *Ibid.,* Jan. 7, 1968.
[6] Evan Hill, "Newport, N.H. (Pop. 5,800) Is Ready to Vote," *New York Times Magazine,* March 10, 1968, p. 34. © 1968 by The New York Times Company. Reprinted by permission.

stay with the President. "I can still support a man," he said in January, "even though I disagree with him."

Still, McCarthy continually exerted public pressure for support on both Robert Kennedy and Senator Edward Kennedy of Massachusetts. Robert Kennedy did say he considered McCarthy's candidacy a "healthy influence" which would allow people "to take out their frustrations in talk instead of violence," but that was as far as he would go. In a question-and-answer session with a group of New York students the following exchange took place:

> STUDENT: *Don't you think your influence behind McCarthy would make all the difference and give us a means of channeling our protests?*
>
> KENNEDY: *I also have to analyze on the basis of whether I could do more good by taking a step such as that or make a better contribution in some other way. It is my judgment at the moment that this (backing McCarthy) doesn't further the cause. I give this answer with a great deal of effort. I don't think it is completely satisfactory. But I must examine the issue in relation to my concern about my own future, to my own conscience, and my judgment on what can be most useful. My feeling at the moment is that what I'm doing is the most useful, but perhaps not accomplishing a great deal.*[7]

In February McCarthy published his reactions to the rumors about what Kennedy might do in an article in *Look*:

> *It has been suggested that after I have fought through all the primaries and it gets close to convention time, Sen. Robert Kennedy of New York will step in and pick up all the chips. I doubt it. If that is his plan, he will have a fight on his hands. . . . I will not step aside voluntarily. . . . This is my campaign. I am not a stalking-horse for anybody.*[8]

Although Kennedy was still a self-declared Johnson supporter, he was becoming increasingly critical of the war. "The time has come," he said on February 8, "to take a new look at the war in Vietnam." An administration spokesman told *The New York Times* that Kennedy was "trying to have it both ways"—please the party loyalists by not running and please the liberals by making speeches. But Kennedy's own press representative said his decision not to run had made him free to speak his mind.[9]

[7] *The New York Times*, Jan. 9, 1968. © 1968 by The New York Times Company. Reprinted by permission.

[8] Eugene McCarthy, "Why I'm Battling LBJ," *Look*, Feb. 6, 1968, p. 22. Reprinted by permission.

[9] *The New York Times*, Jan. 9, 1968. © 1968 by The New York Times Company. Reprinted by permission.

In New Hampshire a group of Kennedy supporters led by Eugene Daniell, Jr., was preparing to run a slate of delegates favoring Kennedy and put on a write-in campaign on his behalf, with or without his consent. Elections officials were questioning the legality of an unauthorized campaign. This was a rather delicate issue, since the Johnson write-in campaign did not officially have his permission either. But whereas the Johnson campaign was proceeding with the candidate's tacit consent, the Kennedy campaign was not. Kennedy sent Theodore Sorensen to New Hampshire to inform his supporters there that write-in votes for him would not be welcome. Apparently Sorensen's mission was successful. On February 9 the state Citizens for Kennedy Committee leaders caucused and decided on a "radical change in tactics"—they would back McCarthy instead.

The next day was the deadline for would-be delegates to file, and it was also the day the state Supreme Court handed down its decision that Daniell and his group could campaign for Kennedy without his permission. But Daniell and three other Kennedy supporters decided instead to run as delegates favoring McCarthy. The delegate part of the primary, then, included McCarthy's own slate of 24 pledged delegates, the four Kennedy delegates favoring McCarthy, and a field of 45 Democratic politicians (including Governor King and Senator McIntyre) listed as favoring Johnson. The preference portion of the ballot listed the names of McCarthy and various minor candidates, but not Kennedy or Johnson.

McCarthy had formally opened his campaign in New Hampshire on January 26, and in sampling public opinion at the local level he soon realized that the Johnson write-in campaign had provided him with a valuable local issue. The numbered pledge cards were an obvious attempt to exert pressure, and many Democratic voters resented the state committee's heavy-handed tactics. In a speech at Laconia McCarthy said the whole pledge-card idea was "not altogether inconsistent with administration policy to kind of put a brand on people. It's something they do in Texas. I would hope the voters will react against it. It's a test of the independent spirit of New Hampshire."

The administration supporters, who had at first ignored McCarthy, began to campaign against him. Governor King called him a "spokesman for the forces of appeasement" who was advocating a "policy of surrender which would destroy everything we have been fighting for." Actually, for all the excitement McCarthy had caused with his opposition to the government's policy in Vietnam, his own ideas for handling the problem were not so radical as to frighten the cautious New Englanders who bothered to listen to him, and they were not, by a considerable distance, radical enough for the many Americans who hoped for a dramatic repudiation of the whole containment policy which Vietnam represented. In his *Look* article, for example, McCarthy said:

> *If we shift the main burden of the fighting to the South Vietnamese, still providing the sustaining support, I believe they would be more willing to negotiate. Commensurate with this, we should seek diplomatic help at the UN and the Geneva Conference.*[10]

McCarthy's campaign became, in late February and early March, a far more spirited political operation than it had been at the beginning of the year. McCarthy had been endorsed by the national board of Americans for Democratic Action—at the cost of major dissension within that group, especially from leaders of organized labor—and some of the other liberals and liberal groups who supported him were beginning to raise some respectable amounts of money. He was still underfinanced by presidential-contender standards, but he was able to raise his New Hampshire budget from $80,000 to $120,000.

He bought some television time and hired Richard Goodwin, a former speechwriter for John F. Kennedy—which was a relief to some advisers who were worried about his rather casual speaking style. McCarthy's speeches were sometimes dramatic and forceful, bordering on the kind of Stevensonian eloquence that many of his supporters expected from him, but more often they were low-key, drily humorous, rambling, and had a tendency to leave his listeners with a vaguely unsatisfied feeling; they did not hear quite what they came to hear. Newsmen, especially those who followed McCarthy on his campaign rounds and heard the same speech more than once, reported that his speeches were more like classroom lectures than political orations, and most of the experts thought McCarthy's speech-making manner was one of his greatest liabilities. It did not, incidentally, undergo any great transformation after Goodwin joined the campaign.

The most conspicuous among the McCarthy campaign workers were the college students. McCarthy's daughter had influenced his initial decision to enter the campaign, and college students had been active in his organization from the beginning. In the last weeks of

[10] McCarthy, *op. cit.*, p. 23.

the New Hampshire campaign, busloads and carloads of students were pouring in from Harvard and Brown and Yale and Cornell and other colleges. Sometimes they would come to New Hampshire to work in the campaign over the weekend and return to classes on Monday; others—including a group of students from Michigan who came to work for Romney and switched to McCarthy when their candidate dropped out of the race—were full-time workers. In the last two weeks, there were over a thousand students working out of the campaign headquarters in Concord. Most of them were sent out on door-to-door canvassing assignments, and they were tireless and enthusiastic campaigners, often willing to start early in the morning and work far into the night. Their youth and attractiveness and obvious sincerity made them more effective than the average door-bell-ringing political volunteer, and they were not naive about the kind of impression they wanted to make. "Neat and Clean for Gene" became a kind of internal campaign slogan and rule of behavior: Male volunteers turned out with haircuts and shaves, girls in not-too-short skirts. Students with long hair and beards also helped—but in the office, not as door-to-door canvassers.

While McCarthy campaigned against the war, the war itself had entered a new phase. During Tet, the Vietnamese lunar new year's festival, the Viet Cong launched a major offensive against more than 40 towns, and during the month of February there were serious setbacks to the American image of military superiority in Vietnam. It became easier for critics of the war to question not only its morality but its practicality; people who liked to think of themselves as realists could ask whether the advantages to be gained in Vietnam were worth the cost. The Tet offensive was a factor that influenced the political calculations and fortunes of Johnson, Kennedy, and McCarthy.

As the probabilities of the outcome of the New Hampshire primary were revised, so were the various appraisals of what the outcome would mean. The early polls had indicated about a 10- to 15-per cent vote for McCarthy. But Robert Dishman, a political science professor of the University of New Hampshire who was working on the McCarthy campaign, said about a week before election day that "30 per cent would be not only a moral but a tangible victory for Gene; 20 to 25 per cent would be regarded as a stand-off, and 15 per cent would be a blow to his hopes in other primaries." [11] Governor

[11] *The New York Times,* March 9, 1968. © 1968 by The New York Times Company. Reprinted by permission.

King, at this point, was predicting about a 24-per cent vote for McCarthy; Boutin, a few days later, said that the McCarthy campaign would be a failure if it received anything less than 40 per cent. It was a reversal of the usual campaign tactic of predicting an overwhelming victory; instead, it became necessary for Johnson's backers to revise upward their estimate of the probable McCarthy vote in order to diminish its "moral victory" impact: If the public could now be conditioned to regard 40 per cent as the expected McCarthy vote, it would not regard anything lower as a moral victory; so went the thinking of the Johnson backers.

While McCarthy prospects escalated, so did the "soft on communism" anti-McCarthy campaign. Advertisements signed by Governor King and Senator McIntyre appeared in New Hampshire newspapers with the following message:

> The Communists in Vietnam are watching the New Hampshire primary. They're watching to see if we at home have the same determination as our soldiers in Vietnam.
>
> To vote for weakness and indecision would not be in the best interests of our nation.
>
> We urge you to support our fighting men in Vietnam. Write-in President Johnson on your ballot on Tuesday.[12]

Essentially the same sort of message was contained in radio spot announcements, which repeated the warning about the Communists watching the primary and cautioned the voters against "fuzzy thinking and surrender." Governor King made one widely quoted speech warning that "any significant vote for McCarthy will be greeted with great cheers in Hanoi."

McCarthy called the tactics of the Johnson campaign "McCarthyist"—referring, of course, to the other McCarthy—and said that the kind of campaign King and McIntyre and Boutin were staging was "pretty much in character" with the kind of campaign staged by various Republican politicians in the 1950's. It began to look as though this aspect of the campaign, like the pledge cards, might backfire. The Johnson supporters were criticized from all sides: Senator Kennedy criticized them, a group of pro-Johnson delegate candidates criticized them, saying "We wish to make clear that we do not claim he (Johnson) has cornered the patriotism market," [13]

---

12 *Ibid.*, March 7, 1968.
13 *Ibid.*, March 9, 1968.

and even the leading Republican candidate criticized them. "If we disagree," said Nixon, "let us do it without attacking . . . patriotism and love of country."

Nixon's own campaign in New Hampshire took on a stronger anti-Johnson sound in the last weeks. Nixon—whose only real Republican opposition was a write-in campaign for Nelson Rockefeller —continued to be basically in agreement with the administration's Vietnam policy, but increasingly he reminded voters that Eisenhower's election in 1952 had led to the end of the Korean War. In a speech on March 4 he promised that a new Republican administration would "end the war and win the peace in the Pacific."

Less than a week before the election, there was a new outburst of anti-Vietnam speechmaking in the Senate. Senator Fulbright opened the floor debate, which lasted several hours, and Senator Kennedy, who in previous months had not been one of the strong critics of administration policy, said it was "immoral and intolerable to continue the way we are going in Vietnam."

That night, a CBS news broadcast reported that Kennedy was close to deciding to run—that he would enter the primaries in California, Oregon, and South Dakota. The report said that one of the main reasons for his decision was the signs of new life in McCarthy's New Hampshire campaign. When other newsmen contacted Kennedy for his reaction, he denied the report; he said that under "no foreseeable circumstances" would he become a candidate.

The President had announced that he would stay out of still another primary election, that in Massachusetts—which meant, in effect, giving the Massachusetts delegation to McCarthy. It was a gesture the President could well afford, since he was still assured of the support of party organizations in nearly all the nonprimary states, but McCarthy's Massachusetts campaign manager said: "The President's decision to back off from this contest reveals a very real fear within the Administration, an inability to come to terms with Senator McCarthy's challenge and a reluctance to test its popular strength through the electoral process." [14] In the last days of the New Hampshire campaign, many of the McCarthy workers were beginning to believe that he might even get a majority in the preference vote. He did not do that, but he did get results that no realistic political observer could ignore.

[14] *Ibid.,* March 6, 1968.

The total vote McCarthy actually received was 42.2 per cent: 23,280 votes to Johnson's 27,243. McCarthy also received 5,511 write-in votes in the Republican primary, which was won by Nixon with 80,667. There were 11,241 write-in votes for Rockefeller in the Republican primary, and 600 for Kennedy on the Democratic side.[15]

The excitement over McCarthy's moral victory in the preference vote tended to overshadow his surprising and very real victory in the election of delegates. The Democratic state leadership's decision to allow so many candidates to file as Johnson delegates proved to have been an outstandingly bad tactical error, which can be explained as the result of (a) unwillingness to offend the many important—and in some cases unimportant—politicians who wanted to be delegates, and (b) overconfidence. Because of it, the vote was split among the Johnson delegates, and only four of them were elected. McCarthy, however, had entered only one slate of 24 delegates pledged to him— and 20 of them were elected. Thus, the New Hampshire delegation which went to the 1968 Democratic convention was made up of 20 delegates pledged to McCarthy, four favoring Johnson, and the national committeeman and committeewoman.

The news of the outcome of the New Hampshire primary brought an immediate response from Robert Kennedy. On the day after the election he announced that he was "reassessing the possibility" of whether he would run against President Johnson. The primary, he said, had "demonstrated that there is a deep division within the party. It clearly indicates that a sizable group of Democrats are concerned about the direction in which the country is going." Actually, Kennedy had already made his reassessment and was preparing to announce his candidacy. Where only a few months before there had been no Democratic candidates to challenge the President, suddenly there were two.

The month held one more surprise: On March 31, President Johnson made a nationally televised speech discussing his efforts to find a peaceful solution to the Vietnam war. Near the end of the speech he announced that he would neither seek nor accept the Democratic nomination for another term.

---

[15] 1968 Congressional Quarterly Almanac (Washington: Congressional Quarterly Service, 1969), p. 972. Reprinted by permission.

The New Hampshire primary had momentous consequences, but it did not produce the results for which McCarthy had decided to enter the campaign: a clear dialogue on the Vietnam issue, a reversal of the disaffection of the young with party politics, or a victory for McCarthy himself. The remaining primaries became a series of skirmishes between McCarthy and Kennedy, and on the night of the last primary—California's —Kennedy was assassinated. The Johnson supporters fell into line behind Vice-President Humphrey, who had entered no primaries but picked up his delegates in the state conventions and party caucuses, and as Humphrey inherited the President's political power he also inherited the responsibility for the President's policies; the Chicago convention at which Humphrey was nominated while police battled peace demonstraters in the streets seemed, to many of the same young people who had been so full of optimism in March, the final evidence of the rigidity and unresponsiveness of the old political system. Few of the students who had rung doorbells for McCarthy in New Hampshire took any active part in the November election, when Hubert Humphrey campaigned and lost to Richard Nixon.

INDEX